Toleration

Why should we be tolerant? What does it mean to 'live and let live'? What ought to be tolerated and what not?

Toleration: A Critical Introduction is a comprehensive and accessible philosophical introduction to the theory and practice of toleration. The first part of the book clearly introduces and assesses the major theories of toleration through an exploration of accounts based on scepticism, value pluralism and the demands of reasonableness. Catriona McKinnon also draws on major liberal thinkers – from Locke and Mill to Rawls and Feinberg – in order to examine the relation between harm and toleration.

In the second part of the book, McKinnon applies the theories of toleration to urgent contemporary problems such as female circumcision, the French headscarves affair, artistic freedom, pornography and censorship, and Holocaust denial.

Toleration: A Critical Introduction provides a solid theoretical base for the value of toleration, while considering the detail of challenges to toleration in practice. It is an ideal starting point for those coming to the topic for the first time, and for anyone interested in the challenges facing toleration today.

Catriona McKinnon is Lecturer in Politics at the University of Reading. She is the author of *Liberalism and the Defence of Political Constructivism* (2002), and co-editor of *The Culture of Toleration in Diverse Societies: Reasonable Tolerance* (2003) and *The Demands of Citizenship* (2000).

Routledge Contemporary Political Philosophy

Edited by David Archard, University of St. Andrews
and Ronald Beiner, University of Toronto

Routledge Contemporary Political Philosophy is an exciting new series for students of philosophy and political theory. Designed for those who have already completed an introductory philosophy or politics course, each book in the series introduces and critically assesses a major topic in political philosophy. Long-standing topics are refreshed and more recent ones made accessible for those coming to often complex issues and arguments for the first time. After introducing the topic in question, each book clearly explains the central problems involved in understanding the arguments for and against competing theories. Relevant contemporary examples are used throughout to illuminate the problems and theories concerned, making the series essential reading not only for philosophy and politics students but also those in related disciplines such as sociology and law. Each book in the series is written by an experienced author and teacher with special knowledge of the topic, providing a valuable resource for both students and teachers alike.

Also available in the series:

Theories of Democracy
Frank Cunningham

Forthcoming titles include:

Rights
Tom Campbell

Equality
Melissa Williams

Public Reason and Deliberation
Simone Chambers

Toleration

A critical introduction

Catriona McKinnon

 Routledge
Taylor & Francis Group

LONDON AND NEW YORK

First published 2006
by Routledge
2 Park Square, Milton Park, Abingdon, Oxon, OX14 4RN

Simultaneously published in the USA and Canada
by Routledge
270 Madison Ave, New York, NY 10016

Routledge is an imprint of the Taylor & Francis Group

© 2006 Catriona McKinnon

Typeset in Goudy and Gill Sans by Taylor & Francis Books
Printed and bound in Great Britain by
Antony Rowe Ltd, Chippenham, Wiltshire

British Library Cataloguing in Publication Data
A catalogue record for this book is available from the British Library

Library of Congress Cataloging in Publication Data
McKinnon, Catriona.
   Toleration : a critical introduction / Catriona McKinnon.
    p. cm. -- (Routledge contemporary political philosophy)
   Includes bibliographical references.
   ISBN 0-415-32289-8 (hardback : alk. paper) -- ISBN 0-415-32290-1
(pbk. : alk. paper)
   1. Toleration.   I. Title. II. Series.
HM1271.M39 2005
179'.9--dc22

                       2005015347

ISBN10: 0-415-32289-8   ISBN13: 978-0-415-32289-8 (hbk)
ISBN10: 0-415-32290-1   ISBN13: 978-0-415-32290-4 (pbk)

Taylor & Francis Group is the Academic Division of T&F Informa plc.

For Matt, with love.

Contents

Acknowledgements   *viii*

PART I   1

1 Toleration: a call to arms   3

2 Opposition and restraint   18

3 Toleration from scepticism   35

4 Toleration from value pluralism   52

5 Toleration from reasonableness   67

6 Political harm: the liberal paradigm   81

PART II   99

7 Culture and citizenship: headscarves and circumcision   101

8 Artistic expression   119

9 Pornography and censorship   137

10 Holocaust denial   153

11 Conclusion: new challenges for liberal toleration   172

Notes   *175*
Bibliography   *202*
Index   *211*

Acknowledgements

This book started life as a series of graduate seminars on *Contemporary Issues in Toleration* that I taught at the University of York in 2000–2. The master's students who participated in the seminars gave me acute comments on the material, and much food for thought; my first debt of gratitude is to them. As a result of conversations about toleration and its problems, Dave Archard – as an editor of the series in which this book appeared – suggested that I undertake the project. I would like to thank him for his advice, support, and encouragement, all of which have been heartening and sound. Similarly, Tony Bruce at Routledge has been a great help and source of guidance; my thanks to him, the three anonymous readers of the original proposal and all at Routledge.

All that is really necessary for writing a book like this is access to a good library, correspondence with people who are thinking about the same things, and time. On the latter front, I have incurred a number of debts. The bulk of my writing was done while on leave from the University of York; I would like to thank the university, and my ex-colleagues in the Department of Politics, for granting me a sabbatical term as part of this leave. During this sabbatical term I spent a wonderful month as a Fellow in Philosophy at the Liguria Study Centre in Bogliasco near Genoa. I would like to thank the Bogliasco Foundation in New York for this award, and Sue Mendus and Hillel Steiner for their support in making the application. At the study centre itself, Alan Rowlin was the perfect host; I thank him for his company. In addition, I would like to thank the other Fellows whose company during my month in Genoa made the experience even more memorable; in particular, Danny Anderson, Jeffery Cotton, Bob and Florence Fogelin, and John and Brigitte Reader (and special thanks to Bob for very helpful discussion of chapter 3).

I acquired further time to work on the book through the award of a Study Abroad Fellowship from the Leverhulme Trust; for their references for this award, and their cheerful toleration of my seemingly incessant requests for their support, I would like to thank in the warmest terms Iain Hampsher-Monk, Hillel Steiner and Jo Wolff. My Fellowship was originally to have been spent at the Centre for Applied Philosophy and Public Ethics in the Department of Philosophy, University of Melbourne, and I would like to thank Tony Coady, Jeremy Moss and all at CAPPE for helping to make the necessary arrangements.

However, I was unable to enact my original plans due to poor health, and instead spent the period of the Fellowship as an Associate Research Fellow in the Philosophy Programme of the School of Advanced Study, University of London. I am extremely grateful to the staff at the Leverhulme Trust – in particular, Jean Cater and Bridget Kerr – for enabling me to change the arrangements for my Study Abroad Fellowship with the minimum of fuss; they prevented what was a very stressful time from becoming impossibly so. The same is true for Tim Crane who, as Director of the Philosophy Programme, arranged a Research Fellowship for me at short notice without hassle. My sincere thanks to all of them. Finally, on the time front, I would like to thank my new colleagues in the Department of Politics and International Relations at the University of Reading for securing a workload which made it possible for me to finish the book (almost) on schedule despite taking up a new contract there, and for the friendly welcome they have given me.

With respect to correspondence on the material in the book, I have been lucky in having detailed written feedback from Gideon Calder (on chapter 11), Paula Casal (on chapter 8), Bob Fogelin (on chapter 2), John Horton (on virtually the whole manuscript), and Cécile Laborde (on chapter 8). In addition, Alan Haworth and Stephen Newman provided very helpful comments on the penultimate draft. I would like to thank them all for taking the time to think about what I think, and for having the generosity to share their thoughts with me. In particular, I would like to thank John Horton for his extremely acute and constructive comments, and for his continuing support. Material from the book has, in one form or another, been presented in research seminars at the following institutions: the Universities of Brighton, Exeter, Manchester, Oxford, Reading, York, and the London School of Economics. I am grateful for the invitations to speak at these venues, and to the audiences who attended for their comments.

My final set of debts are personal. The experience of writing this book was marred by a serious health scare when I was far from home. At times like that you learn who you can rely on, and I would like to thank Havi Carel, Karen Chung, Cécile Laborde and Nigel Pleasants for their friendship. My family – my dad, Jim; my sister, Fiona; my brother-in-law, Pete; and my lovely niece, Mads – stick by me with love whatever the circumstances, but over the last two years have been the best family anyone could hope for. Finally, I would like to thank Matt Pittori, whose reappearance in my life brought me up for air, and whose daily presence makes my heart race: I dedicate this book to him with more love than I used to think possible.

Part I

Chapter I

Toleration: a call to arms

Society needs to condemn a little more and understand a little less.
(John Major, 1993, while Prime Minister of Britain)[1]

Introduction

Toleration is a matter of putting up with that which you oppose: the motto of the tolerant person is 'live and let live', even when what she lets live shocks, enrages, frightens, or disgusts her. As such, toleration is a controversial value. The secular righteous on the left reject it as the pet indulgence of a pampered liberal elite whose self-interest it serves by providing them with convenient excuses for blocking any agitation aiming at real social change. The secular righteous on the right reject it as the corrupt policy of the morally spineless who lack the insight and strength of will to improve the moral character of society and their fellow citizens through zero tolerance. And the religious righteous treat arguments for toleration with suspicion in the face of the eternal damnation to be meted out to those who will inevitably stray from the path to salvation once other paths are made available to them through the practice of toleration.

The erstwhile defenders of toleration thus attacked by the righteous have fallen asleep at their posts. Like freedom and equality, toleration is a value that no democratic politician would dare to repudiate, and the political zeitgeist has it that we democrats are all agreed, more or less, on the questions of why it is a good thing to be tolerant, what ought not to be tolerated, and how the value of toleration is best realised in political principles and procedures, the law, and personal behaviour. And the fact of putative agreement on apparently justified answers to these questions has encouraged neglect of the arsenal of arguments available in the defence of toleration. This complacency in democratic communities with respect to the principles and practice of toleration renders the attacks of the righteous – albeit often under cover of defences of democracy, freedom, justice, and 'our way of life' – perhaps more of a threat than at any time since the middle of the last century. To get a sense of the dangers, consider the following cases.

On 2 November 2004 film-maker Theo van Gogh was murdered on an Amsterdam street by a suspect who, the Dutch justice minister claimed, 'acted out of radical Islamic fundamentalist convictions'. Van Gogh had recently collaborated with the Dutch MP Ayaan Hirsi Ali, a self-described 'ex-Muslim', on a film exploring Islam and women, which was broadcast on Dutch television in August 2004. In the film a Muslim woman was shown being forced into an arranged marriage, beaten by her husband, raped by her uncle, and then punished for adultery; verses from the Qur'an relating to the status of women were then shown projected across the woman's beaten shoulders. Hirsi Ali's suggestions for combating the misogyny she perceives in Islam are for fundamentalist Islamic books to be banned, and for Muslim Mullahs to be expelled from the country. The murder of Van Gogh shows the worst kind of intolerance in action: the kind that ends with death. But can the solution to that terrible intolerance – in a country that is arguably the birthplace of toleration – really be more intolerance, in the form of book-banning and banishing?[2]

Race relations in Holland are deteriorating, with polls showing increased support for anti-immigration policies. The popularity of Rotterdam-based politician Pim Fortuyn (who stood on a strong anti-multiculturalist and anti-green platform, and was murdered by an animal rights activist in May 2002) is testament to this. And the Dutch 'List Fortuyn' is not an isolated example in Europe. 'New populist' political movements are gaining popularity (and, in some cases, political power) across the democracies of Europe: witness Le Pen's Front National in France, Jörg Haider's Freedom Party in Austria, the Alleanza Nazionale in Italy, the Progress Party in Norway, and the Danske Folkeparti in Denmark. These movements are united by their self-described commitments to speak for 'the common man', to oppose immigration and restrict multiculturalism as an aspect of this speech, and to unapologetically resist what they see as overstated and misguided 'politically correct' policies guided by a concern for human rights, climate change, and multiculturalism. Their emergence on the political scene serves as a call to arms for the defenders of toleration.

The British experience with respect to its most prominent new populist party, the British National Party (BNP), is more muted; their successes are limited to a few seats in local elections. However, the relative failure of the BNP in formal political arenas does not show that Britain is free from racial intolerance. A recent Council of Europe survey on racism and xenophobia ranked the UK the European state most hostile to political refugees.[3] And statistics show that, relative to resident population in a police force area in 1997–8, black people were five times more likely to be stopped and searched by the police than white people;[4] that black Caribbean pupils were five times more likely (in 1995–6) to face permanent exclusion from schools than white pupils;[5] that (according to studies conducted by the University of Brighton and the University of Sussex) 'covert racism exists almost everywhere' in the state school system;[6] and that (in 1995–6) the unemployment rate for ethnic minorities (18 per cent) was more than double that for whites (8 per cent), with four in ten young black women unemployed in that period compared to one in ten young white women.[7]

Of course, statistics can tell a thousand stories, and interpretations of those offered here can be given so as to avoid the conclusion that racism is endemic in the British police force, education system, and employment market. Perhaps more telling, then, are statistics relating to the perception of racial intolerance held by members of racial minorities. In 1995, an estimated 15 per cent of all offences against Asians and blacks were seen as racially motivated, compared to 1 per cent against white people.[8] 1996 statistics further confirm this perception of racial violence in the UK: one in fifteen white people was very worried about 'being subject to a physical attack because of their skin colour, ethnic origin, or religion', whereas one in three people from an ethnic minority expressed such a worry.[9] And in this period people from ethnic minorities were twice as likely (26 per cent) as white people (13 per cent) to say they avoided events or activities – such as football matches, nightclubs and pubs – because of fear of violence or crime. Finally, among 16–24-year-olds, 85 per cent of black Caribbeans and 50 per cent of Asians did not feel they could rely on the police for protection from racial harassment.[10] Either Britain faces genuine problems of racial intolerance, or the worries and distrust consistently expressed by large numbers of its ethnic minorities do nothing but articulate a mass delusion with respect to the incidence of racial discrimination and violence in Britain.

Finally, and moving west, the state of the culture of toleration in the US can be seen by considering the gay marriage debate there. The current furore about gay marriage in the US can be traced back to the Supreme Court's 1986 interpretation of Bowers v. Hardwick as a case about whether there exists a constitutional right to sodomy.[11] The court decided that no such constitutional right existed, and thereby made it possible for states to criminalise homosexual sex, and discriminate against homosexuals on the basis of their criminality (for example, Alabama denies custody of children to gay people on the grounds that gay relationships are criminal). However, the decision in Bowers was recently struck down by a Supreme Court decision in Lawrence v. Texas (26 June 2003).[12] Here, the court ruled that Texas' anti-sodomy laws violated the constitutional right of all persons to privacy, thereby directly contradicting the decision in Bowers (the court stated that 'Bowers was not correct when it was decided, and it is not correct now'), and opening the door to legal challenges to all subsequent legislation drawing upon Bowers. In response to Lawrence (just three days after the decision), Senate Majority Leader Bill Frist (with bipartisan support) endorsed the Federal Marriage Amendment to the US Constitution, which states that:

> Marriage in the United States shall consist only of the union of a man and a woman. Neither this constitution or the constitution of any state, nor state or federal law, shall be construed to require that marital status or the legal incidents thereof be conferred upon unmarried couples or groups.

This amendment denies to gay couples the right to marry as recently established by the decision of the Massachusetts Supreme Judicial Court in Goodridge v. MA Dept of Public Health (a case in which seven gay and lesbian couples challenged the decision of the Massachusetts Department of Public Health to deny them licences to marry).[13] President Bush voiced his support for this amendment, stating that, 'Marriage is between a man and a woman, and I think we ought to codify that one way or another'.[14]

A key ground on which the Marriage Amendment is claimed to be intolerant is that the denial to gay people of the right to marry violates their constitutional right to privacy. However, those opposed to gay marriage, such as the Alliance for Marriage, claim that permitting it in law would devalue heterosexual marriage and undermine the role of women.[15] On this view, it is often claimed that gay marriage is to be placed outside the limits of toleration because the practice of marriage historically belongs to the heterosexual community, and is a signal of commitment peculiar to heterosexuals and valued by them as such. An analogy here is with all-male clubs. Men join these clubs because they are all male; if such clubs are forced by law to open their doors to women then they lose their value for existing members. To avoid this harm, provision should be made for women to open their own clubs. Applied to the question of gay marriage, the analogous argument is that homosexual couples should be permitted to join together in legally recognised civil unions – as they currently are in many US states, and may soon be in the UK – but not in marriage. The principle at work here is: 'separate but equal'. This principle was, famously, struck down in 1954 by the US Supreme Court with respect to racial segregation in schools in *Brown v. Board of Education*, and this decision is held up by all as a landmark on the road to racial equality and toleration in the US.[16] Fifty years on from *Brown*, can toleration permit that 'separate but equal' be written into the US Constitution with respect to the rights of homosexual people to enter into the marriage contract, with all its attendant benefits?

We do not live in a tolerant world, and claims that we democrats are all tolerant now should be treated with suspicion: either we are not as democratic as we like to think, or our democratic commitments at best underdetermine the choice of different practices of toleration, or at worst generate practices that directly conflict. Furthermore, the way the world is means that any sane politician has no choice but to pursue policies of toleration. If anything is a fact about human nature and its operation on a bounded planet with limited resources, then this is: conflict between persons is a permanent feature of their interaction in social contexts. Many such conflicts are open to solution without remainder through negotiation using procedures agreed to by parties to the conflict; for example, conflicts about territory, contracts, or reparation can have this character. However, many other conflicts cannot be resolved without remainder via procedural means: when persons come into conflict on questions about the best way to live, the right things to think, the ideal political society, and the true road to salvation, no amount of negotiation and bargaining will bring them to agreement without at least one party relinquishing the commitments that created the conflict in the first place.

Such conflicts provide the circumstances of toleration. The record of history aside, there are many reasons to think that such conflicts are endemic in human society: for example, that they are the normal result of the exercise of reason in conditions of freedom; that they are a consequence of the incommensurability of the values involved in such conflicts; or that they reflect the fact that the truth of the beliefs, and the significance of the values, manifest in such conflicts are relative to the point of view of the believer and the moral system of the valuer. These explanations of the permanence of pluralism will be explored in due course (in chapters 5, 4 and 3 respectively).[17] For the moment, note that the fact that such conflicts stand as circumstances of toleration does not entail that toleration is the only solution to such conflicts. Other routes to the resolution of such conflicts more common in history are war and oppression. For those who cannot countenance toleration of their ideological opponents, napalming their villages, pointing nuclear warheads at them from a nearby island, or flying aeroplanes into their landmarks, are real, practical alternatives. And for those who win such wars, or who already have power over those they oppose, an Inquisition, a committee for un-American activities, or two years' hard labour in Reading jail serve the end of conflict resolution just as well as toleration.[18] The circumstances of toleration are here to stay, but the practice of toleration is not a given. If a peace fit for justice is our goal – that is, social organisation according to non-oppressive principles which mediate hot and cold conflicts so as to prevent their deterioration into war – then toleration is our only option. With toleration secured, further measures to achieve justice – however conceived – are possible. Insofar as everyone ought to care about justice, everyone has a reason to value toleration.

Two philosophers who saw clearly the imperative to be tolerant as issuing from the nature of human beings inhabiting a world in which avoidance of one another is not an option were John Locke and John Stuart Mill. Before entering the current debates we would do well to recall their lessons.

Avoiding jihad and the tyranny of the majority: Locke and Mill on toleration

John Locke (1632–1704) published his famous *A Letter Concerning Toleration* in 1689.[19] Locke was a very political political philosopher, and was involved in struggles to establish limited government throughout his life. The arguments of the *Letter* set limits on the authority of governments and priests with respect to religious belief, and are addressed to these agents of intolerance.

Restoration England was not a safe place in which to be non-Anglican. The post-Civil War Restoration settlement of 1660–2 saw Anglicans gain control of (the 'Cavalier') Parliament, and thenceforth use their power to enact legislation (for example, the 'Clarendon Code', the Toleration Act, and the Act of Uniformity) to enforce religious uniformity, quash the dissent of Baptists, Presbyterians, Independents, Quakers and – as a matter of course – Catholics, and fine, imprison, and deport members of these denominations. The settlement also saw the Anglican Church itself become more non-latitudinarian and insistent on uniformity of belief and religious practice.

Religious tensions simmered in Restoration England and the threat of revolution, or a return to civil war, was constant. During this period (in 1667) Locke became personal physician to the Earl of Shaftesbury, and soon thereafter also became his friend, confidante, and political ally. In 1679 Shaftesbury attempted to pass through Parliament the Exclusion Bill, which would have denied the throne to Charles II's Catholic brother, James II. Because Charles had no legitimate heirs, the success of the Exclusion Bill would have, in effect, overturned the principle of hereditary succession upon which the whole monarchy rested. Charles reacted by dissolving Parliament. Shaftesbury was then associated with the seditious activities of the Duke of Monmouth (one of Charles' illegitimate sons), and implicated in the 1683 Rye House plot to assassinate Charles and his brother, James. Upon discovery of the plot, Shaftesbury fled to Holland. Although the extent of Locke's direct involvement with Shaftesbury's political activities is not clear, Locke also sought exile in Holland, where he remained until the year after the 1688 Glorious Revolution in which James II was replaced on the throne by Protestant William of Orange and Mary (James II's daughter).[20]

Locke wrote the *Letter* during his exile, but never acknowledged authorship of it. Living in these times, Locke must have been keenly aware of the circumstances of toleration, and the ever-present bellicose and/or oppressive solutions to the conflicts constitutive of it. The *Letter* insists on the distinction between church and state: the former is a voluntary association concerned with the spiritual welfare of its members,[21] and the latter a non-voluntary association concerned with temporal, civil matters and the common good.[22] As such, it is impermissible for either institution to use force to impose conformity in religious belief and practice: these matters lie outside the scope of the state's legitimate concerns, and even though the church ought to facilitate worship and offer guidance, ultimate responsibility for the spiritual welfare of each person lies with the person herself. This distinction, however – and the religious toleration it implies – is the conclusion of the *Letter*. The arguments that deliver it are as follows:[23]

1   The argument from the irrationality of imposition: by its very nature, faith cannot be imposed, therefore the intolerant religious oppressor acts irrationally.
2   The argument from scepticism: rulers cannot know which form of worship is the path to salvation, which counsels them to practice toleration with respect to this aspect of faith[24] (although note that this argument assumes that some form of worship provides this path: Locke did not extend the limits of toleration to include atheists).[25]
3   The argument from pragmatism and rulers' self-interest: there is no alternative to toleration if stability is to be secured; such stability is in the interests of any ruler. '[T]here is only one thing which gathers People into Seditious Commotions, and that is Oppression'.[26]

By far the most well-known and powerful of these arguments is the first, and I shall focus just on this. The argument is simple.

The care of Souls cannot belong to the Civil Magistrate, because his Power consists only in outward force; but true and saving Religion consists in the inward perswasion of the Mind, without which nothing can be acceptable to God. And such is the nature of the Understanding that it cannot be compell'd to the belief of any thing by outward force. Confiscation of Estate, Imprisonment, Torments, nothing of that nature can have any such Efficacy as to make Men change the inward Judgment they have framed of things.[27]

Coercive force acts on the will; religious belief is not subject to the will; there-fore, coercive force cannot secure religious belief. The wielders of such force act irrationally in attempting to achieve an end which cannot be secured with the instruments at their disposal.[28] Generalising the argument to all forms of belief, would-be oppressors cannot achieve the ideological conformity they aim at through the use of force and so – insofar as they are rational – ought to practice toleration with respect to those they oppose. On this argument, toleration is required in virtue of the reasons for action available to potential oppressors, rather than the desirable consequences of toleration for those tolerated.[29]

Is this a good argument? There are at least four sites of weakness. The first relates to the key premise that belief is not subject to the will. This seems true: regardless of how much I will myself to believe that $2 + 2 = 5$, that I have a guardian angel, or – looking out over a December London skyline – that it is sunny and 70 degrees today, I cannot do it. However, as Jeremy Waldron notes, the direction of our attention with respect to materials that influence belief-formation is (often) subject to the will, and so can be manipulated by coercion.[30] This, surely, is part of the practice of schooling children, and makes sense of prohibitions on materials such as those imposed by the Vatican's list of banned books (the 'Index Expurgatorius'). We may not be able to coerce belief directly, but we can control access to the materials upon which belief is formed, in which case the scope of toleration recommended by Locke's argument from rationality may be far more limited than it at first appears: it may permit book-banning, Newspeak, and heavy gagging orders.

Second, we might attack the *prima facie* plausibility of the key premise. It is not true that we cannot secure belief by coercion: if I tie you down and hypno-tise you I can manipulate your will so as to force you to believe that you are a 5-year-old child. In that case, the key premise should be interpreted as stating that coercion cannot secure the right kinds of belief:[31] beliefs acquired in this way are not genuine, because they are not acquired freely, and *ipso facto* cannot deliver salvation to the believer. The problem here, as Waldron notes, is that few of our beliefs meet what appears to be a very demanding test for genuine-ness: that the belief should be acquired free from external influence. And it is anyway not clear why this test is a test for genuineness: what does it matter to the genuineness of my belief that King Canute existed that a trusted historian friend told me this, or that I established it through my own independent research?[32]

Next, and relating to the argument as a whole, we might doubt whether the outward profession of belief in the absence of inward conviction is as valueless as Locke assumes. Would-be oppressors may not care a jot for what the oppressed really believe, so long as they go through the appropriate external motions. Again, this qualification to the argument means that the limits of toleration may be far more narrow than we democrats are comfortable with: if the qualification holds, then there may be no justification for freedom of religious practice, association or expression (*qua* practices external to belief) in the name of toleration.

Finally, as many commentators have noted, the argument from rationality seems to miss the mark with respect to what is wrong with intolerance.[33] According to this argument, intolerance is wrong because it is irrational; but this fails to register the harm that intolerance visits upon the oppressed. Surely intolerance is wrong because it is in some way immoral, rather than just in virtue of being a failure of practical reasoning on the part of oppressors?

Notwithstanding these problems, Locke's *Letter* contains a powerful acknowledgement that the circumstances of toleration are here to stay, and a classic statement of why oppression and war are misplaced resolutions to the conflicts constitutive of these circumstances. But Locke's arguments are limited to religious belief and practice, and addressed to agents of intolerance with tangible coercive powers. For arguments for toleration that extend beyond matters of belief, and address the intangible culture of intolerance as well as the power of institutional authorities, we must turn to John Stuart Mill's *On Liberty*.

Although not participant in Lockean seditious politics, Mill was nevertheless a political animal; indeed, he served as MP for Westminster in 1865–8, during which time he agitated for women's suffrage. Born in 1806 (to James Mill, an intellectual companion of Jeremy Bentham, who was the leader of the influential 'British Radicals'), Mill wrote his major works at the height of the Victorian Empire, and the themes they contain reflect the dangers – and the benefits – of this political climate.[34] With respect to questions about the advantages of toleration, and its limits, Mill is the most powerful thinker in the philosophical canon, and his influence permeates across all aspects of liberal theory and practice.

Mill's reflections on toleration start with a characterisation of the circumstances that call for it that immediately distinguishes his approach from Locke's. He claims that although the emergence of representative government has successfully addressed the injustice of tyrannical elite rule, it has created a new danger: the tyranny of the majority. This is because the will of the people represented in this form of government

> practically means the will of the most numerous or most active part of the people; the majority, or those who succeed in making themselves accepted as the majority; the people consequently may desire to oppress a part of their number; and precautions are as much needed against this as against any other abuse of power . . . the "tyranny of the majority" is now generally included as among the evils against which society requires to be on its guard.[35]

This reflection makes the scope of toleration far wider than in Locke: toleration is a potential political palliative in any arena of human life in which the majority might tyrannise, and we know from bitter experience that this is possible with respect to anything human beings do, say, or believe. There are two agents of majority tyranny: the law (which exerts coercive influence through the direct and tangible threat of physical force; law breakers can be arrested, sentenced, and physically detained or otherwise punished); and social mores (which exert moral coercion through the less tangible channels of public opinion and social disapproval; those who run against the social grain can be ridiculed, marginalised, shunned, and made socially dead). To counter both these forms of tyranny Mill famously offers 'one very simple principle, as entitled to govern absolutely the dealings of society with the individual in the way of compulsion and control', which is that,

> the sole end for which mankind are warranted, individually or collectively, in interfering with the liberty of action of any of their number is self-protection. That the only purpose for which power can rightfully be exercised over any member of a civilised community, against his will, is to prevent harm to others. His own good, either physical or moral, is not a sufficient warrant. He cannot rightfully be compelled to do or forbear because it will make him happier, because, in the opinion of others, to do so would be wise, or even right. These are good reasons for remonstrating with him, or reasoning with him, or persuading him, or entreating him, but not for compelling him, or visiting him with any evil in case he do otherwise. To justify that, the conduct from which it is desired to deter him must be calculated to produce evil to some one else. The only part of the conduct of any one, for which he is amenable to society, is that which concerns others. In the part which merely concerns himself, his independence is, of right, absolute. Over himself, over his own body and mind, the individual is sovereign.[36]

Mill's 'Liberty Principle' (LP) lays down two necessary (and jointly sufficient) conditions for the interference of society (through law or public opinion) with the individual: that the action interfered with is (a) other-regarding and (b) harmful. In Mill's view, (a) is lexically prior to (b) in any consideration of whether interference is permitted; that is, if (a) is satisfied, then consideration of whether (b) applies is appropriate and, if (b) does apply, then interference is required. In other words, social interference with individual action is never permitted when the action is self-regarding, regardless of whether or not the action is harmful to the agent. According to Mill, the LP protects individual liberty in three key areas of human life.

(a) 'liberty of conscience in the most comprehensive sense; liberty of thought and feeling; absolute freedom of opinion and sentiment on all subjects, practical or speculative, scientific, moral, or theological'.[37]

(b) 'liberty of tastes and pursuits; of framing the plan of our own life to suit our character; of doing as we like, subject to the consequences that may follow: without impediment from our fellow creatures, so long as what we do does not harm them, even though they should think our conduct foolish, perverse, or wrong'.[38]

(c) 'liberty . . . of combination among individuals; freedom to unite, for any purpose not involving harm to others'.[39]

In proscribing grounds on which one set of agents may act on its opposition to another set of agents through interference with their practices, or attempt to alter their beliefs and values, the LP functions as a principle of toleration. What are the benefits of setting the limits of toleration in this way? Mill claims that the LP is justified in virtue of its utilitarian benefits; that is, in virtue of how practice according to it would increase the greatest happiness of the greatest number of people in society. (Note here the contrast with Locke: for Mill, toleration is required in virtue of its morally desirable consequences, rather than in virtue of the irrationality of intolerance on the part of oppressors.) To get the real measure of Mill's justification of the LP, however, requires more precision with respect his conception of utility.

> It is proper to state that I forego any advantage which could be derived to my argument from the idea of abstract right, as a thing independent of utility. I regard utility as the ultimate appeal on all ethical questions; but it must be utility in the largest sense, grounded in the permanent interests of man as a progressive being.[40]

According to Mill, utility lies in the realisation of our natures as progressive beings: for Mill, any happiness worth the name is achieved through the development and exercise of 'faculties more elevated than the animal appetites',[41] and these faculties require the oxygen of liberty to flourish. In particular, to have a 'progressive nature', according to Mill, is to be 'capable of being improved through free and equal discussion' (which explains the level of attention Mill devotes to arguments for freedom of expression within the bounds of the LP);[42] and to be capable of learning from experience (which explains Mill's insistence that progress requires that people be free to conduct 'experiments in living', and to develop individuality).[43]

Mill's defence of the LP and the individual freedoms to be derived from it is a beautiful and formidable liberal classic; we shall return to many of the arguments of On Liberty in the discussions to come. For the moment, let me signal the two most commonly noted problems with the argument which relate to: (1) Mill's conception of harm; and (2) the putative distinction between self- and other-regarding actions. With respect to (1), Mill permits that both acts and omissions can cause harm,[44] and that the concept of harm can extend beyond direct physical damage (as evinced in his claim – in the discussion of the well-known example of the mob outside the corn dealer's house – that incitement to violence 'may justly incur punishment').[45] As we will see in Part II of this book, much debate about the practice of toleration takes the form of disputes about the harms from which persons have a right to be protected in law. For the moment, however, note that H.L.A. Hart's interpretation of Mill on harm in terms of 'rule-utilitarianism' is surely correct: harmful acts are those in violation of rules which would maximize utility were they to be followed universally.[46] Mill's LP provides a normative framework within which those attempting to formulate such rules in law and policy are required to work.

The problem in (2) is connected to (1): in order to assess whether an act is harmful in a way that requires the attention of the law we need to determine whether it is an other-regarding act. But the distinction between self- and other-regarding acts is *prima facie* spurious. Mill puts the objection thus: 'No person is an entirely isolated being; it is impossible for a person to do anything seriously or permanently hurtful to himself, without mischief reaching at least to his near connections, and often far beyond them.'[47] As J.C. Rees notes, the key to addressing this objection is that '[t]here is an important difference between just affecting others and affecting the interests of others'.[48] It is true that no act of mine is entirely self-regarding: every action I perform requires that I take a breath, and in breathing I deplete the stock of oxygen available globally and to that extent I affect every other person. But this trivial observation does not undermine the self-/other-regarding distinction once we understand the distinction in terms of the effect actions have on the interests of others, where these interests are to be understood in terms of the conditions necessary for the realisation of the nature of persons as progressive beings. Reading Mill in this way, only acts which damage others in terms of these interests lie within the scope of legitimate social interference; insofar as their effect on the interests of persons as progressive beings is indifferent or positive, all other other-regarding acts lie outside the scope of social interference. The effect of this reading is to enlarge the set of individual freedoms derived from the LP: all self-regarding acts, and other-regarding acts indifferent or positive in the way just mentioned, are to be kept free from interference in the name of progress. Rules for the protection of individual liberty have significant utilitarian advantages for progressive societies; such rules, for Mill, set the limits of toleration.[49]

Toleration: contemporary problems

Locke and Mill give us good reasons for preferring toleration to holy war and stifling social conformity. For reasons they saw clearly, politicians must keep toleration in the forefront of their minds when making policy. That said, this is not a book of political analysis. Rather, this book aims to reassert the significance of toleration by exploring the best current theoretical answers to the following questions: How is toleration possible? Why is toleration required? And, what are the limits of toleration? The dangerous complacency about toleration in the political zeitgeist is mirrored by a mysterious quiet in the Academy: with a few key exceptions, the subject of toleration has been largely absent from the academic literature for the last twenty-five years, and the questions just listed have rarely been addressed directly.[50] Before embarking on discussion of these questions let me lay out some structural features of toleration on which (most) contemporary theorists agree. As we will see in subsequent chapters, disagreement about the interpretation of some of these features marks out distinct conceptions of toleration, and different theories of toleration can help-fully be seen as offering divergent interpretations of various of these features. The six essential structural features of toleration are as follows:[51]

1   *Difference*: what is tolerated differs from the tolerator's conception of what should be done, valued, or believed.
2   *Importance*: what is tolerated by the tolerator is not trivial to her.
3   *Opposition*: the tolerator disapproves of and/or dislikes what she tolerates, and is *ipso facto* disposed to act so as to alter or suppress what she opposes.
4   *Power*: the tolerator believes herself to have the power to alter or suppress what is tolerated.
5   *Non-rejection*: the tolerator does not exercise this power.
6   *Requirement*: toleration is right and/or expedient, and the tolerator is virtuous, and/or just, and/or prudent.

Features (1)–(4) lay out the circumstances of toleration; that is, the conditions in which it is meaningful to describe one agent as tolerant of another. The first (1) states an obvious condition of toleration: unless a person, group, or practice differs from me, I cannot be said to tolerate them or it. There is no sense to be made of the idea of tolerating oneself (beyond understanding this idea in terms of hyperbolic expression of self-loathing, or lethargy) because of the truth of (1): everyone is self-identical, in which case no one can tolerate herself.

With respect to (2), we only tolerate what we take to be important or signifi-cant; what we take to be unimportant or insignificant we simply ignore, if indeed it succeeds in registering with us at all. Many problems in the practice of toleration arise because of a divergence of opinion on the importance of a feature or practice between a tolerator and the person she tolerates; a practice that is of deep significance to a tolerator can mean little to those who engage in it, and this causes yet more friction between them, in addition to the fact of difference stated in (1). For example, take the issue of Sunday shopping. To the devout, this practice violates the sanctity of the day of worship and risks infecting other areas of life with a godless consumerism. However, to Sunday shoppers, the fact that shops are open is merely convenient, and such conve-nience is something they mildly approve of, if they think about it at all. The Sunday shoppers differ from the devout on this question on the axes of content and quality of belief: they believe that Sunday shopping should be permitted, but most of them do not burn with the fire of conviction on this issue.

Turning to (3), it must be the case that the tolerator is opposed to what she tolerates, and this opposition can take the form of dislike and/or disapproval. That toleration is a response to opposed differences explains why, in the example given above, we would only describe the devout as being in a position to tolerate the Sunday shoppers, and not *vice versa*, because only the devout have deep and strong views on the value of Sunday shopping. The Sunday shoppers' commitments to the value of the convenience of Sunday shopping are too weak, in most cases, to generate disapproval or dislike of the devout; instead, most Sunday shoppers are simply indifferent to the protestations of the devout. The question of whether toleration is best understood just as a response to disliked differences, or as a response to disliked and/or disapproved of differences may seem of little consequence, as both dislike and disapproval are ways of being opposed to something, and it is this that really matters for toleration. However, as we will see in chapter 2, this is not the case: a great deal hangs on the question of the nature of the opposition which serves as a condition for toleration, and different conceptions of toleration are generated according to the account of opposition offered. For the time being, however, I shall simply use the generic term 'opposition' to describe this circumstance of toleration.

Features (4) and (5) relate to the control the tolerator believes herself capable of exercising over what she tolerates: (4) states a circumstance of toleration, and (5) describes the tolerator's reaction to it. A person's first impulse when confronted with something she is opposed to is to attempt to rid herself of it, to remove it from her experience. In some cases, a person will know that she lacks the power to do this: in that case, her failure to intervene to eradicate what she is opposed to cannot be called toleration. Rather, she puts up with what she knows she can do nothing about: prisoners do not tolerate their guards, or slaves their masters. However, when a person does believe herself to have the power to make at least some headway in eradicating what she is opposed to, then she is in a position to tolerate it. If she does not exercise this power (on principled grounds), then she tolerates what she opposes. Taking the example of Sunday shopping again, if a small group of devout people in a secular society believe that, whatever they do, they will never defeat the drift to an ever-increasing consumerism, then in not lobbying against Sunday shopping they are not thereby tolerating it: rather, they have resigned themselves to it. In contrast, if the same group believes that making sufficiently large donations to a political party will translate into that party's allegiance to their cause, and yet does not make these donations, then the group tolerates Sunday shopping, given that the other conditions for toleration are satisfied.

The final aspect of toleration in (6) reflects a schism in the history of theorising about why toleration is required. On some accounts, toleration is required because the alternative to toleration is war, and war is too costly – in all sorts of ways – as a method for negotiating disputes and disagreements. On this view, toleration is a practical strategy to be adopted by wise and canny people who realise that the attempt to convert all others to their cause can never succeed: the tolerant person is prudent. A parallel strand of interpretation has it that toleration is morally required: the tolerant person is virtuous, and/or the tolerant state is just. These two views of toleration can be held in tandem, because there is no reason to think that the counsels of prudence and the laws of morality must always pull in different directions. However, it is always possible that they might pull in different directions such that what prudence dictates is what morality disallows, which is why the two interpretations are best kept apart. For instance, if a person previously limited in her power over others suddenly gains much more power then prudence might dictate that she no longer tolerate people she hitherto restrained herself from interfering with. However, if toleration is a moral requirement then arguably the requirement that she continue to tolerate these people remains in place even when her power increases. The question of whether toleration is a moral or a prudential requirement cannot be answered until the question of whether toleration responds to disliked differences, or disliked and/or disapproved-of differences, has been addressed in chapter 2. For that reason, I shall refer here simply to the 'requirement' of toleration.

The approaches to toleration to be discussed in what follows start by offering different accounts of its structural features, and thence different accounts of its limits. It is notable that all these approaches lie within the purview of liberalism, broadly conceived. Along with freedom and equality, toleration is one of the great values associated with the liberal tradition in political philosophy. From Locke onwards, liberals have agreed that, whatever else the state ought to do, it ought to enforce political principles of toleration. What marks out the liberal conception of toleration from non-liberal conceptions is its aspiration to inclusivity: liberals aim to defend principles and practices of toleration which permit as wide a range as possible of lifestyles, communities, and practices to coexist. What makes toleration so central to liberal conceptions of justice is that such conceptions acknowledge the fact of pluralism, that is, the fact that it can be legitimate for people to differ on questions of value, religion, morality, politics, and the good. This makes toleration an indispensable part of ideal liberal political practice. However, the liberal commitment to toleration, as just stated, is very thin: without further specification of what toleration demands and how it is to be understood, this commitment gives no practical guidance whatsoever.

This book addresses different conceptions of the theory and practice of toleration in the contemporary philosophical literature. It examines the roots of liberal thinking about toleration in different conceptions of pluralism, explores contemporary philosophical debates about the justification and the value of toleration, and explores how these philosophical controversies have mapped on to some recent real world examples of problems in the practice of toleration. Although the book aims to provide an introduction to the dominant ways that toleration can be theorised and its practice defended, and to indicate the most important philosophical and practical challenges to these theories, it also mounts an argument for one particular approach to toleration (the 'reasonableness defence') along the way. The practical challenges to toleration laid out in Part II are presented in part as challenges to the reasonableness defence argued for in Part I; however, the discussion in Part II stands free of the reasonableness defence and is thus accessible to those who do not follow me in taking this approach to be the best bet for the defence of toleration on the contemporary scene.

The need for toleration has not disappeared; far from it. The fact that political and military power is concentrated in fewer hands than it ever was makes the call to toleration more insistent, more urgent. Political theory by itself can never solve real world political problems. But unless defenders of toleration have some good arguments to show why we should be tolerant, and a proper understanding of the implications and costs of making those arguments, then any hope that real world problems will be dealt with through the use of reason and argument rather than force is doomed. And whatever else is true of democrats, they have always preferred the debating chamber to the sword.

Chapter 2

Opposition and restraint

The peak of tolerance is most readily achieved by those who are not burdened with convictions.

(Alexander Chase)

Introduction

In chapter 1 I laid out six structural features of toleration, on which contemporary theorists are agreed. These are: (1) difference, (2) importance, (3) opposition, (4) power, (5) non-rejection, and (6) requirement. When a situation is characterised by (1)–(4), toleration is possible. Toleration can only be required in response to features of situations or persons to which the tolerator is opposed in significant ways, which the tolerator believes herself to have the power to alter, suppress, or eradicate, and which the tolerator – as a result of all this – is disposed to interfere with so as to alter, suppress, or eradicate. The question of when, exactly, toleration is required (that is, the question of when, exactly, a person ought not to act on the disposition just mentioned) will depend on the details of the situation. I postpone discussion of this question until Part II, where different situations exhibiting features (1)–(4) will be considered as a way of exploring the limits of toleration. Discussion in this chapter will continue to focus only on the question of what toleration is, rather than on the question of what ought to be tolerated.

In what follows I survey some interpretations of one key circumstance of toleration, and their consequences for our understanding of toleration and the theoretical challenges that any account of it has to face. This circumstance is opposition: in order to be tolerant of something a person must be opposed to it. I shall consider three interpretations of the nature of opposition. First, the 'weak' interpretation allows that toleration can be a response both to disapproved-of differences *and* to disliked differences; however, this interpretation has some unpalatable consequences for our understanding of what it is to be a tolerant person. In contrast, and second, the 'strong' interpretation has it that toleration is properly thought of as simply a response to differences evaluatively disapproved of by the tolerator. However, in giving an account of what constitutes evaluative disapproval that does not generate the counter-intuitive consequences of the weak interpretation, the strong interpretation creates a notorious (but putative) paradox of toleration. According to this paradox, what the requirement to be tolerant demands is impossible to deliver: making evaluative disapproval one of the circumstances of toleration means that toleration is never appropriate.

A third approach – the 'wide' interpretation – takes a different tack. Here, the claim is that the 'cut' between dislike and disapproval is the wrong one for the characterisation of opposition; rather, toleration should be thought of as a response to judgements of dislike or disapproval for which the tolerator takes responsibility, and thereby genuinely takes to be justified. This interpretation of opposition *prima facie* has significant advantages over the other two accounts insofar as it avoids some of the counter-intuitive consequences of the weak interpretation, and the intractable form of the putative paradox generated by the strong interpretation. However, as we will see, to be convincing the wide interpretation must be backed up by a full account of what it is about the commitments that ground opposition that makes them suitable as one of the circumstances of toleration. That is, the wide interpretation must be accompanied by an account of why it is that commitments informing opposition for which a person takes responsibility nevertheless ought not to be acted upon by that person in the name of toleration. What is needed is an account of the status and nature of these commitments such that a wedge can be driven between a person taking these commitments to be justified and taking other-regarding intolerant action in the name of these commitments to be justified. What requires explanation, on the wide interpretation, is how it can be possible for a person opposed to others on the grounds of commitments she genuinely takes to be justified nevertheless to reject as unjustified (on principle) the other-regarding action *prima facie* demanded by these commitments. If such an account is available then the tension between having the commitments constitutive of opposition, and overruling the practical demands of these commitments so as to practice toleration, is resolved. Presenting the central challenge to any account of toleration in this way explains why the major contemporary theorists of toleration have attempted to justify its practice by reference to scepticism about values, reflections on the nature of pluralism, and analyses of the requirements of reasonableness. Each of these theories provides the focus for the three chapters subsequent to this one. For the moment let me give a fuller account of the three interpretations of opposition just sketched.

Toleration and opposition: the weak interpretation

According to the weak interpretation of opposition as a circumstance of toleration, a person is tolerant when she refrains on principle from acting on her disposition to oppress or interfere with another person or group in order to prevent them from engaging in practices or exhibiting properties which she dislikes *and/or* of which she disapproves. The key difference between the weak and the strong interpretations of opposition is that the former includes dislike as a possible circumstance of toleration, whereas the latter excludes it: the weak interpretation thereby allows for a wider range of cases of restraint in the presence of opposition to be accurately described as cases of toleration. For example, according to the weak interpretation, a person is tolerant when she refrains on principled grounds from acting on her most deeply held religious beliefs in order to prevent, say, the legalisation of homosexual adoption; but she is also properly described as tolerant if she refrains (on principle) from lobbying for compulsory elocution lessons for Yorkshiremen, given her aversion to the Yorkshire accent. Questions related to the interpretation of opposition simply in terms of evaluative disapproval will be addressed in the next section. For now, the focus will be on the stipulation that dislike can provide a circumstance of toleration.

On the weak interpretation the circumstances of toleration can include dislike as well as disapproval. We might think that not much hangs on the question of whether toleration responds only to evaluative disapproval, or to disapproval and dislike. Indeed, we might think that putting up with things one dislikes is a paradigm case of toleration. Consider, for example, the putative instances of toleration described by Mary Warnock in the following passage.

> I am tolerant if one of my daughter's boy-friends wears sandals with his suit or a stock with his tweed coat, and I not only make no mention of this outrage, but actually express myself pleased when they announce their intention of getting married. I am exercising the virtue of toleration if I am still on good terms with my son, though when he stays in the house I can never clear the breakfast before lunchtime, nor be certain that there is any whisky left in the bottle for when the Chancellor calls.[1]

It might strike us that Warnock's restraint in these circumstances shows her to be an exemplary tolerator: toleration involves putting up with things one dislikes for the sake of greater values or rewards (in Warnock's case, presumably, continued good relations with her daughter and son). However, allowing dislike *per se* to be a form of opposition to which toleration can be properly said to respond has the following two counter-intuitive consequences which should dilute any initial enthusiasm for the weak interpretation.

The first consequence is related to the fact that not all dislikes are as benign as those in Warnock's example. If the circumstances of toleration are understood to include disliked differences then people who dislike different others out of sheer prejudice or mindless hatred, but who refrain from acting on their prejudice or hatred for whatever (principled) reason when they believe they have the power to do so, will count as tolerant.[2] Consider a rabid racist who hates non-whites, but restrains himself when it comes to discrimination and violence against them. His reasons for restraint might be that his Grand Wizard has decreed that the time is not yet ripe for the exercise of white power to successfully and finally expel and eliminate all non-whites,[3] that he doesn't want to upset the delicate sensibilities of his ageing mother, or that he believes that the best way to subvert the liberal egalitarian political zeitgeist is from the inside by presenting racist policies in the manifesto of a legitimate political party (such as the British National Party) whose members can gain access to public office via success at the ballot box. According to the weak interpretation as we have it so far, this rabid racist – whatever his reasons for restraint – is properly and accurately described as tolerant.

Some people accept this consequence: anyone who exercises principled self-restraint with respect to action expressive of their strong feelings of dislike for others is tolerant, even if we think that the grounds for their dislike are unjustified, mistaken, or reprehensible. Note, however, that this is not to say that *every* inactive racist qualifies as tolerant. For example, a racist who does not join a lynch mob because he is too lazy and apathetic to leave the house is not tolerant; rather, he just can't be bothered. But the racist described in the last paragraph is not like this; rather, he exercises self-restraint with respect to his dispositions to oppress non-whites on the grounds of his commitment to some other principle (respectively, in the examples given above, obedience to a revered leader, respect for the feelings of a loved mother, and commitment – moral and/or prudential – to democratic decision-making procedures as a way of achieving nefarious political goals). This principled restraint – regardless of the contents of the principle – is sufficient for toleration, on the weak interpretation. In that case, the weak interpretation allows that toleration can be a morally neutral disposition or character trait: to say of a person that she is tolerant is not necessarily to praise her morally, for the grounds of the opposition to which her toleration is a response (and, indeed, the principles according to which she exercises restraint) may themselves be morally objectionable, as in the case of the racist given above.

However, a second consequence of this characterisation of toleration as morally neutral stretches the intuitions of some people to breaking point. Consider again our racist. Imagine that this person is introduced, through his racist friends, to members of far-right political groups, who not only hate blacks, but also Jews and homosexuals. By association with these people the racist acquires some more prejudices: he becomes anti-semitic and homophobic in addition to being racist. However, again, he does not get involved in the production of anti-semitic literature, or go on gay-bashing excursions with his new-found friends, again, for any number of possible (principled) reasons. On the account of toleration as morally neutral, a racist who acquires new prejudices which he refrains from acting upon thereby becomes *more* tolerant, regardless of the content of the principles from which his reasons for restraint are derived.[4] Is this an acceptable conclusion?

There are at least two ways to respond to this example. First, we might simply bite the bullet and insist that the rabid racist who restrains himself, for whatever principled reason, is indeed tolerant and, furthermore, is less tolerant than a rabid racist who is also anti-semitic and homophobic but exercises restraint, regardless of his principled reasons. On this account, toleration is a morally neutral method for negotiating conflict – regardless of what the conflict is about or which party is in the right – as opposed to a virtue, and the principles according to which toleration is practised need not be moral principles, or be morally acceptable. Here, toleration mediates hostilities to ensure a degree of peace between the parties who oppose one another.

The characterisation of toleration as morally neutral means that there are two grounds on which to question the coherence of the idea of a tolerant racist: (1) that his beliefs, preferences, and desires are morally obnoxious; and (2) that the principles which govern his disposition to act on these beliefs, preferences and desires are morally obnoxious. With respect to (2), the objection is that only a person whose self-restraint is rooted in moral principles can qualify as tolerant. In order to cash out this objection much would have to be said about what makes principles moral (as opposed, say, to prudential), and what makes them morally acceptable. But even granting the existence of acceptable accounts addressing these issues, there remains a further (and, I think, more fundamental) objection as follows. Even when self-restraint is rooted in morally acceptable principles – such as respect for a sensitive mother – this is still insufficient for toleration because what the restraint responds to is morally unacceptable. Thus, and with respect to (1), the objection is that toleration is a virtue which cannot be exhibited by someone in virtue of their morally obnoxious oppositions to others.

Every decent person agrees that a racist ought not to act upon his prejudices, and that racists have a moral obligation to exercise restraint with respect to their obnoxious preferences. However, the question is not whether people *ought or ought not to act on their prejudices*; the question is whether we *accurately describe* people who refrain from acting on their prejudices *as tolerant*. One reason why we might balk at such a description is that we think of toleration as a virtue, and consequently we think of tolerant people as virtuous. In that case, it jars to claim that people with racist prejudices who exercise self-restraint with respect to these prejudices – even when this restraint is rooted in morally acceptable principles – are thereby virtuous, and can become more virtuous by acquiring more prejudices and exercising similarly principled self-restraint with respect to these new prejudices. Rather than heaping moral praise on such people by calling them tolerant, we ought to require not only that they refrain (on morally acceptable principled grounds) from acting on their prejudices but, further, that they rid themselves of these prejudices altogether in the name of toleration. This explains Peter Nicholson's remarks that:

> Toleration is not a second best, a necessary evil, a putting up with what we have to for the sake of peace and quiet, but a positive good, a virtue distinctive of the best people and the best societies.[5]

Nicholson's point here is that we ought not to think of toleration as a remedial virtue required of morally flawed people because we cannot expect any better of them, either in terms of the oppositions they have to others, or in terms of the principles – if such they have – that govern their disposition to act on these oppositions. Rather, in his view, the virtue of toleration is a mark of moral excellence possessed by persons whose other features do not qualify them as morally vicious.

If we think of toleration as a virtue, then it can seem that the way forward is to insist that the opposition to which toleration responds is evaluative disapproval: the tolerator is a person who has a genuine evaluative objection to what she tolerates and does not act upon it, and to restrain oneself on principled grounds with respect to one's evaluative objections to others is – within limits – virtuous. Let us turn now to this view of toleration and its problems.

Toleration and opposition: the strong interpretation

According to the strong interpretation of opposition as a circumstance of toleration, a person is tolerant when she refrains on principled grounds from acting on her disposition to oppress or interfere with another person or group in order to prevent them from engaging in practices or exhibiting properties of which she evaluatively disapproves. Nicholson draws on the strong account in his definition of toleration in terms of moral disapproval:

> toleration is the virtue of refraining from exercising one's power to interfere with others' opinion or action although that deviates from one's own over something morally important and although one morally disapproves of it.[6]

If this interpretation is to avoid the counter-intuitive consequences of the weak interpretation then it must be possible to distinguish evaluative disapproval from dislike. Consequently, one way to nip the strong interpretation in the bud would be to deny that any meaningful distinction can be made between dislike and disapproval. Taking moral disapproval as an example of the evaluative judgements to which this interpretation refers, consider Warnock's rejection of the distinction:

> I simply do not believe that a distinction can be drawn . . . between the moral and the non-moral, resting on the presumption that the moral is rational, or subject to argument, the non-moral a matter of feeling or sentiment. So far is this from being true that the concept of morality itself would wither away and become lost in the concept of expediency if strong feelings or sentiment were not involved in the judgement that something is morally right or wrong.[7]

Warnock's point is not simply that most, if not all, moral judgements are attended by strong emotions and feelings. Rather, her point is that part of what it is to make a moral judgement is to experience a certain feeling of opposition or an emotion of disgust etc. towards what is judged to be morally unacceptable. Without this, she thinks, moral judgements would cease to matter to us in the way that they do; without this, our moral judgements would be a matter of making cool calculations and assessments to which we would feel no particular attachment. Warnock thinks that this picture of moral judgement is alien to human beings.

If Warnock is right, and if her comments about moral disapproval generalise to all forms of evaluative disapproval, then the strong interpretation cannot get off the ground. However, even if emotional reactions are partially constitutive of evaluative disapproval, it is still the case that evaluative disapproval differs from *mere* dislike. In which case we still need an account of what marks the difference between moral disapproval and mere dislike.

Prima facie, one promising strategy is to focus on the form, as opposed to the content, of any instance of opposition serving as a candidate for evaluative disapproval.[8] We might think that what makes a judgement an evaluative judgement is that it must be possible to state the judgement in such a way that it can become a matter of *public dispute* between the judger and anyone who disagrees with her. This does not mean that the judgement of opposition ever has to be actually stated in this way; rather, the requirement is that it must be possible to state the judgement such that it can be used as a public criticism of those to whom it applies, against which they can attempt to defend themselves. So understood, there are many types of evaluative judgements. For example, the moral judgement that persons ought always to keep their promises, the aesthetic judgement that Beethoven was a better composer than Brahms, the teleological judgement that boats ought to float and helicopters hover, and the customary British judgement that queue jumping is unacceptable.

Let us take some examples to make this clearer. Consider two statements that a person P is willing to state in public: (A) 'I find strawberry ice cream so much tastier than vanilla ice cream', and (B) 'I believe that a woman's place is in the home.' Imagine that P states (A) at the end of a dinner party, having just polished off a dish of strawberry ice cream. The hostess replies, 'You know, I disagree. I find vanilla to be much nicer. I really should have served that instead.' How is P likely to respond to her hostess? Is she likely to say: 'No, no, I must dissent. You are wrong about how tasty I find strawberry ice cream, and here's why . . . '? What could she offer by way of an argument to establish that her experience of strawberry ice cream as more tasty than vanilla ought to be shared by her hostess, who has made some kind of mistake in her experience of vanilla as nicer than strawberry? What could she latch on to in what her hostess said in order to refute her hostess' statement? P is far more likely just to say: 'Well, there you go. It's all a matter of taste', and move on to a more interesting topic.[9]

In contrast, consider P, again at the end of a dinner party, stating the following to her hostess: 'That was a magnificent meal – you're a fantastic cook. I'm so glad that you share my view that a woman's place is in the home.' The hostess replies: 'I didn't cook this – my husband did – and my place is not in the home. My place is in the market, earning a better wage than him, doing a harder job, and getting less credit for it, thanks to people like you.' Sensing her *faux pas*, P may respond by saying, 'Well, it's all a matter of taste', and quickly change the topic. But if P is bolshy she may say, 'Your resentment of how little praise you get for doing your job shows that it makes you unhappy. You would be far happier staying at home, as I do. It's just in a woman's nature to be a carer; we've evolved that way. You'll never get real satisfaction from being a wage slave.' Or she might say, 'Well, I'm sorry you disagree, but according to my religion a woman has a role, and it's to stay at home.' Or perhaps, 'Well, you must be the last feminist in London. Do you really still buy all that bullshit about burning bras?' The point here is that P could back up her judgement (B) with any number of statements which purport to do more than simply express her feelings about the question: she could invoke some cod evolutionary psychology, religious doctrine, or attack the feminism she takes to be implicit in her hostess' objection.

In sum, the proposal is that dislike should be distinguished from evaluative disapproval because judgements constitutive of the latter can be disputed by reference to arguments, stories, or claims which do more than simply restate the facts of the disagreement and, rather, function as grounds for the judgement that are putatively independent of any person's opinion of the judgement, or of them. In contrast, judgements of dislike lack such support. Instead, a judgement of dislike is an expression of a person's feelings or tastes, and these are not the sorts of things about which people can disagree without either in some way simply restating their disagreement, or invoking grounds for the dislike which do not purport to be objective.

With this account in hand we can assess whether the strong interpretation avoids the problems of the tolerant racist that beset the weak interpretation. Does this purely formal description of what constitutes a judgement of evaluative disapproval disqualify racist etc. statements of opposition as cases of evaluative disapproval, and so rule out the possibility of tolerant racists?

It does not. It is true that many racists, homophobes, and anti-semites are motivated by mindless hatred of, and sheer feelings of disgust with respect to, non-whites, gays, and Jews. However, not all – perhaps, not most – racists etc. hold their views in this way. Many anti-semites have elaborate theories about the genetic inferiority of Jews, or stories about the existence of a world-wide Zionistic conspiracy to manipulate power to the advantage of Jews and disadvantage of non-Jews: witness Hitler's eugenics programme, and the doctrines of many far-right, neo-fascist groups.[10] Many racists have developed accounts of the physical and mental limitations of non-whites, or of the great social benefits of segregation: witness Richard Herrnstein and Charles Murray's book, *The Bell Curve: Intelligence and Class Structure in American Life*, in which they claim that black people are genetically inferior to white people, as illustrated by their lower IQs.[11] And many homophobes appeal to religious convictions, or to the 'findings' of evolutionary psychology, to establish that homosexuality is an aberration, or is abnormal:[12] witness Louis Farrakhan's statement in a 1997 speech in Boston that, 'it seems like being gay or whatever sin you wish to be a part of is okay . . . but I have the duty to lift that gay person up to the standard to ask if they want to live the life that God wants them to or live the lifestyle that they want to live'.[13] When racists etc. of this type express opposition to non-whites etc., they do more than express disgust for members of the group they oppose; and sometimes, when they appeal to science to support their views, they do not express disgust or similar feelings at all. Rather, they appeal to arguments, stories, or claims about which people can disagree, and which purport to be objective. In other words, their judgements take the form of evaluative judgments, and the opposition they express counts as evaluative disapproval, given the proposal just considered. In that case, just as we found in the weak interpretation, the strong interpretation as we have it so far entails that a rabid but (on principle) self-restraining racist can count as tolerant, and can become more tolerant by acquiring more prejudices and not acting upon them on principled grounds, so long as his judgements can be backed up with publicly disputable and putatively objective arguments, stories, or claims. So far, the strong interpretation is no improvement on the weak interpretation.

One way forward is with the claim that what makes a judgement evaluative is a matter not just of its form, but also of its content. It might be argued that not only must it be possible for a judgement to become the subject of public dispute but that, furthermore, the judgement – and the stories, arguments, and claims which support it – must be *justified*. This qualification rules out the judgments of racists etc. as instances of evaluative disapproval because these judgements – and the stories, claims, and arguments associated with them – are not justified. In that case, in virtue of their unjustified beliefs, racists etc. can never qualify as tolerant, and the status of toleration as a virtue is safe. The conclusion we should reach is that racists etc. ought to abandon their unjustified opposition to those they hate, along with the spurious grounds they cite in support of this opposition.

This certainly avoids the problem of the tolerant racist, but the solution carries a high price for any defender of toleration by giving rise to a strong version of a notorious 'paradox of toleration'. D.D. Raphael takes moral disapproval to be the type of evaluative disapproval to which toleration responds, and he characterises judgements of moral disapproval as justified when they conform to the 'principle of respect for persons'. Given his characterisation, he describes the paradox of toleration as follows:

> If toleration implies moral disapproval of what you tolerate, and if the criterion of moral approval is conformity to the principle of respect for persons, then toleration presupposes that what you tolerate does not conform to the principle of respect for persons. But on the other hand, so it is suggested, we ought not to tolerate whatever contravenes the principle of respect for persons. Then how can there be toleration at all? We cannot, as a matter of logic, tolerate anything unless it goes against respect for persons, and yet we ought not to tolerate anything which does that.[14]

The revised criteria for evaluative disapproval relate both to the form and to the content of a statement: the statement must be publicly disputable, and be justified (in Raphael's case, by conforming to the moral principle of respect for persons).[15] Any judgement that satisfies these criteria is an instance of evaluative disapproval, and this generates the putative paradox as follows: (a) what is disapproved of must be deserving of evaluative disapproval, otherwise the judgement – which is justified – would not oppose it; (b) but if something deserves evaluative disapproval, then it is morally wrong (or otherwise evaluatively flawed), and so deserves opposition; (c) in that case, it ought not to be tolerated. The problem for this strategy is that the only people who qualify as potential tolerators – those whose judgements are justified – are people who ought not to tolerate those they oppose through these judgements. The strategy lays down such stringent conditions for the possibility of toleration in its account of opposition that it appears to leave no room for the practice of toleration. On this account, a person who tolerates others who are genuinely deserving of evaluative disapproval is not virtuous, but rather objectionably permissive of their evaluatively unacceptable behaviour.[16]

Any interpretation of opposition that makes it a requirement that evaluative judgements are justified (or true) in order for them to provide the circumstances of toleration will face an intractable version of the paradox of toleration insofar as it follows from the fact that a judgement is justified that it ought not to be acted upon (by the agent or her representatives). But herein lies a problem with respect to the generation of the putative paradox: the judgement that x is deserving of evaluative disapproval does not entail the judgement that the judger, or her representatives, ought to coercively enforce the judgement of evaluative disapproval. The tight connection between judgements of disapproval and action upon them from which the paradox emerges only holds for moral fanatics and fundamentalists, for whom every moral judgement is an overriding practical imperative. For the rest of us, the connection is often not so strong, and certainly not uniform across all our evaluative judgements. If the strong interpretation incorporates an account of evaluative judgement that generates the 'paradox' of toleration then it is a theory about the *impossibility* of toleration, and not the contrary. However, if we eschew this interpretation we need (1) an account of what makes it possible for us to make genuine judgements of evaluative disapproval without judging that those judgements ought to be coercively enforced by ourselves or our representatives. This makes it possible for us to consider (2) which evaluative judgements ought to be so coercively enforced. In the next section I address (1) by modifying the strong interpretation in what I call the 'wide' interpretation; different answers to (2) focusing on features shared by all judgements that ought not to be coercively enforced will be addressed in chapters 3, 4 and 5; and in Part II I address some real world problems of toleration arising from particular substantial judgements possessing these features.

Toleration and opposition: the wide interpretation

The challenge now is to find a characterisation of the opposition to which toleration responds which creates space for its practice by permitting that not all judgements of opposition have the imperatival force that created the intractable version of the paradox of toleration, but which avoids the problem of the tolerant racist which besets the weak interpretation. The best way to start is to reject the cut between dislike and disapproval in the debate about what constitutes the right form of opposition for toleration. What matters is not whether opposition is constituted by dislike and disapproval *per se*; rather, what matters is the way in which the potential tolerator makes her judgements of dislike or disapproval, which reflects the extent to which we think she genuinely takes these judgements to be justified. This differs from the weak interpretation by stipulating that the tolerator must take her opposition to be justified by taking responsibility for the judgements constitutive of it: the weak interpretation, remember, allowed that any dislike could serve as a circumstance of toleration, whatever its genesis and however it figures in a person's network of other beliefs and commitments. And it differs from the strong interpretation by stipulating that (a) dislike can be a form of opposition to which toleration responds, and (b) that a tolerator must (as I shall argue) take responsibility for her judgements of opposition, and to that extent show that she genuinely takes these judgements to be justified, which is weaker than the requirement that the opposition *actually be* justified. On this account, a person is tolerant when she refrains on principled grounds from acting on her disposition to oppress or inter-fere with another person or group in order to prevent them from engaging in practices or exhibiting properties to which she is responsibly opposed.[17] Before considering how this interpretation fares when faced with the problems encoun-tered by the weak and strong interpretations, let me say some more about what is involved in the idea of responsible opposition, and why this makes the wide interpretation more attractive than the strong and weak interpretations.

The best way into these questions is via examples. Consider two people who share the belief that homosexuals ought not to be permitted to marry in civil law. The first person, Anna, is a devout and practising Roman Catholic. Anna believes that homosexuality is a sin – an offence against God – and she cites what she takes to be biblical evidence for this. She has attended discussion groups in which homosexual Catholics made their case for the recognition of same sex marriage in the church and in law, and keeps up on the political debate in the media. Anna's belief about the sinfulness of homosexuality supports her belief that the Catholic Church should not sanction same sex marriage. Given that part of Anna's faith also includes a concern for the spiri-tual well-being of others, she is not only opposed to same sex marriage within her church, but also in civil law, for she believes that to permit same sex marriage in law is tantamount to state encouragement of spiritual degradation. However, although Anna lobbies against movements within the church supportive of homosexual marriage, she does not do so with respect to similar movements in civil society, even though such movements are well organized and have won some important political battles in the past. Anna's reasons for avoiding such engagement are that she believes that the best route to spiritual salvation for those outside of the church is a completely free and independent acceptance of the church's moral authority. She abhors homosexuality out of concern for the souls of the sinners who practice it, but she believes that enforcing spiritual purity using law would not increase the likelihood that such sinners would turn to God. So, the best Anna can do, in her eyes, is to hope that the good example of those within the church rubs off on those outside of it, and leads them to change their ways.

Now consider Betty, who is also opposed to homosexual marriage in law. Betty's opposition originates not in religious belief, but in her upbringing in a male-dominated, macho culture. In her formative years Betty was surrounded by people at home and school who, as a matter of course, would use homophobic terms of abuse against one another, and where being subject to one of these taunts was taken by everyone she knew to be sufficient grounds for an attack on the victim. When Betty reached university she shared a house with psychology students, who told her about a theory which, they claimed, established that homosexuality 'goes against nature' because homosexual unions are infertile and do not permit those in them to achieve genetic survival. This information stayed with Betty, and seemed to her to confirm everything she already knew about homosexuality. This prompted Betty to get involved in groups lobbying against homosexual marriage. However, after a while, Betty decided that it was best for her not to lobby against homosexual marriage because – if the theory that had so impressed her was true – then permitting homosexuals to marry would allow them to pair off with one another and not infect the heterosexual gene pool with their defective genes. Hard as it was for her, given her disgust for homosexuals and their lifestyles, Betty kept her mouth shut when the issue came up in the pub, and crossed the street when anti-gay marriage protestors approached her with petitions to sign (although she could not bring herself to sign petitions put up by the gay lobby supporting homosexual marriage).

Anna and Betty are similar in many respects. For both of them, their opposi-tion to same sex marriage is important, they both believe themselves to have the power to influence the law so as to prevent this practice, and they are both disposed to interfere with – or to empower their representatives to interfere with – homosexual practices so as to prevent them, *ceteris paribus*. But *ceteris* is not *paribus*, because each of them reins in her disposition to interfere on the (consequentialist) principled grounds that the aim they share of eradicating homosexual unions will be best achieved by such action. However, would we want to claim that Anna and Betty are both, or equally, tolerant?

Intuitively, I think that even if we would want to claim that Anna and Betty are both tolerant, we would want to claim that Anna is more tolerant than Betty. How are we to explain this intuition?[18] The weak interpretation lacks the resources for such an explanation: that Anna's opposition might be said to be a clearer case of evaluative (in this case, moral) disapproval than Betty's opposi-tion makes no difference to the candidacy of each as a tolerator. The strong interpretation is also inadequate here: if either Anna's or Betty's opposition is a genuine case of moral disapproval (and so a justified form of evaluative disap-proval) then in failing to act on this opposition they are morally lax rather than tolerant. And if their oppositions are not genuine cases of moral disapproval then they ought to rid themselves of their oppositions to homosexuality altogether.

In contrast, the wide interpretation offers an explanation of why we might think that Anna is more tolerant than Betty. This is that Anna takes responsibility for her opposition to same sex marriage in such a way that we are willing to believe that she genuinely takes this opposition to be justified. In contrast, Betty's opposition is not grounded in judgements for which we think she has taken responsibility, and so we are less willing to believe that she genuinely takes this opposition to be justified. Anna has spent time and effort reading the Bible and consulting books on theology to attempt to settle the matter for herself. Betty, however, is opposed to homosexual marriage as a consequence of having been brought up in a homophobic environment. It was not until she reached adulthood that Betty stumbled across the cod theory that she took to be fit to support her opposition, and even then she made no effort to find out more about it. The difference between Anna and Betty, according to the wide interpretation, is in our assessments of the responsibility each takes for the judgements of opposition each makes, which makes a difference to how genuine we believe each of them to be in their claims to take their opposition to be justified. We are willing to believe Anna, but we have our doubts about Betty. (Note, however, that this is not to say that we are doubtful of Betty's *sincerity* in claiming to take her oppositional beliefs to be justified. But the genuineness of a belief and the sincerity with which it is held and voiced are distinct.)[19]

What counts as taking responsibility for a belief is unavoidably a matter for delicate judgement on a case by case basis: hard and fast criteria for judging cases are likely to be either too coarse-grained to do the trick, or too stringent to generate the right answers in all cases. However, we can make some general remarks. To take responsibility for one's beliefs is to reflect – and remain willing to reflect – on them through exposure to sources of information and different perspectives which have the potential to alter those beliefs. One way of holding beliefs responsibly is to read and study around their subject matter. However, responsible belief is not the prerogative of academically inclined people: cross-cultural, inter-class, and inter-generational conversation with others, immersion in popular culture, travel,[20] enjoyment of the arts, and experimentation with pleasurable and painful experiences are all forms of experience which can answer the call for responsible belief formation.[21]

It might be objected that these ways of coming to have and hold beliefs are the privilege of the affluent and educated classes. It may well be true that the routes to responsible belief track economic, political, and social advantage (although caution is advisable here: middle-class patronisation of others can easily be taken to be received wisdom by those who so patronise). If this is true, then the wide interpretation entails that economically, politically, and socially disadvantaged people are less likely to be tolerant than members of more advantaged groups. Two reflections are important here. First, that a person is not in a position to exhibit the virtue of toleration does not justify holding that person responsible for this failure. Even if irresponsible belief formation tracks class disadvantage, the wide interpretation does not generate judgements of blame with respect to members of disadvantaged classes who are *ipso facto* not in a position to practise toleration. The same is true, for example, of members of groups who – because of geographical or cultural isolation, or political oppression – do not have access to the routes to responsible belief. Second, if irresponsible belief does indeed track class disadvantage then a political commitment to toleration provides yet further justification (in this case, not related to considerations of equality or distributive justice) for the eradication of class privilege.

To return to Anna and Betty, comparison of them suggests how the wide interpretation might deal with the problem of the tolerant racist that dogs the weak interpretation. On the wide interpretation, mindless thugs who acquire prejudices as a way of making friends and influencing people, or unlucky adolescents brought up in a culture of racism and homophobia who acquire these prejudices in order to satisfy peer pressure, will not count as tolerant on this account, even if they can back up their prejudices with a few dog-eared scraps of spurious theory, or a half-read copy of *Mein Kampf*, and even if they refrain from acting on their prejudices for reasons derived from laudable moral principles, such as that whenever possible one ought not to act so as to upset one's mother. This is because the beliefs of such people are irresponsibly formed and held, and thus we doubt the genuineness of their claims – if they make them at all – to take their oppositions to be justified.

However, the wide interpretation makes it possible that self-restraining racists who take responsibility for their beliefs, and whom we thus judge to be genuine in taking their opposition to be justified, can be tolerant. Furthermore, a little reflection on what is being claimed here softens the counter-intuitiveness of the idea of a tolerant racist as it appears in the weak interpretation. To claim that such a person has the virtue of toleration is not to claim that she is virtuous. That a person possesses one virtue does not establish that she is a good person, as attested to by the phenomenon of honour among thieves. In cases such as those of the tolerant racist, the wide interpretation permits us – *pace* Nicholson[22] – to think of toleration as a remedial virtue. It would be best if racists rid themselves of the prejudices they take to be justified through responsible reflection on their racist beliefs; but such reflection does not guarantee this, and in the meantime their principled restraint qualifies them as tolerant. *Prima facie*, the wide interpretation improves on the weak interpretation by allowing for distinctions between different kinds of racist before recommending a judgement as to whether they are candidate tolerators.[23]

How does the wide interpretation fare with respect to the paradox of toleration as it is faced by the strong interpretation? If advocates of the weak interpretation can offer explanations of why some commitments – racist etc. commitments included – do not automatically generate an obligation to act upon them, or at least are trumped by the obligation of toleration not to act upon them, then the 'paradox' is diluted. The problem that these explanations address is a weaker form of the paradox of toleration, and is nicely laid out by Bernard Williams:

> If we are asking people to be tolerant, we are asking . . . [them] to lose
> something, their desire to suppress or drive out the rival belief; but they will
> also keep something, their commitment to their own beliefs, which is what
> gave them that desire in the first place. There is a tension here between
> one's own commitments and the acceptance that other people may have
> other and perhaps quite distasteful commitments. This is the tension that is
> typical of toleration, and the tension which makes it so difficult.[24]

When a person genuinely takes her opposition to be justified through responsible belief it takes the form of a commitment, and toleration requires that she
does not act upon this commitment. As Williams describes it, this problem is a
tension rather than a paradox, and he is right to say this. There is nothing
formally paradoxical or impossible in the idea of a person having a commitment
and yet not acting upon that commitment. Unlike any account which takes a
judgement to be sound only if it is backed up by an overriding 'ought' (which
makes toleration impossible), this account allows some room for toleration by
opening up space between having a commitment and judging that it ought to
be acted upon.

The wide interpretation improves on the strong interpretation in this respect
by abandoning the cut between dislike and disapproval in its account of opposition. The retention of this cut in the strong interpretation, and its exclusive
focus on judgements of evaluative disapproval, can encourage the thought that
toleration is impossible because judgements of disapproval – especially judgements of moral disapproval – can appear, insofar as they are justified, to
dominate or exclude all other judgements in practical reasoning. Giving a more
diffuse account of opposition discourages this way of thinking about it, thereby
opening up room for the practice of toleration.

What is needed to flesh out this account is an explanation of when a person
with a commitment C which she genuinely takes to be justified through responsible belief ought not to act upon C, and so practise toleration.[25] What is
needed to open up space for toleration is an account of why some commitments
do not generate an obligation to act upon them (or to empower representatives
to act upon them) for the person who has them; or, at least, do not generate an
obligation to act upon them which trumps the obligation not to act upon them
and so to practise toleration.

Importantly, in order to avoid the paradox associated with the strong interpretation, this explanation cannot be that the content of the commitment does
not pass some test of what it is for a commitment to generate a moral obligation. If the explanation takes this form then the space for toleration is closed:
commitments informing opposition either ought to be acted upon, in which
case toleration is inappropriate, or ought not to be acted upon, in which case
opposition ought to be abandoned. As John Horton puts it:

> There are, so to speak, two directions from which toleration can cease to be
> a virtue: on the one hand, some things should not be tolerated, because

they should not be permitted; on the other, some things should not be objected to, hence are not the appropriate objects of toleration.[26]

Conclusion and prospect

The attempt to meet the challenge of opening up space for toleration faced by the wide interpretation motivates the three justifications of liberal toleration that dominate the contemporary philosophical literature to be considered in the next three chapters. Respectively, these accounts draw on scepticism with respect to value, theses of incommensurability, and a characterisation of pluralism as reasonable. The challenge is to find a characterisation of the commitments constitutive of opposition which allows that persons can genuinely take these commitments to be justified through responsible belief and yet accept, with respect to at least some of them, that other-regarding action in line with them is not justified. At this point, we should be optimistic about the prospects for finding such an account. Although we do not yet have a theory of how this is possible, the phenomenon itself appears to surround us: most of us – barring fanatics and fundamentalists – have first-hand experience of standing opposed to other people and their practices and yet at the same time judging that it would be wrong, on principle, to act on this opposition. In brief, the three approaches to be canvassed are as follows.

First, scepticism with respect to value severs the connection between taking a commitment to be justified and taking other-regarding intolerant action demanded by that commitment to be justified, in two ways. First, sceptics might claim that no imposition of the values embedded in such commitments upon unwilling recipients is ever justified because there are no ('universal') values which all people ought to share. *Ipso facto*, intolerant other-regarding action on commitments any person takes to be justified is ruled out, and toleration is required in all cases where people's values and commitments clash. Second, the sceptic might claim that taking a commitment to be justified does not entail or require taking knowledge of it to be certain. This sceptic argues that the appropriate attitude for a person to adopt towards her commitments is doubt, and that this is consistent with her taking these commitments to be justified through responsible belief. If it is true that we ought not to impose on others commitments towards which we ourselves ought to have an attitude of doubt, then toleration is justified.

The second way of understanding the commitments constitutive of opposition so as to flesh out the wide interpretation is in terms of incommensurability. When commitments are incommensurable they cannot be compared or ranked in terms of their value. If some of the commitments constitutive of opposition are incommensurable with commitments to which they are opposed then a person's belief that these commitments are justified does not entail that she ought to impose them on others. When incommensurability holds between commitments in opposition then it is illegitimate to judge one set of commitments to be superior to the other; indeed, it is illegitimate to attempt to compare the sets of commitments in terms of their value at all. If intolerant other-regarding action on the basis of commitments taken by the agent to be justified involves such judgements, then the truth of theses of incommensurability makes toleration appropriate and required whenever the theses are true of commitments that stand opposed. The key to this approach is the suggestion that a person who judges (through responsible belief) her set of commitments to be superior to another set with which they are incommensurable makes a mistake about the nature of these commitments, and the values that inform them.

The final approach gives an interpretation of the commitments constitutive of opposition in terms of their reasonableness. On this view, it is possible for a person to take her own commitments to be justified and oppose others in the light of them while also rejecting as unjustified the imposition of these commitments on others insofar as the disagreement between the person and the others she opposes is reasonable. On this account, persons ought to accept that in conditions of political freedom human reason will naturally operate so as to make disagreement between people on the big questions of morality, religion, politics, and philosophy inevitable, permanent, and not to be regretted. Once a person accepts, say, that those who practise a different religion from hers have reached their conclusions through the correct use of reason – that is, that responsible belief formation and maintenance is possible with respect to a plurality of beliefs which differ in content – then she cannot take the imposition of her own (equally reasonable) commitments on these persons to be justified. On this account, opposition can only justify intolerance towards unreasonable persons and disagreements. Let me now turn to these arguments.

Chapter 3

Toleration from scepticism

> The trouble with the world is that the stupid are cocksure and the intelligent are full of doubt.
>
> (Bertrand Russell)[1]

Introduction

The question addressed by the theories canvassed in this chapter and the next two is: what makes it possible for persons disposed to oppress or interfere with others to whom they are responsibly opposed to practise toleration by not acting on this opposition for principled reasons? More crudely, if opposition is heartfelt and genuine, how and when can toleration with respect to the object of opposition be practised? This chapter considers whether various forms of scepticism establish that toleration is possible and (within limits) required.

The forms of scepticism to be considered here relate only to moral and ethical matters, and can be broadly categorised into three divisions: metaphysical scepticism, pragmatism, and epistemological scepticism. Metaphysical ethical scepticism relates to *what there is*, morally speaking, and what we mean when we talk about what exists in the moral universe. Pragmatism models the nature of moral discourse in terms of *its relation to the ends and purposes* of the collectivities who use it; it also maps the limits of moral discourse by reference to such collective purposes and without recourse to metaphysics. Finally, epistemological scepticism relates to *what we can know* about morality, and the extent to which we can hold our moral beliefs and make our moral judgements with certainty. Arguments for toleration can be mounted on the back of these three forms of scepticism. Let me begin with a few words about metaphysical scepticism.

Metaphysical ethical scepticism can be divided into at least two further camps: subjectivism and relativism. Subjectivist sceptics claim that when we make moral judgements we do no more than express an opinion on the matter of the judgement, or emote with respect to the issue addressed by the judgement.[2] For example, when I state that 'torturing cats is wrong', either I express a belief of the same type as my belief that Rome is a more charming city than Naples, or I give vent to an emotion in the same way as when I swear at my computer for its refusal to obey my instructions. Of course, the subject matter of my judgement that torturing cats is wrong – that is, the torture of cats – matters to me more than the subject matter of my judgement of Rome and Naples (i.e. the comparative attractions of Italian cities), and my insistence to an errant toddler that torturing cats is wrong is more likely to achieve the end aimed at by that judgement (i.e. the cessation of cat-torturing) than will my cursing at my computer (i.e. my computer's complete subjection to my will). Nevertheless, the subjectivist claims, moral judgements are of the same type and perform the same function as expressions of opinion and emotion, albeit that their subject matter is often deemed by the judger to be more significant than that of other expressions of opinion and emotion.

The argument for toleration from subjectivism is as follows. If subjectivism is true then toleration is possible and required because each person ought to recognise that, regardless of how strongly she is opposed to others, and how responsibly she has formed the beliefs constitutive of this opposition, her judgement of opposition is nothing but one opinion or emotional response among many, and that its strength or her genuine conviction that it is justified does not, therefore, legitimise other-regarding intolerant action upon it, either by the agent herself or by her representatives.

In philosophical circles the sceptical argument for toleration from relativism has been far more influential than this argument for toleration from subjectivism, and it is not hard to see why. The argument from subjectivism just laid out is invalid.[3] From the fact (if it is one) that moral judgements do nothing but express a person's opinions and/or emotions nothing follows about whether the person ought to act on those opinions or emotions. If subjectivism is true then the judgement 'people ought to practise toleration' is nothing but an opinion or an emotion which is on the same footing in terms of its authority in practical reasoning as all the judgements of opposition it is supposed to rein in. If subjectivism is true then we have no reason to believe that any putative moral requirement to be tolerant has more imperatival force than any other moral judgement; in fact, if subjectivism is true then we must conclude that such a judgement about the requirement to be tolerant has no more imperatival force than the judgements of opposition it is supposed to overrule. In that case, we cannot move from subjectivism to toleration (or, for that matter, to any other moral requirement). Given this, my focus in the next two sections will be only on arguments for toleration from two forms of relativism: anthropological and philosophical.

The focus of relativism is not on moral language and its uses, but rather on the existence of moral facts and truths, and consequently on the scope and imperatival force of moral judgements.[4] There are many ways to be a relativist, and little can be gained from trying to provide one catch-all definition of relativism. It is more useful to adopt David Wong's suggestion that a relativist can be identified according to whether she rejects one or more of the following propositions:

1   Moral statements have truth values [i.e. moral statements can be true or false].
2   There are good and bad arguments for the moral positions people take.

3   Non-moral facts (states of affairs that obtain in the world and that can be described without the use of moral terms such as 'ought', 'good', and 'right') are relevant to the assessment of the truth value of moral statements.

4   There are moral facts (that may or may not be claimed to be reducible in some way to non-moral facts).

5   When two moral statements conflict as recommendations to action, only one statement can be true.

6   There is a single true morality.[5]

The form of relativism with which I shall mostly be concerned here is that which rejects (6) and, consequently, (5) above; that is, that there is more than one true morality, in which case the statements of opposition made by parties to a moral conflict can both be true even though they require incompatible courses of action. Given this form of relativism, the argument for toleration is as follows. If there is more than one true morality then it is always possible that a person's opposition to others is opposition to a form of life informed by a morality just as true as her own. If that is the case, then regardless of how justified she takes her own moral judgements of opposition to be, and regardless of how responsibly she has formed her beliefs, she cannot infer that it is legitimate for her to act on these judgements so as to interfere with others she opposes. In that case she ought to practise toleration, at least with respect to people whose ways of life are informed by a morality that might be just as true as her own.

In the next two sections I shall work through arguments for toleration from relativism before turning to the arguments from pragmatism in the fourth section and from epistemological scepticism in the fifth. I shall conclude that the prognosis for such sceptical arguments for toleration is not good. The relativistic arguments considered will be shown to be invalid; the pragmatist arguments will be shown to carry very high costs with respect to our allegiance to cherished democratic values; and the argument from epistemological scepticism will be criticised for its underdeveloped account of why doubt with respect to our evaluative beliefs entails toleration, whereas doubt with respect to our non-evaluative beliefs does not. These conclusions open the door to discussion of arguments for toleration from incommensurability in the next chapter.

Anthropologists' relativism

Whereas subjectivism is a view about what we do with moral language, relativism is a view about what there is, morally speaking. Relativism as it is found in and inspired by the work of cultural anthropologists is a view about the scope of moral judgements, statements, prescriptions and principles, which is derived from the observation that moral practices and norms differ enormously across cultures, traditions, and time. This relativism is best understood as an explanation of the views laid out in the last section: that there is more than one true morality and, consequently, that statements of opposition requiring incompatible courses of action can both be true. Anthropologists' relativism starts with the reflection that at no point in history have all people converged in their moral judgements, and that study of the different peoples of the world shows this convergence to be as unlikely as ever. For this reason, it is held to be false that there are any moral terms with universal application: all moral terms have force relative only to the groups who use them.

Some philosophers have objected that this characterisation of relativism is a parody.[6] This may be fair with respect to relativism as it is found in philosophical circles, but it is not fair with respect to anthropological circles. For example, in 1947 the Executive Board of the American Anthropological Association voiced its opposition to the United Nations Universal Declaration of Human Rights on the grounds that application of the universal moral standard of rights to cultures not possessed of the concept of a right violates the integrity of those cultures.[7] Since then, relativism has thrived in anthropological circles (although there is, admittedly, disagreement among anthropologists as to whether relativism ought to be adopted as a methodology for field work, or rather accepted as a truth about the nature of morality).[8] Describing the true project of 'romanticism' (by which he means 'relativism'), Richard A. Shweder writes that,

> the aim of romanticism is to revalue existence, not to denigrate pure being; to dignify subjective experience, not to deny reality; to appreciate the imagination, not to disregard reason; to honor our differences, not to underestimate our common humanity.[9]

According to Shweder, the value of relativism – insofar as it blocks the attempt to use power to interfere with the practices of groups and cultures to which we are opposed – is that it enables us to 'stay on the move between different worlds, and in that way become more complete'.[10] The thought here is that by practising toleration we can expand our horizons and show respect for the subjectivity of others.

It is not my purpose here to evaluate relativism as it is found in anthropology, and it may well be the case that the practice of toleration brings the benefits Shweder identifies. However, that is not to the point. Our question is, rather: does anthropologists' relativism deliver toleration? In order to answer this question we need to lay out with more precision the anthropologists' relativistic argument for toleration, as follows:

1 Anthropology shows that moral principles and practices fundamentally differ across time, place, and culture.
2 Therefore, there are no moral principles with universal scope; that is, there are no moral principles which apply to all persons in all places at all times.
3 Therefore, we ought never to interfere with persons whose moral practices we oppose, even when we have the power to do so; that is, we ought to practise toleration.

The first problem with this argument lies in the move from premise (1) to premise (2): the fact of non-convergence among persons on moral principles is irrelevant to the question of whether there are any moral principles with universal application. The fact of non-convergence could be explained by the ignorance of mankind, or by their wilful refusal to think carefully about moral problems and the principles fit to address them. Or it could just be bad luck that no persons or groups have yet discovered the moral principles that apply to all of us. The irrelevance of convergence on moral matters to the existence of universal moral principles is further confirmed once we recognise that even if all persons did come to converge on a set of moral principles, this convergence would not be sufficient to establish that these principles had universal application, that is, that they were the right principles for all persons in all places at all times. Dystopian fiction – such as George Orwell's *1984* – thrives on this possibility, and it is easy to imagine a morally horrific alternative history whereby Hitler's Nazis achieved the world domination they sought.

This problem aside, the best objection to this relativistic argument remains that given by Bernard Williams (who calls relativism 'possibly the most absurd view to have been advanced even in moral philosophy').[11] Referring to the argument as laid out above, Williams' criticism is that it is self-defeating: the argument has as its conclusion (3) a principle with universal scope which it denies the possible existence of in one of its premises (2). If premise (2) is true then it is just as justified for us to impose our values on those we oppose as it is for us to tolerate them: there is no universal standpoint from which this imposition can be criticised. The heart of the problem with the argument is that relativism is a *meta-ethical* doctrine; that is, it is a view about what morality *is*. However, any principle of toleration can only be justified by a *normative* argument; that is, by an argument about what *ought* to be done. But, as Williams observes,

> it cannot be a consequence of the nature of morality itself that no society ought ever to interfere with another, or that individuals from one society confronted with the practices of another ought, if rational, to react with acceptance.[12]

Anthropologists' relativism cannot justify toleration. To do that requires the insertion of a normative premise into the argument laid out above. And for the justification of toleration to remain genuinely relativistic it must be the case that *relativism itself* delivers that normative premise. So let me turn now to relativism as it is found in philosophical circles, and to an argument for toleration mounted on the back of this form of relativism.

Philosophers' relativism

Moral relativism as defended by philosophers does not draw only on reflections about the astonishing diversity of moral principles and practices among mankind. Rather, the best philosophical defences of relativism posit it as the best theoretical explanation for the existence of this diversity. For example, J.L.

Mackie claims that relativism,

> has some force simply because the actual variations in the moral codes are more readily explained by the hypothesis that they reflect ways of life than by the hypothesis that they express perceptions, most of them seriously inadequate and badly distorted, of objective values.[13]

The best explanation for the fact of non-convergence on moral matters is that there is nothing to converge upon: diverse moral principles are products of diverse ways of life (and only have validity within these ways of life), rather than cock-eyed approximations to a true morality independent of these ways of life. David Wong echoes Mackie's 'inference to the best explanation' strategy of argument for relativism; however, he makes explicit what he claims to be a philosophically respectable connection between relativism and toleration. Let us consider his argument.

Wong's relativism takes the form of a denial that there exists a single true morality; or, put positively, he permits that there can be more than one true morality. However, *pace* the anthropologists, he realises that this reflection *in itself* is not sufficient to generate a moral requirement to be tolerant. What the critics of the anthropologists' relativistic arguments for toleration have failed to register, according to Wong, is that 'the relativist arguments of nonphilosophers also can be interpreted as arguments from moral relativism and one or more ethical premises to toleration'.[14] In other words, and as was noted above, what Wong proposes is the insertion of a normative premise into the relativistic argument in order to generate the conclusion that we ought to practise toleration. The normative premise Wong makes use of is inspired by Kant's ethics and is, he claims, central to the European tradition of thinking about ethics. He calls this premise 'the justification principle':

> one should not interfere with the ends of others unless one can justify the interference to be acceptable to them were they fully rational and informed of all relevant circumstances. To do otherwise is to fail to treat them with the respect due to rational beings.[15]

Wong thinks that combining the justification principle with relativism yields the following argument for toleration.

> If moral relativism is true, two persons A and B can have conflicting moralities that are equally true and that therefore may be equally justified. Suppose B is required or permitted by his morality to bring about a state of affairs X. A can bring about some other state of affairs Y that precludes the coming about of X. It would be a violation of the justification principle for A to bring about Y, because she could not justify to B the preventing of X. We thus have an argument for A tolerating B's action according to his moral beliefs.[16]

Wong's thought here is that, for any person A who is committed to the justification principle, their morality forbids them to act so as to prevent another person B from achieving ends required by B's morality, and that this can be true of A even if, as relativism has it, her morality and the morality of B with which it conflicts are equally true and justified.

This argument establishes that A ought to tolerate B if and only if the following conditions hold:

1   A endorses the justification principle; and
2(i) A does not have any other moral commitments which require her to bring about Y; or
(ii) A has other moral commitments which require her to bring about Y, but this requirement is hedged by an 'all else being equal' qualifier, and A's endorsement of the justification principle creates a competing requirement which violates this qualifier and thereby blocks A's requirement to bring about Y.

There are problems with each of these conditions understood as providing circumstances in which A can genuinely be in a position to *tolerate* B. With respect to condition (2i), if A has no moral commitments which require her to bring about Y and thereby prevent B from bringing about X then A is not opposed to B in the way we established in chapter 1 as required for toleration to be possible. If bringing about Y is a matter of indifference to A then she lacks opposition to B; or if bringing about Y is not significant enough to A for her to feel compelled to bring it about, then her opposition to B lacks the quality of importance necessary for her to be a potential tolerator of B. Either way, the conflict – if such it is – she has with B is not to be mediated by toleration but, rather, some other virtue (compromise, perhaps, or canny bargaining).

Turning to (2ii), if A has moral commitments which require her to bring about Y, then *prima facie* she is in a position to tolerate B. However, if these commitments are trumped by her commitment to the justification principle then it again becomes unclear whether A is in a position to tolerate B. The justification principle to which A is committed, in Wong's argument, states a requirement to respect the rational nature in other persons: what prevents A from acting on the commitment she has to bring about Y, on this reading of the argument, is her respect for the rational nature in B. But if A has such respect for B, then it is not clear in what sense she is opposed to B. What is required for this version of the argument to work is a way of distinguishing between a person and the person's beliefs and practices, plus an argument to show that opposition to a person's beliefs and practices can be consistent with respect for the person herself. Unless this distinction and this account of opposition are possible and plausible, A's commitment to respect the rational nature in B, on this version of the argument, disqualifies her as a potential tolerator of B.[17]

This problem is highlighted in an example given by Wong of how the justification principle might operate in a situation in which both A and B accept the principle. The question, in this case, is which of them ought to act on their commitment to the justification principle. Wong claims that,

> if B engages in homosexual activity with another consenting adult and A must decide whether to prevent such activity through the law, it would seem most likely that the justification principle must weigh more heavily against A's intervention than B's abstinence from homosexual activity.[18]

Now, apart from the fact that Wong gives no explanation of why the justification principle ought to weigh more heavily with A than with B – a question I shall return to shortly – this example shows what is required of a tolerant A on the reading of the argument just considered. Being committed to and acting upon the justification principle in practising toleration towards B, A must respect B as a person while at the same time abhorring his homosexuality. It is not uncommon for people to make this distinction: we can hate the sin but love the sinner. However, any argument for toleration must also address harder cases where making a distinction between a person and her practices and attributes stretches credulity. For example, can the distinction be made in the case of religious oppositions so as to generate an argument for religious toleration on the back of the justification principle? Can we say with a straight face to Palestinians that their oppositions to Israeli Jews are premised on a mistaken conflation of the Jewishness of their opponents' practices and their opponents themselves? Any argument for toleration must apply to hard cases like these. Making the separation of the person and the attributes and practices that others oppose the starting point for toleration makes it doubtful that the complexity and difficulty of toleration in hard cases can be adequately captured: Palestinians and Israeli Jews oppose *one another*, not their practices and attributes understood as separable from their essentially 'unencumbered selves'.[19]

Next, and related to (1) above, if A endorses the justification principle then A is committed to respecting the rational nature in other people, and is thereby – according to Wong – committed to the principle that 'one should not interfere with the ends of others unless one can justify the interference to be acceptable to them were they fully rational and informed of all relevant circumstances'.[20] However, is this not just to say that anyone committed to respecting the rational nature in others will be committed to toleration (where its limits are set by what interference can be justified to others, when fully rational and informed)? In that case, what Wong has provided is an argument to show that persons committed to toleration ought to practise toleration. But this is not what we wanted. Rather, the justification of toleration that we seek ought to address those whose opposition may not be tempered by respect for the rational nature in one another, and who may not always (and may be right not to) distinguish opposed practices from their practitioners. What we want is a justification fit to convince an A who hates homosexuals and what they do, and who has the power to make gay sex a crime, that she ought not to wield this power on principled grounds. Wong's argument does not deliver this justification.

The final problem relates to some remarks I made at the end of the previous section. Even if Wong's argument for toleration overcomes the difficulties just outlined, it is not clear what work is being done in the argument by his relativism. The justification principle provides the normative premise in Wong's argument that was missing from the anthropologists' argument. However, the justification principle is not entailed – or even suggested – by Wong's relativism. Just as we saw with respect to the anthropologists' argument, the truth of the meta-ethical thesis of relativism has no implications with respect to action-guiding normative principles: relativism leaves everything where it is, morally speaking. This is not, of course, to impugn Wong's normative premise. But if it is this premise that does the work in Wong's justification of toleration, then the justification is not relativistic, and the premise requires far more by way of defence than what Wong offers.

It seems that we have exhausted the possibilities for metaphysical sceptical arguments for toleration: neither subjectivism, nor relativism à la the anthropologists or the philosophers, will do the trick. In that case, we should turn to epistemological scepticism. However, before we move on it is worth reviewing a final form of scepticism whose advocates reject the label 'relativism', and which, it is claimed, yields an account of liberal toleration fit for a 'postmodern' age: pragmatism.

Pragmatism

Pragmatism is the view that social values and political principles are judged to be the right principles for any given society according to how well these values and principles enable the society in question to achieve its collective goals and realise its shared ends: crudely, for pragmatists, morality is what works. The best known advocate of pragmatism with respect to political questions is Richard Rorty.[21] Although Rorty does not mount an argument specifically for toleration on the back of his pragmatism, he takes it that what he calls 'postmodern bourgeois liberalism' incorporates the value of toleration, and is to be defended with pragmatist arguments.

One of Rorty's key concerns in articulating his pragmatism is to establish that the justification of political principles can and ought to proceed without appeal to foundations in metaphysical truths, moral facts or universal moral principles, an unchanging human nature, or a shared practical reason. I shall return to Rorty's anti-foundationalism shortly. For the moment, let me review the connection between his anti-foundationalism and his vision of a good (*inter alia*, tolerant) liberal community.

Rorty characterises the current state of politics, ethics, philosophy, and culture in general in terms of a breakdown of hitherto respectable dichotomous pairings: 'appearance and reality', 'human nature and cultural nurture', 'analytic truths and synthetic truths', 'morality and prudence', 'science and art'.[22] Rorty claims that in each of these pairs philosophers had taken one of the terms to refer to something ahistorical, objective, and/or unchanging (reality, human nature, analytic truths, morality, science) and the other to refer to something culturally relative, context-bound, and/or subjective (appearance, cultural nurture, synthetic truths, prudence, art). Rorty claims that various movements across the continental/analytic philosophy divide – and outside of philosophy in art, literature, anthropology, sociology, psychology, and history – have conclusively undermined these dichotomous pairings. With respect to the practice of political justification, the rejection of the distinction between an ahistorical human nature and its culturally informed manifestation, and the distinction between morality and prudence, has left political justification without foundations.

In a world bereft of these foundations, professional philosophers and political scientists ought no longer to be the experts to whom people turn in search of political justification (if indeed they ever were). Rather, those who have a deep understanding and strong vision of the values of liberal society (such as toleration) through artistic and cultural activity and analysis – people Rorty calls the 'strong poet' and the 'culture critic' – ought to be the people turned to when liberal principles and institutions are under attack or require reaffirmation.[23] According to Rorty, poets and culture critics undertake this form of political justification by comparing current principles and institutions to historical and utopian (or dystopian) counterparts. The task of political justification so conceived is redescription 'in the hope of inciting people to adopt and extend [the new] jargon'.[24] Pragmatist political justification aims at the inculcation of values through the replacement of one vocabulary with another.

Rorty thinks that when political justification aims at liberal principles the key value to be inculcated in people is solidarity around the set of liberal values. When liberal principles lack foundations, the best (i.e. most effective) way to ensure their future survival is to get people to come to share the values expressed by these principles by seeing one another as fellow members of a liberal community: on this picture, the practice of toleration is supported by getting people to see one another as bound by ties of solidarity in a liberal community all of whose members are deserving of toleration.[25] Poets and critics use persuasion to create such solidarity through 'redescribing ranges of objects or events in partially neologistic jargon, in the hope of inciting people to adopt and extend that jargon'.[26] For Rorty, we achieve solidarity not through argumentative appeal to defunct philosophical foundations, but through art and literature which persuades us to see one another as co-members of a political community.

The danger here is that without an ahistorical account of human nature, or a true moral theory, we lack the means by which to judge the values embedded in competing vocabularies. The danger is that all vocabularies are then as good as one another; consequently, political justification becomes redundant and violence is as good a means as any for political change. Rorty attempts to avoid this picture of political change with the idea that the direction of change should be guided by values which embody the 'we-intentions' of members of liberal societies bound together in solidarity. 'We-intentions' are,

[T]hose beliefs and desires and emotions which overlap with those of most other members of some community with which, for purposes of deliberation, [a person] identifies herself, and which contrast with those of most members of other communities with which hers contrasts itself. A person appeals to morality rather than prudence when she appeals to this overlapping, shared part of herself, those beliefs and desires and emotions which permit her to say 'WE do not do this sort of thing'.[27]

Political justification by poets and critics is driven by we-intentions, and is addressed only to members of the political community to which the poets and critics belong. The similarity here between the relativistic arguments for toleration already considered and Rorty's argument is striking. For the anthropologists, the validity of moral principles is always relative to the existing norms and practices of particular groups: Rorty's claim above about how morality is constituted by we-intentions seems very close to this. And if Rorty is right that political change in any community must be directed by the existing we-intentions of that community, then toleration is justified in any given political community only if the we-intentions of that community are already directed towards toleration; this looks remarkably similar to the problem I identified with Wong's arguments for toleration, that is, that they can only get off the ground if a normative commitment to practise toleration is already present. Is Rorty's pragmatism simply a sophisticated version of one or both of the relativisms already considered, and in that case subject to the same difficulties that they face in justifying toleration?

In my view, the answer to this question is 'yes'. However, Rorty disagrees. He claims that 'to accuse postmodernism of relativism is to try to put a metanarrative in the postmodernist's mouth' (which, however, makes it very odd that Rorty chose to call one of the most prominent collections of his essays *Objectivity, Relativism, and Truth*).[28] In order to avoid putting anything in Rorty's mouth to which he might object, let us consider some other grounds on which to criticise his pragmatist defence of toleration.

First, consider the response recommended by this approach to people who do not see themselves as members of a solidaristic liberal community, and who reject its we-intentions: Rorty's examples are Nietzsche and Loyola.[29] With respect to them, Rorty states that,

To refuse to argue about what human beings should be like seems to show a contempt for the spirit of accommodation and tolerance, which is essential to democracy. But it is not clear how to argue for the claim that human beings ought to be liberals rather than fanatics without being driven back on a theory of human nature, on philosophy. I think that we must grasp the first horn. We have to insist that not every argument needs to be met in the terms in which it is presented. Accommodation and tolerance must stop short of a willingness to work within any vocabulary that one's interlocutor wishes to use, to take seriously any topic that he puts forward for discussion.[30]

Rorty's strategy for dealing with dissenters in a liberal society – the people to whom toleration is most commonly claimed to be owed, and of whom it is required by liberal society – is to ignore them. Rorty worries that such exclusion might show contempt for the spirit of accommodation and toleration that characterises democracies. It is true that Rorty's solution for dealing with dissenters is not accommodating, but our concern here is with toleration rather than inclusion. Is Rorty right to worry about the democratic credentials of his account as regards toleration? Does toleration as it has so far been understood require that one engage in some way with those one opposes? As things stand, it does not. But as we move through discussion of some of the practical issues in Part II it will become clear that many parties to these debates believe that the demands of toleration ought to be expanded so as to require some engagement with opponents on pain of toleration becoming an impotent – or worse, desta-bilising – political value.

A key area for concern in Rorty's pragmatist defence of toleration relates to his characterisation of the strong poets and culture critics as the catalysts of political change. Rorty insists that these people ought to undertake the task of inculcating new vocabularies with a sense of contingency and irony. A sense of the contingency of liberal values has two aspects. First, it is a recognition that these values have no foundation in a mind-independent reality, a divine order, or an essential ahistorical human nature; this much is familiar. Second, and relatedly, it is a recognition of the fragility of these values: history need not, and easily might not, have produced any liberal cultures, and the future survival of these cultures is not assured (Rorty reads Orwell as asserting this aspect of contingency in *1984*).[31] Because of their acceptance that 'anything can be made to look good or bad by being redescribed' the strong poet and culture critic read Orwell and others, and recognise the importance of asserting and defending liberal values.[32] But because of their recognition that that the vocabulary in which they express their liberal hopes and values is not a 'final vocabulary' – that it may be replaced by another more expressive, more persuasive vocabulary – the strong poet and culture critic have doubts about the expression of their liberal hopes as they express them. This makes them ironists. However, and crucially, this is not true of the poet's and critic's audience: Rorty claims that these people ideally are not suffused with doubt about the vocabulary of their convictions.

> In the ideal liberal society, the intellectuals would still be ironists, although the nonintellectuals would not. The latter would, however, be commonsensically nominalist and historicist. So they would see themselves as contingent through and through, without feeling any particular doubts about the contingencies they happened to be.[33]

The private irony of Rorty's intellectuals in the ideal liberal society should be a cause for concern: the division of labour and distribution of knowledge about the real purposes of political justification on this picture echoes that associated with act-utilitarianism, and is distasteful from a democratic point of view for the same reasons. In crude terms, act-utilitarianism understood as a political philosophy is the view that a political authority ought always to act so as to maximise the greatest overall happiness of the greatest number of people. In some cases this will require that the authority sacrifice the happiness of (perhaps a large) minority (or even majority) of the governed in order to achieve maximum total happiness. For example, the total happiness of the political community might be maximised if a segment of the community were secretly spirited away by government agencies to become test subjects for drugs which might cure cancer. However, if the governed were to become aware of the grounds on which the political authority made its decisions then the fear and insecurity engendered in them by this knowledge would damage the authority's ability to achieve maximum overall levels of utility. In that case, such an authority would have to keep the act-utilitarian nature of its decision-making procedures secret, and present a different picture of these procedures to the governed. The act-utilitarianism of the political authority would have to become 'government-house' only.

Rorty's depiction of the ideal liberal society in which the irony of poets and critics is private echoes government-house utilitarianism: if the non-intellectuals were to become aware of the private irony of the intellectuals who undertake the task of political justification, then they would no longer have the appropriate mindset to accept the justifications offered to them by these people. Why should I change my vocabulary when I know that the poets attempting to induce me to do so have deep doubts about the new vocabulary they offer? Such poets are very far from Orwell, and even Swift. The reason why this is a problem for Rorty – and indeed any liberal who advocates his version of pragmatism – is that this vision of the distribution of knowledge and the division of political labour is deeply undemocratic. Of course, toleration is possible in undemocratic societies; but the abandonment of democracy is a very high price to pay for toleration. If this is what pragmatist toleration requires then we are justified in looking elsewhere for a defence of toleration.

With these problems noted, let us turn now to the final form of sceptical argument for toleration: epistemological scepticism.

Epistemological scepticism: fallibility and doubt

In contrast to metaphysical ethical scepticism, epistemological ethical scepticism relates to our knowledge and certainty of moral and ethical matters. As we saw in chapter 1, and as we will review in detail in chapter 8, John Stuart Mill employs such sceptical arguments for toleration when he claims that because we cannot be sure that we always form and hold true beliefs, we ought not to take our genuine conviction that our opinions are justified as evidence that they are true.[34] In that case, the genuine conviction that our opinions are justified does not support the imposition of these opinions on others through intolerant action. My concern here will be with a revived form of this argument given by Brian Barry.[35]

Remember that what we seek in a justification of toleration is an argument to show that a wedge can be (and ought to be) driven between genuinely taking one's opposition to others to be justified, and taking other-regarding action on the commitments constitutive of that opposition to be justified. Barry attempts to provide this wedge with the claim that 'no conception of the good can justifiably be held with a degree of certainty that warrants its imposition on those who reject it'.[36] If we ought to have an attitude of doubt towards our own beliefs, then toleration becomes possible. Once the attitude of doubt is combined with what Barry calls 'the agreement motive' – that is, 'a desire to reach agreement with others on terms that nobody could reasonably reject'[37] – toleration becomes more than possible: it becomes required. For people who have the agreement motive, an attitude of doubt towards the beliefs constitutive of their opposition to others is sufficient to establish that they ought to practise toleration towards those they oppose.

The obvious first question here is: why ought we to hold our beliefs and convictions about the good life in doubt? Barry offers three considerations in support of his scepticism. First, that reflection on the history of conflict – especially religious conflict – shows that all the means of rational persuasion used by one party to a disagreement to convince the other to convert have failed to eliminate the disagreements.[38] But, he asks, '[i]f I concede that I have no way of convincing others [to share my views], should that not also lead to a dent in my own certainty?'[39] Barry's suggestion is that it should, and that it is appropriate that it does. Second, Barry claims that the degree of voluntary religious conversion in history and the present suggests that in fact people have held, and still hold, their conceptions of the good with the attitude of doubt he describes: if most people were dogmatists with respect to their beliefs then these changes would be far less commonplace.[40] In that case, Barry is simply proposing that the justification of principles of toleration be made to reflect the way in which people already hold their beliefs. Barry's final consideration is strategic: that nothing other than his form of scepticism can provide a justification of toleration.[41]

The third consideration just mentioned must be set aside until we have completed our discussion of the possible justifications of toleration; if there are better non-sceptical justifications of toleration available then Barry's claim here is false. Turning to the second consideration, we might make the general observation that – post the 11 September 2001 attack on the World Trade Center – dogmatism, not scepticism, seems to be the order of the day. We might even claim that that event and its consequences simply revealed a dogmatism that was already widespread both in rogue elements within Islam, and in the religiously inspired political zeitgeist of the US. At the very least, it seems false that we all hold our views about what is good, true, beautiful and just with an attitude of doubt: it may be true that we hold some of our beliefs in this way, but it is surely rare to find a person of whom it is true across the board. And with respect to converts, they are often more dogmatic and fanatical than extant believers: invoking the presence of such people among us is an odd way to lend support to the view that we are (mostly) epistemic sceptics.

Finally, with respect to the first consideration, is it not possible for me to conclude that my failure to convince others of my views reveals their irrationality, and spurs me to hold even more fast to the truth of my beliefs? Isn't it the failure to hold fast in this way that spells Winston Smith's psychological destruction when he finally concedes that 2 + 2 = 5? These general observations relate simply to Barry's claim that doubt is the appropriate attitude to be adopted towards beliefs and convictions about value. However, we might also criticise his argument by granting that doubt is appropriate, and by questioning whether it justifies toleration, as he claims it does. Let us consider these forms of criticism.

Matt Matravers and Susan Mendus make two key points along these lines.[42] The first relates to what the doubt at the heart of Barry's argument for toleration entails in practical terms; that is, in terms of how a person with such an attitude of doubt ought to act. It is crucial to Barry's argument that doubt with respect to a conception of the good ought to prevent the person who holds it from imposing it on others, either directly or through political means (this is where the wedge is driven). However, as Matravers and Mendus point out, it is not the case that doubt in every area of shared human life – even when it is appropriate – is taken to make political inaction appropriate. As they state,

> Consider the case of the sustainable use of resources. Any proposal for the use of political power to restrict current consumption in order to provide a just distribution of the Earth's resources over generations must confront the problem that we lack certainty about the consequences of current levels of consumption. We cannot know with certainty what the consequences of continuing to consume at current rates will be, and yet we do not deem that lack of certainty to be disabling in arriving at decisions about public policy.[43]

If we do not take doubt to require political inaction in cases such as these, then why should we take it to require the inaction characteristic of toleration, as Barry claims it does? One answer is that there is a qualitative difference between the beliefs about the good life ('evaluative' beliefs) and beliefs – such as those outlined in the passage just quoted – about matters of fact ('factual' beliefs). It might be claimed that doubt with respect to factual beliefs either is not appropriate or, if appropriate, does not require inaction, whereas the doubt that ought to attend evaluative beliefs does require inaction (in the form of toleration). There are at least two grounds on which this claim might be made: (1) that decisions on matters about which we have factual beliefs are urgent and unavoidable; and (2) that political action to address such matters does not impact on people's lives in the same way, or to the same extent, as political action matters about which we have evaluative beliefs. In that case, doubt about our factual beliefs should not disable us in practical terms, whereas doubt about our evaluative beliefs should.

There are two grounds for worry about this response. First, as Matravers and Mendus highlight, there is no clear-cut, uncontroversial way of making the distinction between factual and evaluative beliefs upon which this reply relies.[44] For example, some educators in America insist that creationism ought to be taught to children in schools alongside Darwin's theory of evolution, as an alternative scientific view of how we got to where we are. Is creationism a set of factual beliefs? A set of evaluative beliefs? A mixture of the two? Which bits are factual, and which evaluative?[45]

However, even if we grant the distinction between factual and evaluative beliefs, it still has to be shown that this distinction is salient to the argument for toleration, and here there are further problems. Two reasons for thinking that the distinction is salient were given above. However, it is not clear that either of them is sufficient to justify political action with respect to factual but not evaluative beliefs. As regards the first point, the urgency of political action in matters related to evaluative beliefs is very much a matter of where you are standing: for those who believe that they have a duty to save the souls of their fellow human beings, and that a failure to see the light means eternal damnation, decisions to enact policies of religious education etc. may be the most urgent items on the political agenda.[46] As regards the second point, it is hard to think of an example of a decision about a 'factual' matter which does not impact on people's lives and is not trivial: what seems to matter here is not the 'evaluative' or 'factual' quality of the decision but, rather, its details and significance.

Of course, there may be ways not considered here of making the distinction between factual and evaluative beliefs, and of explaining the salience of that distinction, which escape these criticisms, and make arguments from doubt the best candidates for the justification of toleration. However, even if such arguments emerge, it remains the case that this form of doubt is not widespread in many – perhaps most – political communities. In that case, the mindset of most people – the way in which they form, conceive of, and hold their beliefs – would have to undergo radical change before the practice of toleration becomes possible. To avoid this daunting project, one strategy would be to restrict the claim about the appropriateness of doubt to apply only to intellectuals: if these people can be brought to see that they ought to adopt an attitude of doubt towards their key evaluative beliefs then the task of justifying the imposition of political principles of toleration on the dogmatic majority can be left to them. But here, again, worries about the democratic credentials of this division of labour and the distribution of knowledge depicted in this vision of political life are appropriate.

Conclusion

In conclusion, none of the varieties of scepticism considered here clearly provides a successful justification of toleration. Relativism *qua* meta-ethical thesis – anthropological and philosophical – lacks the normative punch required to justify principles of toleration which, after all, state how we *ought* to behave. Pragmatism delivers a justification of toleration which carries a very high cost, namely the compromise of democratic ideals of transparency in government and equal access to the real sources of justification for political principles enacted in policy. And epistemological scepticism is false to the lived reality of forming and holding beliefs as experienced by most of us, requires a *prima facie* untenable distinction between evaluative and factual beliefs, and may also compromise the democratic ideals damaged by pragmatism. It is best to look elsewhere for the justification of toleration: let us turn to arguments from incommensurability.

Chapter 4

Toleration from value pluralism[1]

> There never were in the world two opinions alike, no more than two hairs or two grains; the most universal quality is diversity.
>
> (Michel de Montaigne)[2]

Introduction

In this chapter I shall present an analysis of value pluralism in terms of incommensurability, and give a general account of how this conception of pluralism operates in an argument for toleration. A critique of this argument in its general form will show that it requires elaboration. Two ways in which this might be undertaken – as found in the work of Isaiah Berlin and Joseph Raz – will be assessed. I shall conclude that, notwithstanding the attractions of incommensurability as a thesis about the nature of value, and its implications for our understanding of the human condition, defenders of toleration must take a different tack in justifying its personal and political practice. To anticipate, the metaphysical and existential facts constitutive of a conception of pluralism as permanently incommensurable are the wrong place to focus in the search for a justification of toleration. Instead of attending to the *nature of the circumstances* in which potential tolerators exist, we should instead attend directly to *what is required of potential tolerators themselves* in handling the oppositions that place them in the circumstances of toleration. Let me begin with an analysis of incommensurability, and a general account of its role in arguments for toleration.

Incommensurability

What distinguishes value pluralists from other pluralists is that they explain the fact of persistent pluralism in terms of incommensurability. Incommensurability is a relational property exhibited by values as realised in pursuits and ways of life between which human beings choose. The choices we make between different ways of life are often guided by endorsement of, or attraction to, the values realised in these pursuits: incommensurability is a property (claimed to be) possessed by some of these values, insofar as they are in competition by being exclusively embedded in ways of life which cannot all be pursued at once. To the extent that incommensurability is taken to be an ineluctable feature of the nature of the relations that hold between a variety of values that can be realised in individual and collective life, the fact of incommensurability – if such it is – has implications for the fundamental structure and character of human life. I shall construe incommensurability in terms of six theses.[3] The first triplet of theses states putative truths about incommensurability as a property of values, and the second triplet states the consequences of the truth of the first triplet for our understanding of the human condition.

Three theses of evaluative incomparability:

T1: There is no 'master-value' to which all other values can be reduced, and according to which comparisons between all values can be made.

T2: Because of the truth of T1, it makes no sense, or is inappropriate, to think that it must always be possible to rank values – and the practices, ends, and forms of association in which they are realised – as 'better', 'worse', or 'equivalent to' one another.

T2*:Independent of the truth of T1, it makes no sense, or is inappropriate, to think that it must always be possible to rank values – and the practices, ends, and forms of association in which they are realised – as 'better', 'worse', or 'equivalent to' one another.

Three theses of practical incompatibility:

T3: Because of the truth of T1 and T2 (or T2*) the choice of one valuable set of practices, ends, and forms of association can (and often does) permanently preclude the choice of other valuable sets of practices, ends, and forms of association.

T4: Because of the truth of T1 and T2 (or T2*), it is often not possible, or is inappropriate, for collections of human beings to organise their shared lives along a single axis of value without permanently ruling out other valuable forms of shared life.

T5: Because of the truth of T3 it is often not possible, or is inappropriate, for collections of human beings to organise their shared lives so as to eliminate conflict between them in virtue of their different practices, ends and forms of association.

Let me say a little more about these theses, and give some examples by way of illustration for each of them. The theses of evaluative incomparability essentially relate to the possibility of making comparisons between values as they are realised in human practices and pursuits. It is important to note that no incommensurabilist claims that these theses are true of all values; rather, the claim is that incommensurability is exhibited by some set of values. This is why T2 and T2* deny that it is *always* possible – rather than possible *per se* – to compare and rank values. Furthermore, those who assert these theses take it that the members of the set of values that it is not possible to compare and rank are significant in human life; if this were not the case then the theses of practical incompatibility would be so trivial as to be hardly worth stating at all.

T1 states a general proposition about the nature of value *per se*. It is important not to confuse T1 with another, much weaker, thesis, namely that the limits of human understanding make it impossible for persons to discern a 'master-value' to which all other values can be reduced, and according to which comparisons between values can be made. This weaker thesis states a putative truth about what it is possible for human beings to know. In contrast, T1 states a putative truth about the moral universe, regardless of whether it is possible for persons to come to know what is in that universe: T1 is a metaphysical, not an epistemological, thesis.

The significance of T1 can be shown by considering the dominant theory of value which it opposes: utilitarianism. Utilitarianism (as found in the work of Jeremy Bentham),[4] is the view that persons ought to act so as to maximise overall levels of utility in their society (or in the community of sentient creatures as a whole),[5] where 'utility' is to be measured in terms of pleasure and the absence of pain. What Benthamite utilitarians believe is that any set of options faced by a person, and between which she must choose, can meaningfully and properly be interpreted in terms of how they contribute to the realisation of one value – utility – which makes it possible to compare these options along that axis of value, and to choose the one that maximises this value. T1 denies that there must be a value that can and ought to play the role that utility plays for utilitarians. Hence, T1 entails T2: if there is no such master-value, then practices etc. cannot always be ranked according to how much of this value they realise. In sum, whereas for utilitarians there is *always* in principle a procedure for resolving any moral problem or dilemma, for value pluralists there are some moral problems – wherein incommensurable values clash – which no procedure can resolve: if the theses of incommensurability are true then moral tragedy is a real and ineliminable feature of human life. This does not mean that *all* incommensurable values cannot be ranked at all, and consequently that all choices between incommensurable options are as good as one another. For example, saving the life of another person is better than keeping a trivial promise (*ceteris paribus*) when these two courses of action conflict. However, it does mean that there is *some* set of incommensurable values which cannot be ranked (according to a master-value or otherwise); for example, this set might include keeping trivial promises, pursuing one's self-interest, preventing pain being caused to non-human animals, and increasing our knowledge of human genetics.[6]

Finally, T2* is required as a thesis of incommensurability because we might want to affirm an anti-ranking thesis like that of T2 without commitment to T1 and the grand metaphysical claims it makes about the non-existence of master-values. T2* denies that practices etc. can be ranked by comparison with one another while remaining silent on the question of master values and ranking strategies derived from them. T2 and T2* in conjunction state the putative truths that practices etc. cannot be ranked by reference to a master-value, and cannot be ranked *simpliciter*.[7]

An example which is common in the literature will help to illustrate the significance of T2 and T2*. Consider the relation between friendship and money. Each of these things has value: a life without friends is, we think, an impoverished one, and little or no money, we know, frustrates many of life's aims. However, are we able to say meaningfully that any person who judges friendship to be more important than money, or *vice versa*, necessarily makes a mistake? For those who take T2 or T2* to be true of the values of friendship and money, the answer is 'no': the value of friendship and of money cannot be compared. Importantly, this is *not* to claim that, when a person must choose between the value of friendship and of money, she always commits a wrong in choosing money. Rather, the claim is that if she makes an evaluative comparison between friendship and money, then she makes a mistake about the nature of friendship, and thereby shows herself to be incapable of having friends. As Raz puts it, 'Only those who hold the view that friendship is neither better nor worse than money, but is simply not comparable to money or other commodities are capable of having friends.'[8] If friendship is evaluatively incomparable with money then to be capable of friendship – that is, to be capable of appreciating, enjoying, and experiencing friendship as a value – is to refuse to put a price on one's friendships.[9] But note, however, that this does not entail that we all ought to make ourselves capable of friendship by so refusing. The example illustrates the relationship between valuing money and valuing friendship; it does not generate judgements about which of these values we ought to cleave to, or injunctions not to put a price on our friendships.

Turning to the theses of practical incompatibility, these spell out the consequences of the theses of evaluative incomparability for human life. The focus of T3 is an individual life. Here, the thought is not the common and plausible one that the limited and finite nature of each individual human life means that there are only so many ends that a person can pursue, practices that she can engage in, or forms of associational life in which she can participate. Rather, the thought expressed in T3 is that there are certain valuable ends and practices the dedicated and successful pursuit of which rules out the dedicated and successful pursuit of other valuable ends and practices, *and* that this truth is to be explained by the truth of T1 and T2 (or T2*) rather than by the fact that the lives of human beings are temporally limited.[10] For example, however long a person's life, and however versatile and unlimited her talents, it is not possible for her to live the life of a Poor Clare and pursue a career as an investigative journalist: the former requires a renunciation of the world which would make the latter impossible.[11] The truth of T3 means that the choice of one set of valuable ends within a human life sometimes necessitates relinquishing (often permanently) a different set of (incommensurably) valuable ends.

T4 traces the implications of T1 and T2 (or T2*) for human life in its collective (political and social) aspect. Any choice of political principles will embody some set of values to be realised in practices recommended or dictated by the principles: for example, liberal democratic principles embody the values of individual freedom and equality, and dictate – *inter alia* – practices of universal suffrage and non-discrimination in employment and education as realisations of these values. If T2 or T2* is true then commitment to liberal democratic values and practices rules out some sets of alternative political practices which realise incommensurable values.[12] For example, the political and social values of loyalty, honour, obedience, and social continuity that dominated the Heian and Feudal periods in Japan (794–1185 and 1185–1868 respectively) were realised in practices such as submission to a shogun,[13] the development of bushido as an ethical code for the warrior class of samurai,[14] and the practice of shudo (whereby samurai took male lovers from their younger apprentices, and shogun took lovers from their samurai, as a way of reinforcing ties of loyalty). The values realised in these practices are incommensurable with those realised in liberal democratic practices, which instead aim to realise impartiality, equality of opportunity, freedom of conscience, and the conditions of individual autonomy. When we choose a liberal society over a Japanese shogunate, we lose something of value.[15]

Whereas T4 traces the consequences of the truth of theses of evaluative incomparability across societies, T5 addresses the consequences of the first thesis of practical incompatibility (T3) for relations between individuals within any society. T3 tells us that choice between incommensurably valuable practices, ends, and forms of association necessarily (although not universally) involves loss. This is so because the virtues associated with such practices etc. can often necessarily exclude one another: the contemplative virtues of the Poor Clare nun make it impossible for her to cultivate the worldly virtues of the investigative journalist. T5 states the putative truth that such incompatibility will generate conflict; given that the incompatibility is entailed by truths about the nature of value in T1 and T2 (or T2*), this conflict is a permanent fact of human life. As we will see in the penultimate section, it is of great importance how such conflict is characterised: is it hot and hostile, or measured and considered?

The most attractive feature of the incommensurability theses is that they offer an explanation of the diversity of human practices etc., and the clashes that can occur between them, without recourse to the controversial forms of metaphysical scepticism considered in the last chapter. Incommensurabilists do not claim that we do something with our moral language other than what we appear to do, and neither do they claim that moral principles and ethical norms are limited in scope to the cultures which generate them. If the incommensurability theses are true, then we can treat diversity among persons and across cultures as a permanent feature of the human condition without doing violence to our commonsense conception of the demands of morality. A further attraction of the theses is that they explain the lived experience of moral conflict and tragic choices that most people face at some point in their lives, and that we are all familiar with from novels, plays, and films. It may be that the incommensurability theses state profound truths about the nature of value and the human condition. However, our interest here is whether, if true, the theses deliver a justification of toleration; it is to this question that we now turn.

Toleration from incommensurability?

The argument for toleration from incommensurability is as follows:

1   Given incommensurability, conflict between people on significant questions of value is a permanent feature of the world.
2   Given incommensurability, it is illegitimate for some persons or groups to impose at least some of their values and ends on other persons or groups with whom they conflict.
3   Therefore, with respect to at least some practices and forms of association realising significant values with respect to which people conflict, toleration is required of parties to the conflict.

The theses of incommensurability are often taken to deliver premise 1 and premise 2 of this argument in the following way. With respect to premise 1, if people are divided by at least some incommensurable differences then they will inevitably and ineradicably stand opposed to one another on at least some of the big questions. And with respect to premise 2, if there is no master-value according to which at least some ends etc. can be compared and ranked (T1) – or if some ends etc. cannot be ranked *simpliciter* (T2*) – then no person or group is justified in imposing ends etc. on others separated from them by their incommensurable differences to which the person or group is responsibly opposed (and therefore in a position to tolerate).

As it stands, this argument is invalid, for two reasons. First – as we saw in the last chapter – meta-ethical truths about the nature of morality are not sufficient to establish normative truths about the demands of morality or prudence. *Prima facie*, the theses of incommensurability cannot, on their own, establish that toleration is required. This problem is manifest in premise 2, where incommensurability is taken to entail the illegitimacy of imposition. But if meta-ethical truths do not deliver normative requirements then, at best, the theses of incommensurability can establish the requirement to be tolerant only in conjunction with an additional normative premise which explains what it is about imposition that is objectionable.[16] Distinguished liberal accounts of this additional premise are developed in the work of Isaiah Berlin and Joseph Raz, to which I turn in the next two sections.

The second reason why the argument as it stands will not do relates to premise 1. This premise states that the divergence in values etc. which the truth of the theses of incommensurability makes inevitable entails conflict between those who so diverge. This is supposed to show that one of the circumstances of toleration – opposition – is permanent. However, the inference from incommensurability to opposition contained in this premise is invalid. As we saw in chapter 2, toleration is a response to disliked and/or disapproved-of differences. But the argument as just laid out does not establish that incommensurable differences will prompt dislike and/or disapproval between those divided by them: a person can experience conflict with another on significant questions without experiencing dislike and/or disapproval of the other, as is often the case when colleagues, friends, or family members come into conflict. The theses of incommensurability which inform premise 1 of the argument just laid out assert the existence of ineradicable and evaluatively incomparable differences: they address the *nature* of pluralism. What they do not establish is the *character* of the disagreements between people separated by incommensurable differences, and this is what is needed if arguments for toleration are to be mounted on the back of theses of incommensurability. In the work of Raz we find an argument to show that it is inevitable and appropriate that people in conditions of pluralism dislike and disapprove of one another; this argument will be addressed in the penultimate section. However, let me first present Isaiah Berlin's famous version of the argument, which pivots on the value of negative liberty.

Berlin: negative liberty

Berlin is famous for his anti-utopianism; that is, for his opposition to the view that the perfect human society, in which all values are realised in a harmonious whole, without conflict or sacrifice, is achievable.[17] In Berlin's work this opposition is generated by his commitment to a characterisation of the human condition in terms of a pluralism of incommensurably valuable ends, practices, and forms of association, and consequently of human life as punctuated by unavoidable tragic choices between such ends etc. If there are many goods of incommensurate value then the choice of one permanently excludes the choice of others: the human condition is unavoidably characterised by the experience of loss. It is because he believed that not all values are realisable together that Berlin conceived of utopias as dangerous illusions.

> The notion of the perfect whole, the ultimate solution, in which all good things coexist, seems to me to be not merely unattainable – that is a truism – but conceptually incoherent; I do not know what is meant by a harmony of this kind. Some among the Great Goods cannot live together. That is a conceptual truth. We are doomed to choose, and every choice may entail an irreparable loss.[18]

Berlin's commitment to the truth of the incommensurability theses is at the root of his claims that the harmonious realisation of all values is not possible across cultures, within cultures, and within the life of a single person. This much is familiar from the discussion of incommensurability in the second section of this chapter: the theses of evaluative incomparability have consequences for human life expressed in the theses of practical incompatibility. However, it is important to note, *pace* some crude interpretations of Berlin on pluralism,[19] that Berlin's incommensurabilism is not a form of relativism. Berlin's view is not that there are some sets of values which count as such only from the perspective of a particular individual or culture. If this was his view then his comments about the unavoidable collision of values would make no sense. If P is a value only for me, and Q is a value only for you (in which case P does not entail ~Q, and Q does not entail ~P), then we can, at most, acknowledge that we have different values given our different perspectives, but we cannot disagree about them, for we share no value-commitments over which we could disagree. Rather, Berlin's view is that incommensurable values are objective values. That is, their status as values does not depend on whether any person or group takes them to be values; kindness is valuable whether or not anyone believes that it is good to be kind.[20] One of the things that makes Berlin's account of pluralism so interesting is precisely this feature: because the account is not relativistic it cannot be dismissed out of hand on these grounds.[21]

If, as Berlin has it, human life is often a matter of the realisation of great values preceded by tragic choices between these values, then how are human beings to live together? If the great goods are incommensurable then surely the choice of any set of political values cannot be guided by an over-arching value according to which all political values can be ranked. Does this mean that the choice of liberal political principles – including principles of toleration – is groundless, irrational, or unjustifiable? Is this choice just a leap of faith? Is it just an affirmation of existing political commitments for persons already imbued with the spirit of liberalism? This is how John Gray interprets Berlin's commitment to liberalism: in his view, Berlin's liberalism fares best when construed as akin to Rorty's pragmatism.[22] However – and as Gray admits – Berlin himself forswears this 'agonistic' liberalism and, as we have seen, eschews the relativism of a Rortyian pragmatism. Furthermore, Berlin makes it clear that the incommensurabilities that pepper his pluralism do not foreclose on the possibility of the justification of liberal principles in terms of reasons.[23] To reconstruct Berlinian liberalism as abandoning the justification of principles of liberal toleration in terms of reasons and argument will not do (regardless of whether it is claimed that this was Berlin's actual view, or that it is an implication of his value pluralism that he failed to fully acknowledge). Instead, to make the justificatory connection between the truth of the incommensurability theses and a commitment to liberal toleration we must examine Berlin's conception of the nature of the creatures who inhabit his pluralism.

> The world that we encounter in ordinary experience is one in which we are faced with choices between ends equally ultimate, and claims equally absolute, the realization of some of which must inevitably involve the sacrifice of others. Indeed, it is because of their situation that men place such immense value upon the freedom to choose; for if they had assurance that in some perfect state, realizable by men on earth, no ends pursued by them would ever be in conflict, the necessity and agony of choice would disappear, and with it the central importance of the freedom to choose.[24]

For Berlin, human beings in conditions of pluralism have no choice but to make choices between incommensurable goods. In order to make such choices, persons must have freedom and, for Berlin, the form of freedom best suited to protecting persons in the making of such choices is negative liberty.

Berlin's famous distinction between negative and positive liberty can be summed up as follows: negative liberty ensures *freedom from* interference, restriction, impediment etc., whereas positive liberty ensures *freedom to* pursue ends, achieve goals, engage in practices etc.[25] A person who is incarcerated, trapped, shackled, or bound in any way (including being bound by rules or laws), either through the deliberate actions of others, the unintended consequences of their actions, or through the workings of nature, has her negative liberty depleted. In contrast, a person lacking the capabilities, power, self-mastery, or knowledge necessary for the achievement of her goals and purposes — again, either through the deliberate actions of others, the unintended consequences of their actions, or through the workings of nature — has her positive liberty depleted. It is often the case that circumstances damaging to a person's negative liberty are also damaging to a person's positive liberty. For example, a person who is kept prisoner has restricted negative liberty in virtue of being physically behind bars, but she also suffers a depletion of positive liberty insofar as her fate is directed by the will of her captor. However, damage to negative liberty and to positive liberty can sometimes come apart. Persons suffering from drug or alcohol addiction often lack the self-mastery required for the achievement of their goals, even though other persons and nature do not literally force continued consumption of the drug. And persons living in oppressive political systems that deplete their negative liberty can sometimes exercise an astounding degree of self-mastery through artistic or intellectual activity, or religious meditation.

Berlin argues that negative liberty is more adequate than positive liberty to the needs of human beings as choosers between incommensurable goods. If there are many goods, all of value, that in principle cannot be realised in the life of one person, then the space for individual choice between these goods must be protected.[26] Rights to negative liberty protect this space. Moreover, the concept of positive liberty is open to abuse and perversion in a way that the concept of negative liberty is not. Positive liberty, when unperverted, protects the space for self-realisation by ensuring the conditions fit for it. However, it is always possible that one group can claim to have privileged knowledge of the 'real selves' or 'true purposes' of others, and thus to have insight into their 'real interests', in such a way as to justify the imposition of extreme restrictions and hardships on these others in the name of the promotion of their freedom. It is always possible for one group to impose terrible restrictions on others on the grounds that these restrictions would in fact be willed by these others if only they had a clear view of their true interests; or, worse, that such restrictions are actually willed by these others, despite their protestations to the contrary. Berlin rails against this abuse of the concept of positive liberty, claiming that,

> The common assumption of [such] thinkers . . . is that the rational ends of our 'true' natures must coincide, or be made to coincide, however violently our poor, ignorant, desire-ridden, passionate, empirical selves may cry out

against this process. Freedom is not freedom to do what is irrational, or stupid, or wrong. To force empirical selves into the right pattern is no tyranny, but liberation.[27]

If pluralism has the nature Berlin attributes to it, and if persons are, as he claims, thereby doomed to be choosers between incompatible goods then, as a matter of political priority, negative liberty requires protection. Berlin's commitment to negative liberty inserts an additional, crucial normative premise into the argument for toleration from pluralism. Without this normative commitment, the metaphysical fact of incommensurability can give us no guidance as to what we ought to do, politically speaking. With this normative commitment we can establish the requirement to be tolerant, and set the limits of toleration, as follows.

If the protection of negative freedom for all is our fundamental normative commitment, then we ought to permit to persons and groups – at the political and personal level – the choice of any goods, so long as this choice does not prevent other persons or groups from exercising their negative liberty to make similar choices. This constitutes a commitment to toleration, limited (at least in part) by a requirement that no person's negative liberty should avoidably be depleted.[28] The wedge that Berlin drives between having a commitment that one genuinely takes to be justified, and taking the imposition of that commitment on others to be justified, is a further commitment to the value of negative liberty. If negative liberty provides the freedom most adequate to the nature of human beings as choosers of different ends, then I ought to accept that my opposition to others does not justify the imposition of my ends on them, because this imposition violates their negative liberty.

However, here is the rub. In the argument as laid out in the last paragraph no mention was made of the unavoidable choice between goods as being a choice between *incommensurable* goods. It is, of course, true that a commitment to negative liberty will deliver a commitment to toleration. Negative liberty directs us to leave others alone in making their choices so long as these choices do not impinge on the negative liberty of others. And if we offer – as Berlin does – a principled ground for thinking that such choice ought to be respected, and that the choices made are significant, then what we argue for is a principle of toleration: we offer grounds for thinking that the principled refusal to interfere with the pursuits etc. of others is required, and that these pursuits are significant. The problem is that this argument can run without any claims being made about the incommensurable nature of the goods between which people must choose. The argument would still stand even if the fact that human beings are doomed to be choosers were to be explained just in terms of the bland fact that such beings are limited in their capacities and life spans, and so cannot choose everything they might want to choose in a single lifetime; and this is not a thesis of incommensurability. In developing the additional normative premise needed for Berlin's argument for liberal toleration to get off the ground it looks like we have rendered the starting point of this argument – the incommensurability theses – redundant.[29] Is there an account of the pluralist argument for liberal toleration which saves the incommensurability theses from redundancy by making them an essential part of the wedge to be driven between genuinely taking a commitment to be justified, and taking the imposition on others of the ends etc. constitutive of this commitment to be justified? For an attempt at such an account we must turn to Joseph Raz's version of the pluralist argument.

Raz: autonomy and competitive pluralism

Raz's pluralist argument for liberal toleration is in many ways similar to Berlin's. Like Berlin, Raz is committed to the incommensurability theses. He claims that the 'mark of incommensurability' is a failure of transitivity with respect to the value of certain ends, pursuits, practices, etc. realising different values.[30]

> Two valuable options are incommensurable if (1) neither is better than the other, and (2) there is (or could be) another option that is better than one but is not better than the other.[31]

Taking two options, A and B, the failure of transitivity in (1) shows that A and B *per se* cannot be compared in terms of their value (as stated in T2*), and the failure of transitivity in (2) shows that there is no master-value C that enables comparison of A and B in terms of their value (as stated in T1 and T2).

Again, like Berlin, Raz recognises that the fact of incommensurability cannot deliver commitment to liberal toleration without conjunction with some normative commitment. Whereas Berlin's additional premise states a commitment to negative liberty, Raz's additional premise states a commitment to the value of personal autonomy.

> The ruling idea behind the ideal of autonomy is that people should make their own lives. The autonomous person is a (part) author of his own life. The ideal of personal autonomy is the vision of people controlling, to some degree, their own destiny, fashioning it through successive decisions throughout their lives.[32]

That Raz's fundamental normative commitment is to autonomy has important consequences for his conception of politics that differentiate it from that of Berlin. Unlike Berlin, Raz believes that 'governments should promote the moral quality of the life of those whose lives and actions they can affect'.[33] Given the value of autonomy, Raz believes that the state has a duty, and the right, to preserve the 'conditions of autonomy' for its members: to cultivate 'appropriate mental abilities' in them, to provide them with 'an adequate range of options' across which autonomous choice can be exercised, and to encourage them to be independent.[34] Furthermore, because a valueless option is not transformed into a valuable option by being chosen autonomously,[35] the state – in virtue of its legitimate concern with the moral quality of members' lives – has a duty and the right to ensure that the options constitutive of the range across which members can exercise autonomous choice are all valuable. Because Raz holds to the theses of incommensurability, this means that the state has the right and duty to preserve a range of genuinely distinct, but incommensurably valuable, options as a consequence of its duty and right to provide members with the conditions of autonomy. These 'perfectionist' features of Raz's view mean that pluralism as it features in his conception of politics is far more moralised than that which features in Berlin's work. For Berlin, the state must permit the exercise of negative liberty in pursuit of any goal – of whatever moral quality – so long as this exercise is consistent with others doing likewise, whereas for Raz, the state must ensure that the practices, goals, and forms of association at which its members can aim and in which they can participate are all of moral value.

Raz's pluralist argument for toleration is that the state must protect a variety of ways of life standing in opposition to one another as a consequence of its right and duty to cultivate and protect the moral quality of its members' lives. In other words, the state is required, as a matter of principle, to ensure that those opposed to one another on issues significant to them do not act on their dispositions to oppress and interfere with one another that are generated by their opposition. If we think that individuals have a duty to recognise the authority of the just state, we must also think that they thereby have a duty to practise toleration: the just state must enact principles of toleration in policy so as to discharge its duty to provide the conditions of autonomy for all by maintaining a range of valuable options in society, and part of what it is to accept the authority of the just state is to accept its exercise of authority in enacting policies.[36]

In this argument, as in Berlin's version of it, the fact of incommensurability appears to be redundant. If the state has a duty and right to improve the moral quality of its members' lives by ensuring for them the conditions of autonomy, and if the conditions of autonomy require a range of (morally worthy) options between which members can choose, then what does the stipulation that these options are *incommensurably* valuable add to the argument? Isn't it enough for the state's perfectionist duties to be discharged that the options it protects are valuable, whether or not they are incommensurable? And isn't the wedge that is driven between a person genuinely taking her commitments to be justified, and taking the imposition of them on others to be justified, simply the obligation that persons have to recognise political authority, regardless of the truth or falsity of the incommensurability theses?

However, this might be too quick. That the requirement on individuals to be tolerant is generated, in a top-down way, by the state's requirement to enact perfectionist policies is best explained by Raz's characterisation of pluralism as *competitive*, and Raz thinks that the competitiveness of pluralism is connected with the incommensurability of the values realised in options constitutive of it. To say that pluralism is competitive is to say that persons leading different ways of life will, just in virtue of their differences, be opposed to one another in a way that disposes them to intolerance of one another, and this makes the imposition of principles of toleration by the state necessary, if the conditions of autonomy for all are to be preserved. If it is the case that pluralism is competitive if and only if the incommensurability theses are true, then these theses cannot be dispensed with in Raz's pluralistic argument for liberal toleration because they, and only they, ensure that pluralism provides the circumstances of toleration.

In order to assess whether the incommensurability theses are redundant in Raz's argument for liberal toleration we need answers to the following questions: (1) what does it mean to claim that pluralism is competitive? and (2) is pluralism competitive if and only if the incommensurability theses are true? I shall argue that the incommensurability theses do no work in Raz's justification of principles of toleration, and that what does the work instead is his commitment to the value of autonomy and his characterisation of pluralism as inevitably and appropriately competitive.

With respect to (1), Raz states that,

> Competitive pluralism not only admits the validity of distinct and incompatible moral virtues, but also of virtues which tend, given human nature, to encourage intolerance of other virtues. That is, competitive pluralism · admits the value of virtues possession of which normally leads to a tendency not to suffer certain limitations in other people which are themselves inevitable if those people possess certain other, equally valid, virtues.[37]

For Raz, if pluralism is competitive then the disagreements arising out of the differences between people in pluralism will be accompanied by certain 'appropriate emotional or attitudinal concomitants or components' that make these disagreements hot and hostile, and dispose parties to them to intolerance.[38] As Raz states,

> [P]luralists can step back from their personal commitments and appreciate in the abstract the value of other ways of life and their attendant virtues. But this acknowledgement coexists with, and cannot replace, the feelings of rejection and dismissiveness towards what one knows is in itself valuable. Tension is an inevitable concomitant of accepting the truth of value pluralism.[39]

If Raz is right about the hostile character of pluralism then intolerance of ends, practices, etc. that differ from our own must be curbed in law if the state is to discharge its duty of maintaining an adequate range of options across which persons can exercise autonomous choice. Importantly, the ends, practices, etc. which, Raz thinks, are in competition are not only products of major systems of belief such as religions and political creeds. Rather, for Raz, pluralism is competitive both at the edges and at the centre: ordinary vices such as vulgarity, cultural differences, and even professional differences are Raz's examples of characteristics for which 'attitudunal concomitants' of hostility are appropriate.[40] Hostility in Raz's competitive pluralism is not reserved – as it should be – for very bad people. Hostility permeates relations between those with different cultures, religions, professions, and weaknesses.

Turning to question (2) above, is the only, or best, explanation of the competitiveness of pluralism the fact of incommensurability? If the incommensurability theses are true then people will conflict in the ends, practices, and forms of association informed by their incommensurable values. The good life aimed at by a Poor Clare is incompatible with the good life aimed at by an investigative journalist: no person can pursue these conceptions of the good at the same time. The theses of evaluative incomparability entail the theses of practical incompatibility. But Raz's characterisation of pluralism as competitive goes beyond the theses of practical incompatibility. In claiming that persons pursuing practically incompatible ways of life will be – indeed, appropriately are – hostile to one another Raz makes a claim about the *character* of pluralism that is distinct from the claims about the *nature* of pluralism contained in the theses of practical incompatibility. Raz claims that, '[t]ension is an inevitable concomitant of accepting the truth of value pluralism';[41] in other words, once people recognise that the differences by which they are separated are incommensurable, the practical incompatibilities between them will take the form of hostile opposition. But this inference is invalid: facts about the nature of pluralism entail nothing about its character. It could be the case that the incommensurability theses are true and opposition is absent; people separated by incommensurable differences might not dislike and disapprove of one another. Or it could be the case that the incommensurability theses are false and opposition is present; people separated by commensurable differences might dislike and disapprove of one another. Given that the incommensurability theses do not entail opposition, the argument for toleration from pluralism in Raz – as in Berlin – is a red herring. What is doing the work of justifying principles of toleration for Raz is a commitment to perfectionist values in political practice, combined with his characterisation of pluralism as competitive. However, neither of these commitments is entailed by the incommensurability theses.

It might be objected here that my rejection of the characterisation of pluralism as competitive on the grounds that it is not *entailed by* the incommensurability theses imposes a requirement on political argument that is far too demanding. Surely, if it is plausible to claim that the truth of the incommensurability theses makes it *more likely* that pluralism will be competitive then these theses are not redundant in the argument for toleration. However, it is hard to see how this case could be made: does the claim that *knowledge* that the incommensurability theses are true create – or is it likely to create – hostility between parties in opposition? What is it that the truth of the incommensurability theses *adds* to the empirical observation that people with very different ways of life and values often oppose one another in a hostile way? Furthermore, given that, in Raz's view, incommensurability characterises relations both between the great goods and between more mundane values, it is questionable whether the truth of the incommensurability theses does, in fact, increase the likelihood of hostile conflict: for example, most of us separated from others by professional differences do not adopt attitudes of hostility towards one another. As an academic I do not loathe athletes, and I do not feel under threat of hostile attack from gangs of hurdlers and high jumpers. In the absence of a more detailed account of how and why the truth of the metaphysical theses of incommensurability increases the probability that the empirical state of affairs of competitive pluralism will hold, we are entitled to some scepticism with respect to the role played by these theses in Raz's argument for toleration.

Conclusion

In conclusion, we have seen that in the pluralist justifications of toleration offered by Berlin and Raz, the theses of incommensurability are dispensable. Instead, both thinkers appeal to values, or characterisations of pluralism, not entailed by these theses in their justifications of toleration. For Berlin, a commitment to negative liberty makes toleration the best policy; and for Raz, a state commitment to promote the conditions of autonomy, given the competitiveness of pluralism, mandates the imposition of political principles of toleration.

Whether or not pluralism is *inevitably* competitive – and regardless of the nature of pluralism – the fact is that pluralism *is* competitive, and we require personal and political principles to govern this competition: we need to continue to seek a wedge to drive between personal commitments genuinely taken to be justified and the imposition of these commitments on others. In the next section I turn to a justification of toleration which does not rely on any claim about the nature of the values informing the oppositions that place people in the circumstances of toleration. Rather, this approach reflects how individuals ought to conceive of their own commitments independent of the metaphysical properties of the values that inform them. If we can claim that toleration is justified because persons ought to accept that, as individuals, there is a range of commitments which they ought not to impose on others, and that the state is justified in encoding this individual obligation in law, then we might have found the wedge we seek. It is to this 'bottom-up' justification of toleration that I turn in the next chapter.

Chapter 5

Toleration from reasonableness[1]

> The Catholic and the Communist are alike in assuming that an opponent cannot be both honest and intelligent.
>
> (George Orwell)[2]

Introduction

Solutions to the problem of toleration as stated at the end of chapter 2 are not, it seems, delivered by the sceptical and pluralistic arguments for toleration considered in the last two chapters. In this chapter I consider an influential recent approach to the problem that draws on the idea of reasonableness. To recap, what we seek is an explanation of why a person ought to reject as unjustified the imposition (by herself or her representatives) on others whom she opposes of (at least some of) the commitments which she herself genuinely takes to be justified through responsible belief formation,[3] and hence why she ought to defend personal and political principles of toleration prohibiting such impositions. Sceptics and pluralists offer reflections on the *nature* of the values that inform these commitments. But because these reflections are meta-ethical they fail to deliver a normative requirement fit to drive a justificatory wedge between genuinely taking one's commitments to be justified, and taking their imposition on others to be justified. On the approach to be considered in this chapter, toleration is justified by the requirement that each person ought to accept that it is unreasonable for her to attempt to impose her responsibly held commitments on another person or group, so long as the disagreement between herself and this person or group which generates their opposition is a reasonable one. On this view, what justifies toleration is the unreasonableness of intolerance.

The devil of this account is in the detail, and for detail we must turn to the work of John Rawls, its most influential advocate. In the next section I give a brief overview of Rawls' political liberalism, in which reasonableness plays such an important role. In the third section I examine in more detail Rawls' account of reasonableness, and how it functions in the argument for toleration; the fourth section dismisses some common misinterpretations of Rawls' account; and the fifth section outlines a more serious problem with Rawlsian reasonableness and questions the extent to which it is adequate to the task of addressing real world problems of toleration. Although I shall argue that the reasonableness defence (as I shall call it) is the most promising approach to the justification of toleration so far considered, I shall outline a challenge for the approach at the end of the chapter which must be met if it is to fulfil this promise. Subsequent chapters will – in different ways – amplify the strengths and weaknesses of this approach.

Before embarking it is worth noting one fundamental respect in which this form of justification for toleration differs from the pluralist approach as found in Raz. For Raz, toleration is required of persons as a matter of legal duty, given that their hostile and dismissive attitudes towards one another in conditions of pluralism are inevitable and appropriate: the state imposes principles of toleration on opposed citizens as a way of discharging its duty to preserve the conditions of autonomy for all. In contrast, on the reasonableness defence the state's duty to impose principles of toleration is derived from the duty each person has to treat her fellow citizens reasonably in the public arena of political life. Whereas Raz (and other perfectionists)[4] offer a 'top-down' justification of political principles, whereby the duties of the state are informed by values embedded in a true moral theory, and the duties of individuals are to obey the law as laid down by the state, the approach to be considered here is 'bottom-up'. The values informing political principles are those that people exercising their practical reason to solve shared problems of justice in a peaceful and mutually profitable way could be committed to; the role of the state is to legislate in accordance with the principles which are a product of the exercise of practical reason shared by people who seek justice for themselves and one another.[5] The thought at the heart of this approach is that features of the political context give reasonable persons justifying reasons to tolerate other reasonable persons to whom they are opposed:[6] insofar as we are required to find principles to govern our shared political problems, to that extent we are also required to practice toleration.

Rawls: liberalism as political[7]

Rawls claims that liberalism can be conceived of as comprehensive or as political. Comprehensive liberalisms draw on moral, philosophical, or religious doctrines in justification of their principles; such is the liberalism of John Locke, Immanuel Kant and J.S. Mill who, respectively, made God's will for his creatures, the nature of human freedom as rationality, and ideals of human development and happiness the cornerstones of their political thinking. In contrast, political liberalism aims to 'stay on the surface, philosophically speaking'.[8] The justification of principles constitutive of a political liberalism aims to remain silent on the big questions, and instead makes use of ideas of justice implicit in the public political culture, and not unique to any particular creed or way of life.[9]

Rawls characterises the pluralistic conditions of which this political culture must be conceived as a product as permanent and reasonable. In other words, the disagreements between persons on the big – and for that matter, small –

questions are to be thought of as 'the natural outcome of the activities of human reason under enduring free institutions'.[10] Note that Rawls' claim is not that the disagreements characteristic of pluralism in the world we know are reasonable (although they might be).[11] Rather, his claim is a methodological one: our starting point for thinking about which political principles we ought to adopt must be the acceptance that many disagreements between people in conditions of freedom could not be eradicated, just in virtue of the way that human reason operates in these conditions. This ensures that we rule out from the start any vision of justice whereby state power is used to coerce people to unite behind the same creed. For Rawls, principles of justice in a political liberalism will always – *inter alia* – have to address problems of toleration because the circumstances of toleration (in particular, difference, importance and opposition) are a permanent fact of human life. Hence, Rawls expresses the fundamental question for political liberalism as a question about the possibility of toleration:

> [H]ow can we affirm a comprehensive doctrine as true or reasonable and yet hold that it would not be reasonable to use the state's power to require others' acceptance of it, or compliance with the special laws it might sanction?[12]

For Rawls, the answer is that so long as persons with different religious etc. doctrines are reasonable, they can form an 'overlapping consensus' on principles of justice to govern their shared lives, and any such set of principles will include principles of toleration. When thinking about solutions to problems of justice, a reasonable person accepts that, whatever the depth of commitment she has to her own moral, religious, and philosophical views, the power of the state cannot be used to suppress or convert other reasonable persons to whom she is opposed. That a set of principles can be justified to reasonable people who nevertheless differ on the big questions renders them just; and that such people can form an overlapping consensus on these principles ensures their stability. I shall examine the relation between reasonableness and toleration in more detail in the next section. For now, let me briefly comment on the idea of an overlapping consensus on principles of justice.

The stability of principles of justice in an overlapping consensus is explained by the fact that '[a]ll those who affirm [the principles] start from within their own comprehensive view and draw on the religious, philosophical, and moral grounds it provides'.[13] The nature of the commitment that each reasonable person who participates in an overlapping consensus has to the principles of justice distinguishes this consensus from a *modus vivendi*, and from a 'constitutional consensus'. In a *modus vivendi* persons commit to principles only insofar as these principles further their interests. Should the balance of power between persons in a *modus vivendi* change such that one group acquires enough power to impose their commitments on others in a way that promotes their self-interest, then it is no longer in their interests to abide by the principles of justice, and the *modus vivendi* might collapse: *modus vivendii* are politically unstable. An overlapping consensus is not a *modus vivendi* because its participants' commitment to the principles of justice at its heart is a consequence of their commitment to their own moral, religious, or philosophical doctrines. Thus, whatever the balance of power between persons in overlapping consensus, they will remain committed to the principles of justice at its heart because the conception of justice these principles express is a 'module' in each of their comprehensive doctrines.[14]

A constitutional consensus differs from overlapping consensus in terms of the content of its principles. Participants in a constitutional consensus agree on liberal political principles guaranteeing certain limited and basic political rights necessary for safeguarding democratic electoral procedures: participants affirm principles protecting these rights as a good for them and their fellow citizens, regardless of the balance of power between them. An overlapping consensus differs from a constitutional consensus primarily in terms of its scope. Principles of justice in an overlapping consensus address the distribution of the rights to freedom of thought, expression, and association; to economic and material goods; to power and opportunities in society; and to access to the social bases of self-respect.[15]

Principles of toleration can form part of a *modus vivendi* or a constitutional consensus. However, overlapping consensus on principles of toleration is preferable to these other forms of agreement for the following reasons. A *modus vivendi*, as we have seen, is not stable; principles of toleration agreed to in these conditions are not guaranteed. Constitutional consensus improves on *modus vivendi* by guaranteeing toleration through the protection of some basic rights to political participation. But, Rawls thinks, these basic rights do not exhaust the content of justice: a fully developed conception of justice must address the distribution of goods beyond basic democratic rights. However, these wider questions will generate a greater degree of opposition between persons than questions concerning basic democratic rights, because different moral, religious, and philosophical doctrines will dictate – on their own terms – different answers to questions related to freedom of expression and association, distributive justice, etc. Given that justice demands answers to these questions, persons participating in an overlapping consensus must exercise toleration across a wider and deeper range of oppositions than in a constitutional consensus. In an overlapping consensus persons find a way to accommodate their oppositions across a wide range of questions so as to jointly endorse the same conception of justice in which principles addressing these questions are rooted. What makes this possible is the reasonableness of persons who participate in overlapping consensus.[16]

Reasonableness and toleration

According to Rawls, our thinking about principles of justice must start with a set of assumptions about persons and the circumstances in which they find themselves.[17] One such assumption is that persons are reasonable.[18] There are two aspects of reasonableness relevant to our discussion here: *the capacity for a sense of justice*, and *acceptance of the consequences of the burdens of judgement*.[19] The first feature explains why an overlapping consensus on principles of toleration can get, and stay, off the ground, and the second feature explains why participants in such a consensus are committed to toleration across the range of issues of justice as described at the end of the last section.

The capacity for a sense of justice is 'the capacity to understand, to apply, and to act from the public conception of justice which characterises the fair terms of social co-operation . . . a sense of justice also expresses a willingness, if not the desire, to act in relation to others on terms that they can publicly endorse'.[20] When people have the capacity for a sense of justice they want to find publicly acceptable and mutually advantageous solutions to problems of social co-operation: they are not stubborn, manipulative, dishonest, or perverse. That the solutions such people seek are mutually advantageous means that the terms of co-operation they agree upon will ensure that 'all who are engaged in co-operation and who do their part as the rules and procedure require . . . benefit in an appropriate way as assessed by a suitable benchmark of comparison'.[21] This commitment to reciprocity prevents anyone from reaping the rewards of principled social co-operation without themselves appropriately engaging in that co-operation.

That persons with the capacity for a sense of justice seek principles of justice that are publicly acceptable commits them to the use of public reason in the justification of any such principles: it commits them to what Rawls calls 'the liberal principle of legitimacy'.[22] This principle demands that each person strive to 'live politically with others in the light of reasons all might reasonably be expected to endorse'.[23] A commitment to public reason reflects the fact that 'public justification is not simply valid reasoning, but argument addressed to others'.[24] This means that when we engage in political justification we must '[proceed] correctly from premises we accept and think others could reasonably accept to conclusions we think they could also reasonably accept'.[25] However, until we know what people committed to the use of public reason must assume about others with whom they must converse about questions of justice in public reason, the ideal of public reason has no content. At this point the second aspect of reasonableness – acceptance of the consequences of the burdens of judgement – becomes relevant.

It might be thought that rational people seeking mutually advantageous solutions to their shared problems of justice would come actively to share a set of values, ends, or beliefs from which principles of justice could be derived. However, Rawls rejects this assumption as a starting point for thinking about justice, and claims instead that a pluralism of religious, moral, and philosophical views among people is to be assumed as a permanent condition which frames their search for principles of justice, and their justificatory conversations about such principles in public reason. Furthermore, he stipulates, this pluralism is to be conceived of as *reasonable*. In part, this means that people in conditions of pluralism are to be conceived of as possessing the capacity for a sense of justice, as outlined above. But it also means that they are to be conceived of as standing under the burdens of judgement. The burdens of judgement explain why rational people with a sense of justice, and in conditions of freedom, cannot be expected to agree on every important matter involving the use of judgement. The burdens of judgement are features of human reason as it operates in conditions of freedom which make disagreement between persons on religious, moral, and philosophical questions inevitable, expectable, not to be regretted, and reasonable.

The burdens of judgement are as follows:

(a) 'The evidence – empirical and scientific – bearing on a case may be conflicting and complex, and hard to assess and evaluate.'
(b) 'Even where we agree fully about the kinds of considerations that are relevant, we may disagree about their weight, and so arrive at different judgements.'
(c) That our concepts are 'vague and subject to hard cases' makes interpretation in disagreement unavoidable, and reasonable persons can differ in the use of their judgement in such interpretation.
(d) 'The way we assess evidence and weigh moral and political values is shaped . . . by our total experience, our whole course of life up to now; and our total experiences surely differ.'
(e) 'Often there are different kinds of normative considerations of different force on both sides of a question and it is difficult to make an overall assessment.'[26]

A person who accepts the consequences of the burdens of judgement accepts that (*inter alia*) – with the best will in the world, and without epistemic or other failure on anyone's part – agreement between herself and reasonable others on the big (and for that matter, small) questions is not inevitable, and indeed may never be achieved. In sum, that human judgement is burdened means that reasonable pluralism must be assumed to be the context in which persons exercise their sense of justice, and converse in public reason (at least insofar as persons are granted political freedom to exercise their judgement): 'many of our most important political judgements involving the basic political values are made subject to conditions such that it is highly unlikely that conscientious and fully reasonable persons, even after free and open discussion, can exercise their powers of reason so that all arrive at the same conclusion'.[27]

The general upshot of all this is that no reasonable person can expect other reasonable persons whom she addresses in public reason to have reasons for supporting certain principles of justice that are identical to her own: a reasonable person will only support principles of justice which she genuinely and sincerely believes could be accepted by other reasonable people who may, consistent with their being reasonable, differ from her on the big questions.

The specific upshot of this for toleration is that a reasonable person does not treat other reasonable persons' disagreement with her on the big questions as evidence that these others are wilful, obstructive, stupid, or misinformed, even though she retains her opposition to them in virtue of believing them to have false beliefs with respect to the issue over which they disagree, given that for her to believe something is for her to believe it to be true. In a Rawlsian society of reasonable people, pluralism is not competitive and hostile in a Razian sense, even though people remain opposed to one another in their religious etc. outlooks. In a society characterised by reasonable disagreement, a reasonable person realises that, however convinced she is of her own views, to insist that political principles be justified by reference to these views in virtue of their truth appears to other people, with equally reasonable views, to be an insistence that her views have this importance simply because they are *her* views.[28] So a reasonable person will refrain from using state power to impose her preferred political principles on others with equally reasonable views across the range of issues forming the focus of an overlapping consensus: reasonable people who accept the consequences of the burdens of judgement endorse political principles of toleration.[29]

To put this in terms of the problem of toleration as stated at the end of chapter 2, what Rawls is claiming is that insofar as a person is reasonable in the two senses specified, she will reject the imposition on others of commitments she genuinely takes to be justified, because she accepts that others can reasonably disagree with her with respect to these commitments, and is committed to the use of public reason to solve problems of justice. Rawls' justification of principles of toleration turns on the acceptability of his characterisation of the operation of human reason as it addresses problems of justice in conditions of freedom. If he is right about this then any person who takes to be justified the imposition on others of her commitments simply in virtue of the fact that she herself genuinely takes these commitments to be justified engages in flawed practical reasoning.

Rawls' reasonableness defence of toleration forms a part of his overall constructivist project of justifying a political liberalism; I shall say nothing by way of criticism of this project here.[30] Instead, I shall focus (in the next section) on the avoidance of three common but misplaced criticisms of the reasonableness defence; the penultimate section addresses a more serious and worrying attack.

Clarifications

Two common criticisms of the reasonableness defence of toleration interpret Rawls' claims about the burdens of judgement as sceptical or pluralistic claims. If the reasonableness defence collapses into either of these approaches then it shares their limitations with respect to the justification of toleration. However, the interpretations of the reasonableness defence upon which these criticisms rest are flawed.

To address the scepticism reading first, Rawls explicitly denies all the following claims:[31] (1) that there is no truth of the matter with respect to disagreements involving judgement; (2) that the truth of the matter with respect to disagreements involving judgement can never be known; and (3) that persons ought to have a sceptical attitude towards their own beliefs in virtue of the fact that they cannot convince others to share them.[32] That is, Rawls rejects metaphysical and epistemological scepticism.[33] The burdens of judgement only explain why reasonable people cannot be expected to agree in all matters of judgement, and have no implication for the fact of the matter – if there is one – with respect to these disagreements, or for the attitudes that persons ought to have towards their own beliefs.

Once we accept that reasonable pluralism is the outcome of the exercise of human reason in conditions of freedom, we must accept, thinks Rawls, that this fact of human life is not to be regretted.[34] One way of disagreeing with Rawls would be to claim that although reasonable pluralism is indeed the inevitable outcome of the free exercise of reason, this is because human beings are flawed and prone to error, and this fact is to be regretted. This suggestion is made by David Estlund when he claims that '[in] order to avoid relying on the strong sceptical views either that there is no truth on [matters of judgement] or that even if there is truth there is no knowledge of it, one must explain disagreement as an *epistemic failure* of at least some people to know things that may be knowable'.[35]

Estlund's argument is this: if commitment to the burdens of judgement is to avoid the implication (1) that there is *no* truth of the matter with respect to disagreements involving judgement, or (2) that the truth of these matters *can never* be known, then commitment to the burdens of judgement must imply (1´) that there *are* truths of the matter with respect to disagreements involving judgement, or (2´) that the truth of these matters *can be* known. But this argument is flawed. Rawls' claim is not that the burdens of judgement do not entail scepticism because they entail non-scepticism; rather, Rawls' claim is that the burdens of judgement have no implications for scepticism, or any other position on the existence of truths and their knowability. In which case, we need not view the disagreement made inevitable by the burdens of judgement in terms of regrettable epistemic failure.[36]

Another way in which to dispute Rawls' claim that the reasonable pluralism made inevitable by the burdens of judgement is not to be regretted is to interpret this claim in terms of the incommensurability theses. As we saw in the last chapter, the truth of the incommensurability theses means that human life is punctuated by tragic choice between incomparable and incompatible goods: human beings experience the world of value in terms of loss. In which case, if the 'burdens' thesis is a thesis of incommensurability, then the reasonable pluralism it makes inevitable is surely to be regretted because it would be better for us to live in a world where tragic choice was not endemic.

In 'Justice as Fairness: Political not Metaphysical' – a paper which is an important prelude to *Political Liberalism*, and which is recast in large part in that book – Rawls appears to endorse this view.[37] On the account offered there, reason has limits with respect to adjudicating conflicts between competing accounts of what is good, true, just, and beautiful, and, once these limits have been reached, pluralism is permanent because all beliefs sets within pluralism are consistent with reason, although none of them is uniquely demanded by reason. The truth of the incommensurability theses means that reason underdetermines beliefs about value because there comes a point at which reason can specify no value according to which other values can be ranked, and neither can it guide comparisons of values in the absence of a master-value.

'Justice as Fairness: Political not Metaphysical' appears in *Political Liberalism* as lecture 1; however, in this work all references to incommensurability as an explanation of the permanence of pluralism have been excised.[38] Instead, the permanence and reasonableness of pluralism is explained simply in terms of the burdens of judgement laid out in the last section, whether or not the incommensurability theses are true. The reason for this excision – and for Rawls' insistence that the burdens thesis is not a sceptical view – relates to the political nature of Rawls' liberalism. Versions of scepticism and the incommensurability theses are highly controversial philosophical doctrines: if acceptance of the permanence of reasonable pluralism with all its consequences for the public justification of political principles is dependent on acceptance of these doctrines, then liberalism does not 'stay on the surface, philosophically speaking'.[39] Rawls' view is that the assumptions we must make about people in order to conceive of them as solving shared problems of justice through the use of practical reason need not, and should not, include the assumption that they endorse philosophical theses of scepticism or incommensurability;[40] and the burdens thesis can be asserted without entailing either of these doctrines.[41]

A third common critique that rests on a misinterpretation is that the reasonableness defence is acceptable in theory, but of limited use in practice. As Leif Wenar puts it, 'Rawls' presentation of justice as fairness is based on a conception of the reasonable that a variety of comprehensive doctrines, as we know them and can expect them to become, will reject.'[42] Wenar argues that practitioners of the major religions, such as Roman Catholicism, are unlikely ever to accept Rawls' political justifications (*inter alia*, of principles of toleration) because of the requirement (which Wenar imputes to Rawls) that arguments of faith do not enter political justification. Wenar claims that this requirement is tantamount to a demand that 'fundamental aspects of [Roman Catholics'] faith and their attitude towards it' be abandoned.[43] Given that it is a fundamental part of Catholic doctrine that 'those religious truths which are by their nature accessible to human reason can be known by all men with ease, with solid certitude, and with no trace of error, even in the present state of the human race',[44] Wenar argues that the expectation that those engaged in political justification do not conceive of their beliefs as the only reasonable beliefs on that subject *ipso facto* excludes devout Roman Catholics from the scope of reasonableness, which means that they are not in a position to practise toleration. But the justification of toleration we seek is supposed to address people who hold their beliefs in precisely the manner of Catholics, and practitioners of other major religions: 'with solid certitude, and with no trace of error'. Of what practical use is a justification of toleration which, in all probability, will not convince those people who are most likely to be intolerant?

In response, we can start by suggesting that, unlike devout devotees, not all – probably not most – persons have 'fully comprehensive' views held in the manner of an article of faith.[45] Most people have less than comprehensive views that they hold in a more or less loose way. If this looseness means that most people hold their beliefs in a less dogmatic and dramatic way than devotees then the prospects for the realisation of reasonableness in a pluralistic society may be more rosy than Wenar believes. However, even if Wenar is right and it is highly unlikely that people will become Rawlsian reasonable believers, the reasonableness defence of toleration – *qua* justification – stands unscathed. What we seek is a *normative* argument to show that persons *ought* to practise toleration: in Rawls, this is derived from reflections on the operation of practical reason in contexts of justice. That people are unlikely to practise toleration because they often exercise their practical reason in a non-ideal way should not discourage us from searching for a philosophical account of why it would be a good thing if they did; if anything, it should spur us on to greater efforts.[46] The facts of human psychology are one thing, and moral argument is another: that human beings often fail to do – or recognise – what they ought to do does not in itself impugn moral arguments which establish what they ought to do.

Setting aside these misplaced critiques, let us turn now to the worrying suggestion that reasonableness, even when properly interpreted, cannot justify the practice of toleration because it gives insufficient guidance as to the limits of toleration.

The problem of incompossibility

Rawls' solution to the problem of toleration is to propose a requirement that each person exercise her capacity for a sense of justice, and accept the consequences of the burdens of judgement, in seeking principles to govern her shared life with others through mediation of the oppositions that exist between them. One criticism of this proposal is that it does not take seriously the fact that the conditions that are adequate for one reasonable person to pursue her ends may prevent another equally reasonable person from adequately pursuing her ends, and that the two aspects of reasonableness give no guidance as to who is to give way – in the name of toleration – when such clashes occur. This 'problem of incompossibility' threatens to stymie the reasonableness defence of toleration. To fix our thoughts, consider the following example offered by Jeremy Waldron by way of illustration.[47]

Imagine a society populated by three (types of) people. P is an 'entrepreneurial pornographer' who enjoys producing and consuming pornography. Q is a devout Muslim utterly opposed to pornography but unable entirely to avoid the products of P's efforts as he goes about his daily business. R is a secular humanist, who is not disturbed by his occasional exposure to P's products, but does not seek them out. Imagine further that P and Q have, in the past, each made an effort to accommodate themselves to the existence of others to whom they are opposed in their society. P 'was once a fanatical pornographer to the point of rampant exhibitionism and voyeurism' such that both Q and R objected to his activities; but now he agrees that public displays of pornography ought to be limited, perhaps by means of zoning laws, media watersheds, etc.[48] Q used to believe that he could not bring up his children as good Muslims while surrounded by unbelievers like R, but has now come to accept the presence of Rs. In this society P and R live together in toleration, as do Q and R: but there remains a problem of toleration between P and Q. For Q, the moral depravity of P is damaging to him in the practice of his faith – just knowing that P is doing what he does causes Q great moral distress – and he worries that the social environment in which his children must live is polluted: Q calls for pornography to be banned. For P, Q's demands that pornography be banned are demands that he be prevented from pursuing the pleasures of the flesh in the (limited) public way that makes them pleasurable for him: P argues that Q should avoid pornographic publications and displays, turn his mind to matters less distressing to him, and thicken his skin.

What guidance does the requirement to be reasonable give us with respect to this problem? Should the demands of P or of Q be overridden in the name of liberal toleration as delivered by the reasonableness defence? Let us consider the extent to which P and Q might be said to exhibit each aspect of reasonableness. Consider first acceptance of the consequences of the burdens of judgement. P's motto is 'whatever floats your boat': he believes that people who do not enjoy pornography are missing out, but he accepts that some people will always be prudish in their sexual preferences, and that they should not have pornography forced down their throats. P's explanation for this fact of life is in terms of the burden of judgement (d): total experiences differ and affect individual sexual mores. By contrast, Q believes that non-Muslim people imperil their souls, and make grave moral mistakes in the way they live as a consequence of their failure to open their hearts to Allah: he wants nothing to do with such people, even though he accepts the inevitability of their presence in the free society in which he lives. Q's explanation of the inevitable presence of lost souls among us is in terms of the burden of judgement (c): the vagueness of our moral concepts means that we must rely on interpretive powers when deciding how we will live, and people who (inevitably, given the burden of judgement (d)) do not look to the Qu'ran for guidance will often make the wrong choices, even though they exercise their reason correctly. Both P and Q are reasonable insofar as they accept the burdens of judgement and their consequences for pluralism, yet they remain opposed in a way that calls for one of them to practise toleration of the other.

So is there a difference in reasonableness between P and Q with respect to their respective exercises of the capacity for a sense of justice? This requires that a person be willing to propose and abide by fair principles of social co-operation so long as others do so too, and be willing to converse with others about these principles in public reason. From P's point of view, he has done just this: he has accepted that his previously rampant public displays of pornography cannot be justified to Qs and Rs in public reason, and now proposes to abide by principles which permit him to continue producing and enjoying pornography, but which limit the arenas in which it is available. From Q's point of view, he has also shown a willingness to abide by fair principles of justice: realising that reasonable others cannot be expected to share his faith, he no longer insists that state power ought to be used to convert unbelievers, and supports principles of freedom of conscience and association which protect freedom of religious worship. However, he still holds that the very existence of pornography in his society damages his opportunities to live his religious life in a way he conceives of as adequate, and so does not endorse principles of freedom of expression which permit the consumption of pornography in any arenas, however limited.

In Part II we will address the details of such real world debates. For the moment, the problem is that both P and Q – *from their own perspectives* – seem to satisfy the demands of reasonableness. They both accept the consequences of the burdens of judgement, and each of them exercises their capacity for a sense of justice. And yet, they still face a problem of toleration: P insists on his right to produce and consume pornography in limited arenas, but Q refuses to accept the existence of this right. If reasonableness justifies toleration then applying the concept of reasonableness to the P–Q dispute should tell us which of these persons ought to give way in the name of toleration: but, Waldron claims, it fails to do so. The reasonableness defence justifies toleration only for people (like R) whose opposition to their co-citizens can be softened without damage being done to conditions taken by them to be adequate for the pursuit of aims constitutive of their way of life.[49]

To many liberal eyes, a tempting response is that Q should give way because his objection to P's limited production and consumption of pornography is oversensitive. There is nothing in P's activities which literally prevents Q from practising Islam: the zoning laws and watersheds supported by P mean that Q and his children can easily avoid P's pornography. Whether or not this is the best response (or indeed the right way to characterise Q's objections to P),[50] it is not available on the reasonableness defence of toleration. First, as Waldron notes, sensitivity *per se* does not *ipso facto* render a person intolerant: for example, the aims of Islam, pious Christianity privately practised, and pious Judaism privately practised can all be pursued by persons in the same society who are tolerant of the religious differences which separate them, notwithstanding the highly sensitive character of each of these aims.[51] What creates the problem of toleration between P and Q is not Q's sensitivity *per se*, but his sensitivity to what it is, in particular, that P does: P's production and consumption of pornography pollutes Q's social environment in a way that he believes damages his life in Islam.

A second tempting liberal response is that Q is simply wrong in his belief that P's pornographic activities cause him harm by affecting his opportunity to lead a religious life in a way deemed adequate by him. Here we get to the heart of the problem for the reasonableness defence. To claim that Q is wrong in this way imposes an external standard on Q of what it is for social conditions to be adequate for him to practise Islam. To be sure, many liberals have taken this 'aggressive' tack with respect to problems of toleration;[52] but it is not a tack available to *political* liberals who aim, remember, to avoid passing comment on big questions in their political justifications. If justifying a principle of toleration in the P–Q case requires addressing the question of what Islam requires of Muslims, then the political liberalism to which Rawls and his followers aspire is not possible. However, questions about the political character of liberalism to one side, passing judgement on others in the way required by this second liberal response is problematical in its own terms. As Waldron states,

> I don't think there is any way of saying that a set of permissions is adequate for the practice of a religion except by paying attention to how the set of restrictions seems from the internal point of view of the religion. To abandon any interest in that would be, in effect, to abandon any real concern for adequacy.[53]

If liberals are to take seriously the requirement that principles of co-operation must protect social conditions adequate for the pursuit of reasonable but diverse aims, then the criteria for adequacy must in some way incorporate the internal judgements of people for whom these conditions are putatively adequate: to override these judgements 'would be arbitrary and unmotivated'.[54]

Conclusion

In characterising the second liberal response above I claimed that it exceeds the bounds of the political by requiring liberals to pass judgement on what Islam requires of Muslims. One way to salvage the reasonableness defence while remaining within the bounds of the political in the justification of liberal toleration is to be more specific about exactly what liberals are required to pass judgement upon, given this response. We might modify the second liberal response as follows. Even if Q is correct in his belief that P's activities cause him harm, he is incorrect in his belief that this form of harm ought to be addressed by political principles, in which case he must tolerate P. Here, the justification of toleration in the P–Q case requires addressing the question of what Islam requires of Muslims *in their shared lives with others*, that is, in the political arena rather than in personal and associational life. The thought here is that reasonable Muslims must accept that what counts as harm to them given the internal perspective of their faith does not *ipso facto* qualify as a harm to be addressed by political principles: in order to establish this, it must be possible for Muslims to present the harm *as such* to other reasonable persons in public reason. (Henceforth I shall refer to these conceptions of harm respectively as 'internal' and 'political' harm.) On this response, the wedge that is driven between genuinely taking a commitment to be justified and taking its imposition on others to be justified is purely political: insofar as a person exercises her judgement to solve the political problems she shares with others she cannot treat the commitments which she takes to be genuinely justified to be *ipso facto* and thereby justified as the basis of principles to solve shared political problems.[55]

If a person is to appeal to these commitments in arguments for intolerance of the activity of others which putatively causes her harm understood as such in virtue of these commitments then – as a necessary condition – the harm must be intelligible as such to other reasonable people (although it is not required that other reasonable people be brought to share the experience of the harm through discourse in public reason; and it is anyway not clear how this could be achieved). However, making such harm intelligible in public reason is not sufficient for the success of a claim that the activity causing it ought not to be tolerated. Beyond this, the harm must be shown to be *politically salient*. The chapters in Part II consider real world problems of toleration in which parties claiming to be harmed present their cases in this way.

Modifying the liberal response in this way provides answers to hard cases of toleration if and only if arguments are made to show that the conditions under which harms experienced as such from an internal perspective also qualify as such from the public perspective by being intelligible and politically salient. In order to solve hard P–Q-type problems of toleration we need to know which of the parties has a harm-based complaint against the other that ought to be addressed by political principles. If the internal harm experienced by each of them through the actions of the other cannot be presented as a political harm, then both are required to tolerate what they object to in the other's behaviour in the name of reasonableness. If each can present the internal harm suffered by them through the actions of the other as a political harm then each, *qua* reasonable, is either required to keep his opposition to himself and practice toleration with respect to the other, or the activities of each causing harm to the other ought not to be tolerated. And if the internal harm complaint of one but not the other can be presented as a political harm, then the one who fails in this respect is unreasonable if he persists in his demands that the institutions of the state ought to be used so as to suppress what he opposes in the other, in which case he ought to be tolerant.

This is what is required if the reasonableness defence is to provide any way forward for thinking about toleration. In the next chapter I address an important account of the distinction between internal harm (often referred to as 'offence') and political harm, and raise some questions about it. With this account in hand we are then in a position to explore, in Part II, how the abstract philosophical considerations about the justification and limits of toleration laid out so far apply to real world oppositions.

Chapter 6

Political harm
The liberal paradigm

> The only way to make sure people you agree with can speak is to support the
> rights of people you don't agree with.
>
> (Eleanor Holmes North, quoted in the *New York Post*)[1]

Introduction

We saw at the end of the last chapter that the most promising account of why
persons in opposition ought to practise toleration with respect to at least some
of their differences – the reasonableness defence of toleration – can deliver on
its promise only if it is accompanied by an account of when the complaints of
any party against those they oppose ought to be addressed in law (or ought to
register as legitimate in the political zeitgeist) in virtue of a *political* harm having
been done to this party; in other words, the harm can be established as such in
public reason. In the absence of such an account the reasonableness defence
provides no principled way of adjudicating the competing claims of reasonable
people whose opposition constitutes a problem of toleration, such as Waldron's
entrepreneurial pornographer and sensitive Muslim.

In this chapter I shall outline an account of political harm beloved of many
contemporary liberals according to which such harm is exhaustively constituted
by the violation of rights. This account *prima facie* provides the right sort of
supplement to the reasonableness defence of toleration, because each person can
be shown in public reason to have the same set of rights. With an account of
these rights in hand liberals committed to the reasonableness defence have a
principled way of adjudicating in law problems of toleration between people who
genuinely take their oppositions to be justified by taking responsibility for the
beliefs which inform these oppositions in the way outlined in chapter 2: each
right in the liberal set could not be rejected as such by any reasonable person.

If successful, the rights-based account of political harm boosts the appeal of
the reasonableness defence by setting principled limits to toleration that reflect
the liberal heritage of this defence.[2] However, the rights-based account of harm
is controversial, for thinkers both inside and outside of the liberal tradition.
Two thoughts unite these critics. First, that the state might have the right, and a
duty, to intervene in cases of opposition so as to uphold one party's complaint

even when that party's rights have not been violated. On this view, the liberal paradigm wherein political harm is exhausted by the violation of individual rights fails to register the significance, from the point of view of justice, of harms that opposed parties can inflict upon one another that it is not possible to characterise (or to characterise well) simply in terms of violations of their individual rights. The second thought is that the liberal conception of rights is unduly narrow and loads the dice against the claims of people like the reasonable Muslim to protection by the state from harms done to them by people like the reasonable pornographer. The three different attacks on the liberal paradigm of harm I shall sketch in the final section of this chapter are motivated by these thoughts, and provide the theoretical backdrop to problems with the liberal paradigm that emerge once attempts are made to apply it to the real world problems of toleration to be considered in Part II.

Harm and offence

The problem of toleration stated at the end of chapter 5 created the following challenge for liberals: find an account of harm whereby oppositions existing between equally reasonable people can be mediated by the state according to principles of toleration. These sorts of oppositions are widespread in contemporary democratic societies. Participants in many seemingly intractable debates on questions of public policy can be characterised as reasonable in the same way as Waldron's pornographer and Muslim: 'pro-choice' and 'pro-life' advocates in debates about abortion, 'Countryside Alliance' and animal rights lobbyists in the UK debate about the ban on hunting with dogs, and gay rights activists and 'Alliance for Marriage' members in the US debate over the Federal Marriage Amendment (which would deny to homosexual men and women a constitutional right to marry)[3] could all argue their cases consistent with acceptance of the consequences of the burdens of judgement while exercising their capacities for a sense of justice. Making reference to the reasonableness of opposed parties in such debates will only take us so far in finding solutions which realise liberal principles of toleration: oppositions may still exist once opposed parties have satisfied the demands of reasonableness, and the state must mediate these oppositions. In order to proceed we need a way of deciding which parties' claims to have been harmed by – or to be under threat of harm from[4] – those to whom they are opposed provide legitimate grounds for state action in the form of legal protection from harm for the party in question.

One way in which to approach this challenge is to construct an account of harm whereby the claims of one or more parties in reasonable opposition to have been harmed by the other can be dismissed. To return to Waldron's example, we might claim either that the reasonable Muslim's claims to be harmed by the pornographer are mistaken (for example, by claiming that the Muslim's sensitivities are too heightened), or *vice versa* (by claiming, for example, that the production of pornography cannot be a part of any mature conception of the good).

This approach has the virtue of generating quick, clean decisions with respect to problems of toleration characterised by reasonable oppositions, but this is more or less the limit of its attractions. If liberal toleration requires that the state peremptorily dismiss as mistaken the sincere claims of various of its genuinely reasonable members to have been harmed by others then the vision of the state as silent on the big moral, religious, and philosophical questions which inform its members' lives – and to that extent, the vision of the state as the servant of its members – beloved of liberals through the ages is an illusion. What liberals with this vision need is an account of harm which enables the legal adjudication of reasonable oppositions, and which nevertheless acknowledges as meaningful the claims to have been harmed made by reasonable people who do not achieve the outcome they desire through such adjudication. In other words, if the account of political harm justifies overruling the Muslim in his dispute with the pornographer by, say, generating laws protecting freedom of expression which cover the pornographer's activities – perhaps by ranking protection from the harm suffered by the Muslim as subordinate to the protection of freedom of expression in the hierarchy of political priorities – then this account must also register as meaningful, and not mistaken, the Muslim's claims to have been harmed by the pornographer, even though (on this account) these claims are not sufficient to ground legislation protecting people from that type of harm. As John Horton puts it,

> [I]t is important to acknowledge the real possibility, even when we reject for what we take to be good reasons the public or institutional accommodation of a particular claim by a cultural group, that their motivating sense of grievance may still have legitimacy. That for whatever reasons we genuinely believe that we cannot incorporate a particular claim for differential treatment, or cannot do so adequately, does not necessarily mean that we *must* reject the validity of the complaint.[5]

The best attempt at such an account is given by Joel Feinberg, and is founded on a distinction he draws between (political) harm and offence.[6] Putting aside for the moment the question of how best to understand political harm, Feinberg offers a taxonomy of offence consisting of six categories, and gives graphic illustrative examples for each category. In considering the examples the reader is invited to imagine herself as a passenger on a crowded bus trying to get to an important appointment – a job interview, say – for which she is late; in other words, she cannot escape the activity which causes the offence without great cost to herself.[7]

1   *Affronts to the senses*: for example, caused by pungent and unpleasant smells and unbearable noises.
2   *Disgust and revulsion*: for example, caused by witnessing other passengers eating 'live insects, fish heads, and pickled sex organs of lamb, veal, and pork, smothered in garlic and onions', and then vomiting their meal up

before consuming their own and one another's vomit along with the remains of the food.[8]

3   *Shock to moral, religious, or patriotic sensibilities*: for example, caused by violence towards corpses, defacement of the flag, or mockery of religious icons.

4   *Shame, embarrassment, and anxiety*: for example, caused by public nudity, explicit public reference to sex acts, and publicly performed sex acts (including those involving animals).

5   *Annoyance, boredom, and frustration*: for example, caused by the inane chatter of others, or by being trapped by a persistent bore.

6   *Fear, resentment, humiliation, and anger*: for example, caused by racist or sexist images or speech, threatening behaviour or appearance (a youth appears wearing a swastika on an armband, or 'pulls out a fake rubber knife and "stabs" himself and others repeatedly to peals of maniacal laughter').[9]

All of us have experienced situations in which the behaviour of others has offended us in one of the ways Feinberg identifies (although, thankfully, few of us have been subject to the more extreme forms of behaviour he identifies which can cause each type of offence). By considering the following two questions we will see how Feinberg's account of offence can be used to partially flesh out the larger account of harm required by the reasonableness defence of toleration: (1) do any of the categories of offence identified by Feinberg capture the experience of Waldron's reasonable Muslim?; and (2) how, if at all, ought the law to address this and the other categories of offence?

The experience of Muslims in dispute with pornographers – and persons involved in the examples of other reasonable oppositions given above – falls into the category of shock to moral, religious, or patriotic sensibilities. This sort of offence strikes us as qualitatively different from the offences of the other five categories, and as somehow more significant. This difference is registered by Feinberg's classification of the offences in this category as *profound* offences. Other examples of causes of profound offence he gives are voyeurism, the deliberate attempt to frighten and mock Jewish survivors of Nazi death camps by parading through a town heavily populated by them,[10] deviant and execrated religious and moral practices (such as eating pork or slaughtering cows), the mistreatment of venerated symbols, and abortion and the mistreatment of corpses.[11]

Feinberg distinguishes profound offence from other forms of offence as follows:

1   profound offences are non-trivial;
2   the experience of them need not coincide with perception of behaviour that causes the offence (that is, bare knowledge of the behaviour may be enough to cause offence);
3   they occur at the level of a person's higher-order (moral, religious, or patriotic) sensibilities rather than her senses;

4   they offend because they are believed to be wrong (rather than being believed to be wrong because they offend); and

5   they are impersonal (the offended person objects to what is being done *per se*, not just what is being done to her).

The complaint of the reasonable Muslim to be harmed by the pornographer's activities is a clear case of profound offence:

1   the production of pornography in her society is not a trivial matter to the Muslim;

2   the Muslim does not consume pornography, and it is the bare knowledge that others do that offends her;

3   the Muslim's moral and religious sensibilities are offended by the production and consumption of pornography;

4   the Muslim believes, in virtue of her moral and religious convictions, that the production and consumption of pornography is wrong; and

5   the Muslim believes that this would be wrong wherever and whenever it happened, even if she were not aware of its production and consumption, and there was no possibility of her coming to this awareness.

In contrast, Feinberg claims, the other categories of offence are best characterised merely as offensive nuisances, and have the following characteristics: they are trivial; they coincide with the perceptual experience of what causes the offence; they are personal (the perceiver of the offensive behaviour believes herself to be wronged by it); the wrong believed to be done by offensive nuisances consists merely in the offence caused (which generally consists of some affront to the senses); and, finally, they are thought to be offensive just in virtue of the offence they cause to the perceiver, and not in virtue of moral or religious principles. Most examples of offence falling into categories other than shock to moral, religious, and patriotic sensibilities are merely offensive nuisances.[12]

Feinberg's distinction between profound offence and offensive nuisance merely provides us with a way of understanding the Muslim's complaints against the pornographer as significant and qualitatively different from, say, complaints about the irritation caused by the sound of a baby crying, or about the embarrassment caused by standing next to tipsy teenagers snogging at a bus stop. Characterising the Muslim's complaints against the pornographer in terms of profound offence captures the significance of the complaints to the Muslim, and renders meaningful any claims to have been harmed by the pornographer that are made by the Muslim. If the reasonable Muslim's complaints are well characterised in terms of profound offence, the question now is how, if at all, the law ought to address the causes of profound offence.

Turning again to Feinberg, we must start with his recommendation for how the law ought to address the causes of offensive nuisances. Feinberg advocates that 'conscientious legislators . . . will have to weigh, in each main category and context of offensiveness, the seriousness of the offense caused to unwilling witnesses against the reasonableness of the offender's conduct'.[13] When assessing the seriousness of an offence legislators must take into account its *magnitude* (that is, its intensity, duration, and extent), whether it could have been *reasonably avoided* by the offended party, whether the offended party *voluntarily incurred* the offence, and whether the offended party has '*abnormal susceptibilities*' to the behaviour which causes them offence.[14] When assessing the reasonableness of the offender's conduct, Feinberg recommends that legislators consider the following factors: the *importance* of the conduct to the person (for example, is it integral to her religious practice?); the *social value* of the conduct; the extent to which the conduct constitutes *free expression*;[15] whether the person has *alternative opportunities* for engaging in the offensive conduct; whether the motive behind the offensive conduct is *spiteful or malicious* (is the conduct undertaken with no other motive than to cause offence?); and, the *nature of the locality* in which the conduct is undertaken (is it in a district or neighbourhood where such conduct is rare and unexpected?).[16]

Applying these standards (roughly, for the stories can always be complicated by additional nuances) to the examples Feinberg gives, it is clear that – at least on public transport – the following causes of offence can be legitimately prohibited in law on the following grounds. Witnessing a person eating their own (or others') vomit or faeces is intensely disgusting, has no social value, can be done in private, and is not what people expect to see on their journey to work, and so can be legislated against in a liberal state. Public sex acts can be prohibited on similar grounds (although a case might be made for the provision of nudist beaches where such activities can be performed in public, if the practice can be shown to be of sufficient personal importance to the participants). Finally, threatening behaviours – such as fake stabbings with a rubber knife, or loud proclamations that one has a bomb in one's shoe as an airplane takes off – can be prohibited given their malicious intent.

In contrast, it is unlikely – again, at least on public transport – that cases could be made using Feinberg's tests for the prohibition of the following types of conduct. The production of pungent smells: some people cannot help making such smells, and there is no acceptable way to determine which aromatic people this is true of; in any case, offended people can simply breathe through their mouths in the presence of such people, if need be (note, however, that if the smell is produced by a factory and constantly wafts over a nearby residential area, then a case for prohibition may be possible). Mockery of religious icons in the written word and through visual images: Feinberg argues that the value of free expression makes unacceptable any legislation which would prohibit a youth from wearing 'a T-shirt with a cartoon across his chest of Christ on the cross [with the accompanying slogan] "Hang in there, baby!"',[17] or the use of expletives, or racist, sexist or homophobic language. Finally, there is no justification for legislation to prohibit bores from cornering their victims (the social value of permitting persons to choose their conversation partners is too great), nor for preventing couples from kissing in public (only people of abnormal sensitivities would find this more than mildly embarrassing).

Feinberg's balancing tests for the legislation of offensive nuisances merely is *prima facie* a sensible way for political liberals to set the limits of toleration with respect to forms of conduct fit to cause such offence.[18] The values appealed to in assessing the seriousness of an offensive nuisance, and the reasonableness of an offender's conduct, are not embedded in any one moral, religious, or philosophical tradition, and can be defended as values without recourse to theories in any such tradition. However, what guidance do these tests give us with respect to the problem of profound offence that arises for the reasonableness defence of toleration?

Feinberg argues that when profoundly offensive conduct is undertaken in public then legislation to prevent it should be considered using the same balancing tests as those that apply to offensive nuisances merely. However, we saw at the end of the last chapter that the pornographer – insofar as he is reasonable – has already accepted legislation limiting the arenas in which he is permitted to display his wares: he accepts that his magazines should be kept on the top shelf behind screens obscuring their front pages, that zoning laws should govern where he opens his next adult cinema, and that his videos should come with a warning as to their explicit content. The reasonable pornographer claims that the legislation governing the dissemination and display of his pornography means that it can easily be avoided by anyone likely to be offended by it. In that case, there can be no argument for any further legislation banning its production and distribution. However, the reasonable Muslim persists: his objection is not that he is harmed by the actual experience of pornography as he goes about his business, but rather that the knowledge that pornography is being produced and consumed by others in his society causes him profound offence. If the complaints of the reasonable Muslim are to ground legislation banning pornography then it must be the case that the profound offence suffered by the Muslim simply in virtue of his knowledge that others in his society produce and consume pornography is appropriately addressed by the law. Feinberg calls this experience 'bare knowledge' profound offence, and argues that no liberal state ought to enact legislation to protect persons from this form of offence, as follows.

The question is whether activities causing bare knowledge profound offence should be exempted from liberal principles generating legislation to protect the private sphere so that the legislation of such activities can be decided using the same balancing tests as those governing offensive conduct performed in public. One way to argue this case is to claim that, even if so exempted, bare knowledge profound offence is reasonably avoidable because only the morally skittish take offence at the very idea of people doing things of which they morally disapprove, in which case it would never provide grounds for the prohibition of private activities giving rise to it.[19] Although this strategy has the virtue of providing a solution to the dispute between the reasonable Muslim and pornographer without a glib dismissal of either of their claims to suffer harm as a result of the other's activities, it nevertheless does not deliver the sort of solution to the problem desired by most liberals. The problem is that the baseline for moral skittishness can fluctuate over time according to the prevailing norms and cultural values, and thus an argument that bare knowledge profound offence in one place or time provides no grounds for legislation for protection from it because those who experience it are skittish may not hold in another place or time. As Feinberg puts it,

> In Saudi Arabia, it may well be that 90% of the population is morally skittish by our own standards even though 'normal' of course by their own. In the United States almost everyone would be put into intensely disagreeable offended states by the repulsive conduct on the bus . . . but hardly anyone would be put into equally disagreeable and unavoidable states by the bare idea of such conduct occurring somewhere or other. . . . But it is at least conceivable (barely) that almost all Saudis are put in precisely the same intensely unpleasant state of mind by the thought that wine or pork is being consumed somewhere or Christian rites conducted somewhere in their country beyond their perception as they would be by their direct witnessing of such odious conduct.[20]

The argument from moral skittishness (i.e., that only the skittish take bare knowledge profound offence at anything) cannot guarantee that bare knowledge profound offence will never provide grounds for the legal prohibition of forms of behaviour – such as diverse religious or sexual practices – which liberals have historically aimed to protect at the level of principle through commitment to individual rights and freedoms. For this reason Feinberg thinks that liberals should justify their resistance to legislation to protect people from bare knowledge profound offence on grounds other than dismissal of such offence as the nervy penchant of the morally skittish. Let us consider Feinberg's alternative argument for resistance that places the opposition of the reasonable Muslim to the reasonable pornographer within the limits of toleration.

> [T]he argument for criminalization of private conduct to prevent bare-knowledge offense rests either on the offense principle or on legal moralism. If it appeals to the liberal's offense principle it fails, since bare-knowledge offense is not 'wrongful offense' in the sense employed by that principle. But if it appeals to legal moralism, it may be valid on those grounds, but it cannot commit the liberal, since the liberal rejects legal moralism. It follows that there is no argument open to a liberal that legitimizes punishment of private harmless behaviour in order to prevent bare-knowledge offense.[21]

Feinberg's strategy is to isolate two ways in which a bare knowledge profoundly offended person might make her case for legal protection, and to reject each of them as unsuccessful from the point of view of justifying liberal legislation. Returning to our reasonable Muslim, the case that falls foul of legal moralism is this: the production of pornography ought to be prohibited because it is morally wrong. For Feinberg – as for the political liberals who advocate the reasonableness defence of toleration – the liberal state must avoid legal moralism, which he defines in terms of commitment to the following principle: 'It can be morally legitimate to prohibit conduct on the ground that it is inherently immoral, even though it causes neither harm nor offence to the actor or others' ('offence' here refers to offensive nuisance merely).[22] Thus, if the reasonable Muslim's complaint is as Feinberg has it, then the liberal state ought not to legislate as the Muslim wishes. The second case the Muslim might make is this: my knowledge that pornography is being produced is harmful to me – by being profoundly offensive – and so ought to be prohibited. Feinberg's response to this case is that because it is 'a claim to protection from their own unpleasant mental states by those who are offended by a "bare thought" . . . of the occurrence of [some] loathsome behaviour',[23] the liberal state ought not to legislate as the Muslim wishes, because in a liberal state persons do not have the right to such protection. Here we see Feinberg's clear invocation of the liberal rights-based paradigm of harm: on the second, non-moralistic, version of the Muslim's argument, the claim that his *rights* are violated by suffering bare knowledge profound offence cannot (Feinberg claims) be supported.

Does Feinberg's response settle the issue? Problems with this approach will emerge in consideration of real world problems of toleration in Part II. For the moment we should note that there are two further possible ways of presenting the reasonable Muslim's case which Feinberg does not consider. First, that the production of pornography is morally wrong, that this type of morally wrong behaviour harms the Muslim, and that reasonable Muslims have a right to be protected from such harm, in which case the liberal state ought to legislate to protect them. And second, that reasonable Muslims and the like do have a right to be protected from the unpleasant mental states constitutive of bare knowledge profound offence, in which case the liberal state ought to protect them in law. In each of these responses the strategy is to establish that bare knowledge profound offence is a harm from which people have a right to be protected by the liberal state: the appeal to rights avoids the charge of legal moralism, and brings the experience of bare knowledge profound offence into the purview of the liberal state.[24]

As we will see in Part II, it is common for reasonably opposed parties in contested real world problems of toleration to invoke, challenge, and modify the account of rights at the core of liberalism in making their cases for legislation. The success of such approaches can only be judged by considering them in detail. Before turning to this I shall give a brief account, in the remainder of this chapter, of the role and nature of rights in contemporary liberalism, and raise in the abstract four important challenges to the liberal account which the real world cases in Part II can be seen to embody.

Liberal rights[25]

The contemporary literature on liberal rights is massive, and I shall make no attempt to survey it here.[26] Instead, I shall focus on the most persuasive and popular answers given by liberals to the following two questions: (1) what are rights?; and (2) what rights do we have? The first question requires a specification of the basis of rights (that is, the grounds on which persons are claimed to have them) and of their role in political thinking and action. With respect to this question, many liberal thinkers conceive of rights as registering persons' *important interests* in *being treated by the state with equal concern and respect* in a way that reflects their *dignity*. There are three components to this characterisation which combine to give a theory of the basis and function of rights to which most liberals subscribe. Let me say a little more about each of these components.

To claim that rights protect persons' important interests is to claim that a person has a right to x when her interest in x is sufficiently important for other people to be held under a duty to provide her with x, or not prevent her pursuit of x.[27] On this view, other people have duties which correlate with my rights, and these duties exist because what they require of others (non-interference with my actions, and/or the provision to me of goods and services) is necessary for certain important interests of mine to be secured. The attractions of making interests the basis of rights are at least four-fold.

First, this account endows the concept of a right with the elasticity it appears to possess when we debate the rights we have. The fact that we can discuss and disagree about what constitutes an important interest explains familiar disputes about the rights we have, and what to do when they clash. For example, most people agree that we have an important interest in fundamental liberties such as freedom of speech and association such that other individuals and the state ought to be held under a duty not to interfere with our speech or associative activities. However, most people also believe that we all have an important interest in security which justifies holding each of us under a duty to accept restrictions on our liberty, and which has, in recent times, been used to justify legislation such as the US Patriot Act.[28] According to the 'interest-based' (IB) account of rights, when the Patriot Act is objected to on the grounds that it permits unacceptable incursions into individual liberties, at least part of what is being claimed is that the interest we have in these liberties is more important than the interest we have in security.

Second, the IB account is context sensitive: the demands placed on person A by person B's important interest in x will not be the same as the demands placed on person C if A and C stand in different relations to B. For example, the important interest each person has in not being tortured imposes a duty on all people not to torture one another, but it imposes extra 'duties of enforcement' on government officials to investigate and prosecute torturers, 'duties of rescue' on those in a position to save torture victims, and perhaps 'duties of communication' on journalists and educators. As Jeremy Waldron puts it, important interests generate waves of duties for persons differentially placed with respect to the interest-holder.[29]

Next, the IB account accommodates the important distinction between universal and special rights. Universal rights are had by every person with the characteristics providing a basis for rights; special rights are had by a person in virtue of something that distinguishes her from other persons. For example, all persons have a right not to be tortured, but only my husband has conjugal rights against me as his wife, in virtue of the contract I make with him in marriage. The IB account can explain the existence of certain universal rights in virtue of the fact that once an interest shared by all people has been identified as being of sufficient importance to provide the basis for a right, we can claim that all people have a duty to help/not hinder one another in pursuit of this interest. It might seem that the IB account cannot so easily accommodate special rights, because it is hard to see how an interest can be sufficiently important to ground a right unless it is an interest that all people share, in which case the interest grounds a universal rather than a special right.

The way in which an IB approach might accommodate special rights can be seen in Joseph Raz's account of the rights created by promise-making. Raz claims that every person has an interest 'to be able to forge special bonds with other people'.[30] This shared interest (a) grounds the universal right to make promises from which the right to make a particular promise is derived, and (b) grounds the universal right to have promises made to us kept. Given that the second of these universal rights can only be exercised when a person has had a promise made to her, we can derive from it special rights to have this particular promise kept, even if what has been promised is not itself in our interests, The IB approach can account for special rights by deriving them from higher-level universal rights, and linking the exercise of the universal right to a particular set of circumstances which are not common to all people.

Finally, it is important that an account of the basis of rights should guide us to political action even in the absence of institutions which encode these rights in law: it should make possible the construction of rights-respecting institutions from scratch, and thereby also make possible critique of any existing institutions which purport to protect rights. Waldron claims, correctly, that the IB account allows us to detect the presence of rights in the absence of legal or other structures which specify who has a duty to ensure that the right is met.

> I can say . . . that a child in Somalia has a right to be fed, meaning not that some determinate individual or agency has a duty to feed him, but simply that I recognize his interest in being fed as an appropriate ground for the assignment and allocation of duties.[31]

The IB account endows rights with radical political potential by characterising them in such a way that they can be invoked to justify setting up institutions designed to deliver justice, and can be appealed to in debates about how such institutions ought to be structured and ought to function.[32]

The second component of the liberal account of rights suggested above is that rights structure the relationship between the state and the individuals or groups in it: the state has a duty not to treat persons and groups in certain ways in virtue of the important interest each person has in being treated with equal concern and respect.[33] To say that persons have such an interest is not to say that the state is under a duty to treat them identically: equality is not uniformity. But it does mean that there are certain things that the state may not do to persons, and certain goods that it must provide for them, even if not doing these things or providing these goods would, on the whole, increase overall levels of happiness or preference satisfaction in society. This understanding of the role of rights in political thinking is defended by Ronald Dworkin. He states that,

> Individual rights are political trumps held by individuals. Individuals have rights when, for some reason, a collective goal is not a sufficient justification for denying them what they wish, as individuals, to have or to do, or not a sufficient justification for imposing some loss or injury upon them.[34]

Dworkin thinks that when the state treats rights as trumps in political thinking it shows equal concern and respect for all its citizens because it ensures for each of them a set of freedoms and other goods necessary for the pursuit of life plans even when other important social goals – such as maximising overall levels of welfare in society – would be better served by denying these freedoms and other goods to some or all citizens. In this respect Dworkin's account is anti-utilitarian: the fundamental interest each person has in being treated with equal concern and respect rules out justifications for curtailing some persons' freedoms or depriving some persons of goods on the grounds that the majority would prefer freedoms and goods to be so distributed.[35]

But why should we think that persons have a fundamental interest in being treated with equal concern and respect by the state? Here the liberal account intersects with Kantian strands in moral theory whereby respect for the dignity of persons as autonomous agents stands as a constraint on what persons may do to one another. As Kant puts it, 'everything has either a *price* or a *dignity*. If it has a price, something else can be put in its place as an *equivalent*; if it is exalted above all price and so admits of no equivalent, then it has a dignity.'[36] According to Kant, human beings are of incomparable worth; that is, there is nothing else to which they can be compared in worth. Kant's reasons for thinking this – connected with the idea of persons as free insofar as they are self-legislating – are complicated.[37] However, what matters for our purposes here is that the fundamental interest persons have in being treated with equal concern and respect by the state through its respect for, and protection of, their rights (understood as trumps) is an interest in being treated as creatures with dignity. When rights are trumps, no person's interests can be sacrificed on the altar of other persons' preference satisfaction. When persons know that they have such rights, the political conditions for their self-respect are in place.[38]

The account of rights I have outlined here is a composite of aspects of different liberal theorists' accounts, and to that extent does not reflect in its entirety the views of any particular liberal. Nevertheless, it captures the spirit of liberal thinking about rights on the contemporary scene. With this account in hand we can turn to the question of the rights that we have.

It is common in the literature for a distinction to be made between first-, second-, and third-generation rights. First-generation rights protect basic and familiar freedoms and privileges; in Rawls' view:

> freedom of thought and liberty of conscience; political liberties (for example, the right to vote and to participate in politics) and freedom of association, as well as the rights and liberties specified by the liberty and integrity (physical and psychological) of the person; and finally, the rights and liberties covered by the rule of law.[39]

There are two things to note here. First, although there is now near unanimous agreement – both inside and outside of liberal circles – that first-generation rights are to be distributed equally and without regard for sex, race, religion, etc., disagreement remains with respect to the question of how to formulate a principle of justice for the equal distribution of these rights, and what the status of any such principle ought to be relative to principles of justice distributing other goods (for example, income and wealth). The details and significance of one such disagreement will become apparent in chapter 9, where consideration will be given to the feminist argument for the censorship of pornography on the grounds that it undermines an equal distribution of the right to free speech across men and women. Second, it is important to note that, on the account of the basis of liberal rights just given (and *pace* some libertarian accounts of rights), first-generation rights are not derived from a more general fundamental right to liberty, but rather reflect the demand that the state treat its members with equal concern and respect.[40]

Second-generation rights are rights to socio-economic goods: income and wealth, health care, education, employment, housing, etc.[41] These rights are more controversial than first-generation rights, for two reasons. First, they require far more by way of political action than first-generation rights. Securing the right to vote for all persons involves establishing and monitoring appropriate electoral procedures. Setting up and maintaining such procedures is, of course, not a small – and often not an easy – matter, but we have a reasonably clear idea about when political institutions are adequate for the protection of these rights: the denial of the vote to women in the UK up until 1928 was a clear violation of the principle of universal suffrage. But it is far less clear what extent of political action is required in order that, for example, the right to health care is given equal protection. Is the US system of private insurance sufficient for the protection of equal rights to health care? Is the UK system of a National Health Service free at the point of delivery preferable? And what is covered by the idea of 'health care' in any case? Is it consistent with the right to health care that people with smoking-related illnesses be made to bear some of the costs of their treatment? Do people have a right to expensive fertility treatment? That the goods to which people are entitled through the exercise of their second-generation rights can be realised in a diversity of ways, and be provided to different extents, means that making judgements about what is involved in respecting such rights far more difficult than making similar judgements with respect to first-generation rights.

The second reason why second-generation rights are controversial relates to possible clashes between them and other rights. Some theorists of rights have argued that the set of rights persons have must be compossible; that is, it must be possible to perform at the same time all the actions fit to discharge the duties generated by each right a person has.[42] If we take the compossibility require-ment seriously, then we cannot permit the existence of a right respect for which requires the violation of another right. One familiar putative instance of such a clash is between the first-generation right 'to hold and to have the exclusive right of personal property',[43] and second-generation socio-economic rights which *prima facie* require heavy taxation of income and wealth forming part of persons' property. In this case, everything depends on how the first-generation right to personal property is defined: if it is defined so as to include the exclu-sive right to decide how to dispose of one's property, then state taxation looks like a violation of this right.[44] But we may opt for a more limited definition of the right to personal property that avoids this clash.[45] In any case, the possi-bility of such clashes makes the existence and nature of second-generation rights even more controversial (which is not, of course, a reason for denying their existence).

Finally, and most controversial of all, are third-generation rights. These rights attach to communities, groups, or nations and include the right to national self-determination, to secession, language rights, cultural rights, and group rights to traditional territories. What makes these rights controversial is that they attach to groups rather than to individuals: when it is claimed that the Basque people have a right to national self-determination, what is meant is that the Basques as a group have this right (although each Basque may have individual rights derived from membership of the group that has this right). Historically, liberal rights have existed to protect individuals, and almost every political document laying out such rights specifies them in terms of what is owed to each individual. Advocates of third-generation rights challenge this paradigm, in particular in debates about the rights of minority cultures, and nations existing within larger states. Defenders of the individualist paradigm claim that the logic of the language of rights will not bear such an interpreta-tion, which inflates the currency of rights-talk to the point of devaluation. The details of some of these debates will emerge in chapter 7, where questions of religion and citizenship will be discussed.

This, in outline, is the liberal account of rights I shall treat as the starting point for an interpretation of political harm fit to flesh out the reasonableness defence of toleration such that oppositions like those between Waldron's reasonable Muslim and reasonable pornographer can be analysed in a way that does justice to the complaints of each party, and – the hope is – can be settled in a principled and recognisably tolerant way. In the remainder of the book various challenges to this account of rights will be presented through analysis of some real world cases. Importantly, these challenges will be articulated in a way that is consistent with the reasonableness defence of toleration in virtue of the appeals they make to their advocates' important interests in being treated with equal concern and respect in a way that reflects their dignity. Such challenges to the account of rights informing a conception of political harm to be placed at the heart of liberal lawmaking can be made in public reason. In that case they cannot be ignored by political liberals committed to the use of procedures for the construction of political principles informed by and justified in public reason.[46] Before moving on to these detailed worries, however, I shall briefly present some more abstract concerns about the liberal account of rights just sketched.

Liberal rights: some worries

There are three sites of disagreement between liberals and their critics with respect to liberal rights that are relevant to the problems of toleration to be considered in the rest of this book. These are: (1) that the account is excessively individualistic and operates with an ethically impoverished vision of the self; (2) that it reveals a gendered conception of justice; and (3) that it mistakes the moral roots of justice.

The charge of excessive individualism was brought against liberals by communitarians in debates in the 1980s, and took two forms.[47] First, that the liberal emphasis on individual rights fails to acknowledge communities of shared values and practices as providing a necessary social context without which the exercise of rights would be impossible, or meaningless.[48] In addition, not only does this way of thinking about political priorities fail to acknowledge that such communities need political protection, it might also cause them damage by encouraging people to use their rights as a way of distancing themselves from one another, and thereby loosening the bonds of shared membership of a community. (With Margaret Thatcher claiming in the 'greed is good' era of 1980s Britain that, 'There is no such thing as society',[49] this worry was very real.) Second, and at a more abstract level, communitarians claimed that the methodology employed by liberals in justification of principles distributing equal individual rights has an objectionable metaphysical underpinning in a vision of the self as 'unencumbered' by particular social bonds. The fundamental interest protected by liberal rights, it is claimed, is in the exercise of the capacity to revise life plans and rethink the values informing them. But this suggests a conception of individuals as capable of standing back from their attachments, values, and communities in order to critically appraise them.[50] Communitarians argued that this vision of the self is false to the phenomenology of living a life, morally etiolated, and metaphysically incoherent.

These theoretical worries about liberalism are echoed in many criticisms of a rights-based account of the limits of toleration made in debates about multiculturalism, and the right to free speech. Advocates of principles of toleration sensitive to multicultural concerns often argue that liberal rights – both in their structure and their content – fail to register the significance of cultural membership for persons, and that the unfettered exercise of these rights by people without such cultural attachments damages people with such attachments. In particular, it is claimed that placing free speech within the limits of toleration, regardless of what is expressed and how it is expressed, makes possible serious attacks on the identity of members of vulnerable cultural groups which the liberal rights-based approach fails to make politically salient.

The next cluster of worries about liberal rights is feminist. The most trenchant feminist criticisms of the liberal rights-based paradigm of harm insist that an equal distribution of fundamental rights across men and women will only evince real equal concern and respect for its members on the part of the state once men and women are equal in power. In the absence of equality of power, equality of rights at best provides women with merely formal protections and permissions which do not translate into meaningful goods for them 'on the ground', and at worst actually masks deep inequalities of power across men and women: for example, if there is no barrier in law to women pursuing the same careers as men, then – it might be asked – what more is there to do, politically speaking, in order to secure equality of employment opportunity for women?[51]

One ground on which feminists have claimed that inequality of power persists relates to the family. Despite equal opportunities legislation, women in Western democracies still bear most of the responsibility for child-rearing and domestic work. Furthermore, career paths are structured such that women who bear children are likely to exit the workplace at a time in life when employment experience must be accrued if career progression is to follow. This means that women experience a double whammy: if they return to work after bearing children they are *ipso facto* disadvantaged in terms of career progression, and carry extra burdens in terms of child care and domestic work that their male peers do not have, and this further disadvantages them in terms of acquiring the necessary experience to compete with men further up the career ladder, or at the same point but with more experience. And these are just the problems faced by women in stable relationships who have embarked on a career path before having children. For single mothers without the education necessary for a career, the prospects are far more grim.[52] That the employment market accommodates the structure of men's lives and their expectations means that women are disadvantaged in comparison with respect to power, both in this market and inside the family itself, where women are economically dependent on men.

For our purposes this inequality of power, and the criticisms of the rights-based paradigm of harm it generates, will become important in chapter 9, where feminist critiques of arguments for the non-censorship of pornography which invoke the right to freedom of expression will be considered. Here, feminists have argued that, in virtue of various inequalities of power between men and women, a defence of the right to free speech which permits the creation and distribution of pornography undermines an equal distribution of this right across men and women: pornography silences women, and a concern to treat all persons with equal concern and respect should therefore require placing limits on the freedom of speech of pornographers.

The final set of worries about the liberal paradigm relevant here is Kantian. Onora O'Neill argues that the liberal rights-based approach lacks the resources to address the question of what a society in which people cultivate social virtues – such as charity, civility, solidarity, and compassion – as well as respecting one another's rights is morally preferable to a society in which people respect one another's rights but do not exhibit these social virtues. The reason for this is that, according to the liberal account, people only have obligations to perform those actions necessary for the respect of rights; the performance of all other actions, or the cultivation of certain dispositions, however laudable, is non-obligatory.[53] Given that most people would want to say that a society of just and socially virtuous people is preferable to a society of just and socially vicious people, the rights-based approach is incomplete.

The alternative, Kantian approach to justice avoids this problem by making *obligations* as opposed to interests the source of rights. On the Kantian view duties of justice constitute the basis of rights, and these duties, rather than interests, are morally basic. Duties of justice are encoded in principles of justice which specify the content of rights, and their relationship to other social values. The Kantian view is that a person A has a right to x if and only if all other people have an obligation to provide A with x, or not to prevent A from having x, and this obligation is derived from the Categorical Imperative.[54] However, the duties of justice embodied in rights belong to just one category of morally good action. On the Kantian view, morally good actions are categorised as follows:

1   *Perfect duties of justice* are required and are the basis upon which rights are attributed to people.
2   *Imperfect social duties* do not have correlate rights but are nevertheless required: for example, we have a duty to act charitably, but not everyone has the right to charity from us.
3   Finally, *supererogatory acts* are those which it is good to perform, but which we do not have a duty to perform (for example, acts of heroism, or great self-sacrifice).

By creating conceptual space between perfect duties and supererogatory actions with the category of imperfect social duties, the Kantian approach allows that we have some social obligations to which no rights correlate. The Kantian approach thus has the resources to explain why we ought to work towards a rights-respecting compassionate, civil, fraternal society rather than a rights-respecting heartless, aggressive, self-seeking society: we have imperfect, non-justice-related, duties of compassion, civility, and fraternity.

To be clear, the problem with the rights-based approach is not that it is necessarily indifferent between visions of the good and bad just society. The good just society can be endorsed over the bad just society in virtue of its supererogatory value, assuming that liberal theorists can give an account of supererogatory value. Rather, the criticism is that on the liberal paradigm people have obligations to perform only those actions necessary for the protection of certain important interests, but that there are social virtues not related to the protection of such interests which characterise the good society and which, we would want to say, people ought to cultivate. The problem is that supporting judgements about the goodness of societies by reference to their supererogatory values leaves it unclear why people ought to work to create this value in their societies. If the value of a good society is supererogatory, then presumably action fit to create this value is also supererogatory. But supererogatory action is non-obligatory, in which case we cannot say of people who do not work to create the good society that they ought to do so. The Kantian approach avoids this problem because its account of the value of a good just society is given in terms of the performance of actions which are obligatory, albeit imperfectly so.

This worry about the liberal paradigm of harm is echoed across the board in the practical problems of toleration to be considered in Part II. On the liberal view, people have rights to perform actions that are 'stupid, cowardly, tasteless, inconsiderate, destructive, wasteful, deceitful, and just plain wrong',[55] such as the production of pornography, the publication of material profoundly offensive to religious groups, and denial of the Holocaust. If the rights-based account of harm as it stands is used to set the limits of toleration then, it is claimed, it lacks the resources to give an account of why people engaging in these activities ought not to do so, even when they are within their rights to do so, and this means that the moral damage done to people who suffer as a result of these activities is not acknowledged.

In sum, there are serious worries at the theoretical level about the liberal paradigm of harm as rights-violation. In each case to be considered in Part II we will see that the party whose calls for legislation to govern the activities of those to whom they are opposed challenges the liberal paradigm by denying that individual rights are the only, or the most important, consideration in setting the limits of toleration in law. Let us turn now to these practical cases.

Part II

Chapter 7

Culture and citizenship
Headscarves and circumcision

The cricket test – which side do they cheer for? . . . Are you still looking back to where you came from or where you are?
(Norman Tebbit, Conservative MP for Chingford, 1974–92)[1]

Introduction

The cases to be considered in this chapter relate to groups united by religious or cultural beliefs requiring – or expressed in – practices which create oppositions between members of these groups and the state. *Prima facie*, what marks out these groups from other groups (such as 'the group of library card holders at the University of Reading', 'teenagers', or neighbourhoods) is that they are 'communities of meaning':[2] the norms, values, and practices of such groups not only influence the practical rhythms of members' lives, but furthermore inform the way in which members interpret their experiences, relationships, and place in the world. That the practices required by, or associated with, membership can conflict with the requirements of liberal citizenship means that cultural and religious groups are often in the circumstances of toleration *vis-à-vis* the liberal state.

The issues to be addressed in this chapter form part of the ongoing debate between 'multiculturalists' and their critics.[3] The nub of this debate is whether cultural groups are of sufficient significance and value (in themselves or for their members) to deserve special treatment by the state. The multiculturalist focus on the significance of group membership to the good of individual members reflects multiculturalism's ancestry in the communitarian critique of liberalism sketched at the end of the last chapter. For multiculturalists, the significance of cultural groups as communities of meaning confers special rights, or exemptions from rights-based prohibitions, on group members which thereby shifts the limits of toleration with respect to (some of) the practices of these groups: the special rights or exemptions demanded by members of cultural groups mean that they may, *qua* group members, be permitted to engage in practices which would otherwise be intolerable, and be exempted from prohibitions which apply uniformly to non-members. For example, in UK law Sikhs (who wear turbans as traditional dress) are exempted from the requirement to wear motorcycle helmets,[4] and Jewish and Muslim abattoirs

which slaughter animals while fully conscious so as to produce *kosher* and *halal*
meats are exempted from the requirement that animals be stunned and uncon-
scious prior to slaughter;[5] and in the US, the Old Order Amish were exempted
from Wisconsin's compulsory school-attendance law on the grounds that
compliance with the law would, according to their beliefs, endanger their
salvation and that of their children.[6]

Multiculturalist theory and practice now treats a wide range of issues not all
of which are related to toleration, so it is important to be specific about the
questions to be addressed. The discussion here will address problems of toleration as they arise with respect to religious and cultural *immigrant groups*. Such
groups by no means exhaust the possible forms that religious and cultural groups
can take, and the problems of toleration they create are not the only problems
of justice with which multiculturalists concern themselves.[7] However, most
people will have had some contact with members of such groups in going about
the daily business of their lives, and thus consideration of these groups provides
somewhat more vivid case studies than might otherwise be the case.[8]

Kymlicka defines immigrant groups as follows: 'groups formed by the decisions of individuals and families to leave their original homeland and emigrate
to another society . . . [giving rise over time to] ethnic communities with
varying degrees of internal cohesion and organisation', where members of such
groups are actual or prospective citizens.[9] For example, Jamaicans who arrived
in the UK in the 1950s, or Italian-Americans. Crudely, immigrant groups want
integration into the main political, economic, and social institutions of liberal
society. Problems of toleration arise if such groups are required to relinquish
cherished cultural practices peculiar to them as a condition of such integration
(whether this requirement is encoded in law and enforced by the state, or
embodied in the informal mechanisms and social networks of the host society;
what we might refer to as its 'culture'). In general terms, the structure of the
problems of toleration embodied in the claims of immigrant groups is as follows.
As we saw in chapter 1, toleration involves a principled refusal to interfere with
the practices etc. of individuals or groups despite significant opposition to these
practices, the power of interference, and a disposition to use that power. In that
case, intolerance involves a principled interference with the practices etc. of
groups in virtue of significant opposition to them through the exercise of power
over them. The liberal approach to toleration sets its limits by reference to individual rights, the content of which is to be settled through debate in public
reason: on this view, interference with groups is justified only when their practices violate the liberal rights of members or non-members. This means that
genuine problems of toleration arise for liberals with respect to groups in two
sorts of cases that can be differentiated in terms of the direction from which the
opposition giving rise to the problem emanates.

1   The practices of the group violate the liberal rights of members or non-
     members. Here, opposition emanates from the liberal state and is directed
     towards the group.

2   The requirements imposed on all its members by the liberal state are
objected to by members of cultural groups on the grounds that the imposition of these requirements violates their rights, and that these rights ought
to be recognised by the liberal state. Here, opposition emanates from the
cultural group and is directed towards the liberal state.

Sometimes group–state relations create problems of toleration because both (1)
and (2) hold. One of the requirements imposed on all its members by the liberal
state is that rights be respected, and its interference with a group might be a
response to practices which violate this requirement. If the group in question
denies that its practices violate anyone's rights, or claims a legitimate exemption from this requirement, then opposition between the state and the group
runs both ways, with each party accusing its opponent of intolerance. However,
problems of toleration are not always symmetrical. The requirements referred to
in (2) might not relate to respect for rights – for example, they might relate to
conditions for citizenship such as competency in written and spoken English –
such that state interference with groups in order to secure compliance is not
accurately read as a response to state opposition to the practices of *that group in
particular*. Nevertheless, the group may still oppose this interference in the form
laid out in (2), in which case we have an (asymmetrical) problem of toleration.

Two cases of immigrant groups in dispute with the state in one or both of
these ways will be considered in this chapter. Before considering these cases,
however, we need more of an account of what it is about membership of such
groups that requires that we take their objections to interference with their
practices seriously as reports of intolerance.

Communities of meaning

If claims for exemptions from requirements and prohibitions, or claims for special
rights, for members of religious and cultural groups are to be at all plausible then
membership must realise, or further, a significant good for persons. Furthermore,
if these claims are to register given the liberal perspective laid out in chapters 5
and 6, then the good that membership furthers must be a good to which persons
have a distributive claim in the name of equal concern and respect. The place to
start is with the claim that cultural group membership is an intrinsic good; that
is, that it realises a good that is necessary for and integral to the good of individual members, and that this good cannot be realised in any other way.[10]

This case can be made so as to resonate with liberal commitments by
connecting membership of a cultural group with the self-respect of members.
Kymlicka offers such an account:

> cultural membership is not a means used in the pursuit of one's ends. It is
> rather the context within which we choose our ends, and come to see their
> value, and this is a precondition of self-respect, of the sense that one's ends
> are worth pursuing.[11]

A person's self-respect depends in part on being or striving to become the kind of person she values; self-respect requires congruence between a person's normative self-conception and her self-expression, and it depends upon meeting standards with which the person in some way identifies. Self-respect requires that a person act in ways at least consistent with, and preferably supportive of, her self-conception. In failing to act in these ways a person fails to be as she had thought she was or hoped she could be.[12] For Kymlicka, cultural groups provide their members with a context which renders meaningful the ends, goals, and associated standards relevant to the development of their self-respect: membership of a cultural group sets the horizons of value for the self-respect-related activities and judgements of members. To borrow Charles Taylor's phrase, cultural groups can provide their members with a 'vocabulary of worth' necessary for the successful exercise of practical reason in pursuit of self-respect.[13] When a person deliberates about courses of action and how they will affect her self-respect, she reflects – however inchoately – on her normative self-conception; she thinks about the kind of person she is and wants to be, and makes decisions on the basis of these beliefs and desires. Kymlicka's view is that, for members of cultural groups, their normative self-conceptions are couched in a language informed by 'cultural narratives'.[14]

The account of the good of membership of cultural groups in terms of how they stand as communities of meaning required for the self-respect of members makes sense in terms of a key methodological principle in the liberal theory of toleration developed in Part I. This is that political principles are justified if and only if they can be shown to promote justice for, or the good of, individual members of society, which rules out the sacrifice of justice for, or the good of, individuals in order to achieve justice for, or the good of, groups or collectivities (this is the point of Dworkin's insistence that individual rights are *trumps* in political thinking). In other words, what we are not permitted to do, given an individual rights-based conception of harm, is to treat groups *per se* as the beneficiaries of principles of justice. This is not to say that groups must be ignored under this paradigm; however, if they are claimed to have significance from the point of view of justice, then this must be in virtue of how they promote or make possible the pursuit of significant (from the point of view of justice) goods for their *individual members*. By offering an account of cultural groups as communities of self-respect-related meaning for members, Kymlicka and Raz make it possible (although not mandatory) to incorporate groups as beneficiaries of justice from a liberal perspective, and thereby allow us to make sense of the relevance of group membership to demands for toleration made by individuals *qua* such members. Furthermore, the good of opportunity for self-respect is a recognisably liberal good. Indeed, Rawls list the social bases of self-respect as 'perhaps the most important primary good'.[15]

How does the claim that cultural membership realises a liberal good for individuals ground arguments for special treatment (in the form of exemptions from prohibitions, or special rights) for members of cultural groups in the name of equal concern and respect? One claim commonly made in the literature is that when a cultural group is a minority – or is relatively powerless – then its members are disadvantaged in comparison with members of majority or more powerful groups with respect to their opportunities to engage in its practices, live according to its values, act in line with its norms, and follow its customs. Legal frameworks, and the institutions of civil society – it is claimed – are often structured so as to reflect the values and expectations of dominant, mainstream cultural groups in virtue of the fact that the history of these groups is often closely intertwined with that of the state inhabited by many less well-established groups. This means that members of minority or less powerful groups bear costs in pursuing their self-respect in cultural contexts not faced by members of more powerful groups: as Kymlicka puts it with respect to members of aboriginal groups, 'they have to spend their resources on securing the cultural membership which makes sense of their lives, something which non-aboriginal people get for free'.[16] Given that membership of a cultural group is not something for which we can hold people responsible – being a Sikh is not like having a taste for mountaineering or *haute couture*, and is instead (so the argument goes) akin to a physical handicap insofar as it is an unchosen feature of persons which can be disadvantaging – equality requires that we compensate members of groups who bear these costs by securing for them in law appropriate exemptions and special rights which create genuine equality of opportunity for self-respect across persons from all cultural groups, regardless of their power and influence.

There is much to be said by way of criticism of the liberal egalitarian case for multiculturalist rights.[17] However, rather than pitching critique at this abstract level, the best way to see how interaction between immigrant groups and the state takes the form of problems of toleration and raises worries about the liberal paradigm is through consideration of some real world cases. Recall that problems of toleration arise with respect to immigrant groups either when the practices of the group are opposed by the state in which the group has settled, or when the group opposes requirements made of its members as a condition of residency and/or citizenship by the state, or both. I shall consider two such cases: female genital mutilation (FGM) as practised (largely) by immigrant groups from Africa, and 'l'affaire du foulard' ('the headscarves controversy') in France. Liberal responses to each case have seemed *prima facie* obvious and justified (at least to liberals): FGM should be banned because it violates women's rights, and the French ban on Muslim headscarves should be revoked because it violates Muslims' rights. But close consideration of the cases reveals arguments that call into question the obviousness of these responses, and force us to reconsider the content and scope of the liberal rights that set the limits of toleration.

Female genital mutilation[18]

The practice of FGM is ancient and, historically, widespread. Evidence suggests that FGM was practiced in the Nile Valley from 3100 BC onwards; that metal rings were passed through the labia minora of female slaves in ancient Rome so as to prevent procreation; that the wives of Crusaders in medieval England were made to wear metal chastity belts during their husbands' absence so as to ensure fidelity; and that clitoridectomy was practised in nineteenth- and twentieth-century France, Russia, America, and England (in the latter two countries, as a medically recommended cure for 'hysteria', 'deviance', and 'nymphomania').[19] Nowadays, FGM is practised in at least twenty-five countries in Africa, in Indonesia, Malaysia and Yemen, in some parts of South America, and in some immigrant communities in Europe, Australia and North America.[20] It is estimated that over 100 million girls and women in Africa have been genitally mutilated, and that current population growth trends in Africa put two million girls a year – 6,000 per day – at risk of FGM.[21]

The UN High Commission for Human Rights classifies the main forms of FGM as follows.

(a) Circumcision or *sunna* ('traditional') circumcision: This involves the removal of the prepuce and the tip of the clitoris. This is the only operation which, medically, can be likened to male circumcision.
(b) Excision or clitoridectomy: This involves the removal of the clitoris, and often also the labia minora. It is the most common operation and is practised throughout Africa, Asia, the Middle East and the Arabian Peninsula.
(c) Infibulation or Pharaonic circumcision: This is the most severe operation, involving excision plus the removal of the labia majora and the sealing of the two sides, through stitching or natural fusion of scar tissue. What is left is a very smooth surface, and a small opening to permit urination and the passing of menstrual blood. This artificial opening is sometimes no larger than the head of a match.[22]

The instruments with which FGM is inflicted can be knives, razor blades, sharp stones, glass, scissors, or fingernails. FGM can be practised on girls and women of any age, but in traditional communities it is normally performed by an 'excisor', and often occurs at the start of puberty in a secret location, accompanied by ritual celebrations.

The risks to physical health associated with FGM performed in contexts lacking adequate healthcare facilities are serious. Unsterilised instruments carry the risk of infection, with some reports estimating that out of every 1,000 females who undergo FGM, seventy will die as a result.[23] FGM can also create many long-term health problems for women: sexual dysfunction, haemorrhage, painful menstruation, tumours, abscesses, cysts, urinary tract and kidney infections, endometriosis, and infertility have all been reported. Women who have been infibulated face particularly severe risks during childbirth, which requires de-infibulation to permit the second stage of labour; in many places, reinfibulation will be performed on a woman after childbirth (and this process may be repeated up to twelve times). In addition, FGM can have serious emotional and psychological health consequences.[24]

The motives underlying the practice of FGM vary across the countries and cultural groups in which it is performed: control of female sexuality, religious belief, initiation rites contributing to group identity, beliefs about hygiene, and aesthetic preferences occur as explanations of FGM in different contexts. However, it is important to be clear that FGM is not required by Islam, or confined to Muslim women: Catholics, Protestants, Copts, Animists and non-believers have all been found to practise FGM in different countries.[25] FGM is a cultural, not a religious, practice.

FGM is widespread in Africa: up to 30 per cent of Ghanian females undergo clitoridectomy,[26] over 70 per cent of Gambian females undergo FGM,[27] and 95 per cent of Djibouti women and 80 per cent of Somalian women are infibulated.[28] However, regardless of what we might think of FGM in contexts in which it is a traditional practice, our concern here is whether it ought to be tolerated in contexts in which this is not the case in virtue of claims made by members of immigrant groups whose roots are in communities in which it is a traditional practice. No statistics exist to show the extent of FGM among immigrant groups in Europe, America, Canada and Australia. However, there is no doubt that the practice goes on, although it is often shrouded in secrecy so as to prevent prosecution or hostile reactions from non-immigrant members of the dominant country.[29] Perversely, it is likely that intolerance of FGM renders the procedure more dangerous than it has to be, just as back-street abortions pose greater health risks than legal abortions performed by health care professionals.

Progress made in Western countries with respect to equality for women and developments in conceptions of women's sexuality in the last three decades make opposition to FGM in these countries widespread. The practice of FGM by immigrant groups presents a stark problem of toleration to which, it might be thought, there is an obvious solution, given the liberal rights-based paradigm of harm: prohibit FGM.[30] And this is exactly how various international organisations and political authorities have reacted to FGM. In 1982 the World Health Organisation stated that FGM should never be performed by health care professionals; FGM on girls under eighteen is illegal in the US,[31] and is prohibited for women of any age in the UK,[32] Canada,[33] and parts of Australia.[34] The line of thought informing these reactions is that FGM is a life- and health-endangering practice for women below and above the age of consent, and constitutes a form of physical and psychological abuse. It is true that, for some women, FGM allows for full integration into their cultural communities, making them marriageable and socially acceptable. To that extent, it might be argued, FGM forms part of a set of practices which make the cultural groups in which it occurs communities of meaning for female members. However, one of the most fundamental liberal rights is to be free from physical assault. If we think, as most people do, that children have these rights, and if rights are trumps, then the case for non-toleration of FGM in liberal states is closed. No degree of cultural cohesion achieved by FGM can ground a justification for permitting the practice which is powerful enough to challenge a justification for prohibiting it which invokes the right to freedom from physical assault; there is no community of meaning of significance sufficient to justify overriding the rights of female children to be free from genital mutilation.[35]

The argument for non-toleration of FGM with respect to females under the age of consent is hard to refute. However, one implication of this argument is worth noting, and should give liberals pause for thought. By parity of reasoning, male circumcision – or MGM – performed on males below the age of consent ought also to be outlawed. There are at least two reasons to pause here. First, because circumcision is an important religious rite in Islam and Judaism, the practical consequences of legislation outlawing it would be wide reaching and potentially politically destabilising; and second, that MGM is a *religious* require-ment might seem to make a difference with respect to our assessment of how the law ought to treat those who wish to practise it on their children. The thought here is that singling out MGM for legal prohibition treats religious parents unfairly by denying to them rights over their children that are not denied to non-religious parents who, for example, wish to have their babies' ears pierced.

In connection with these reflections – and yielding a further reason for pause – it might be claimed that the logic of a prohibition on FGM and MGM on the grounds of the physical harm these practices cause to children ought to be extended so as to protect children from the long-term psychological and emotional harms that parents can inflict (and, it might be claimed so as to make the case even stronger, these are wounds that do not heal like cuts and bruises). Of course, this aspect of harm is registered in many existing laws to protect children, but psychological and emotional abuse tends only to be cited in prosecutions when physical abuse is also present.[36] The argument here would be that a real commitment to protecting children from harm justifies the prohi-bition of behaviours that cause psychological and emotional damage to children, even when no physical abuse is perpetrated. So, for example, the sexual hang-ups bequeathed to many adults as a result of an upbringing in a Roman Catholic environment in which they were taught that sex outside of marriage, and for any purpose other than procreation, is sinful is, on this line, a matter legitimately to be addressed by law. This third thought could be read either as an endorsement of the argument for the prohibition of FGM and a call for an extension of the argument in order to protect children from other forms of harm; or it could be presented as a *reductio ad absurdum*, as follows. If children have a right to be free from FGM and MGM because these practices constitute parental harm, then they also have the right to be free from emotional neglect. The *absurdum* in this *reductio* is in the thought that children have a *right* to love and affection. Are love and affection the kinds of things to which anyone could have a right?

Subtle and difficult questions regarding the rights of parents and children are raised here that I cannot address.[37] Suffice it to say that one way forward – at least with respect to the argument by analogy for the prohibition of MGM – is to limit calls for the prohibition of FGM only to practices of excision and infibulation, and to insist that *sunna* be performed by qualified medical profes-sionals so as to minimise any health risks associated with it. Exempting *sunna* and male circumcision from more general bans on GM could be justified on the grounds that the long-term consequences of these procedures for health – when they are medicalised – are far less serious and damaging than excision and infibulation; in particular, sexual functioning need not be impaired by these procedures.

These complications aside, such cases do not exhaust the possibilities: FGM is sometimes sought by adult women, for example, prior to marriage to a male member of a traditional community in which FGM is practised, or (in the case of infibulated women) after childbirth. What marks out these cases is that the women involved can *prima facie* consent to the procedure (in the sense that they need not be frogmarched to the circumcisor), and a fundamental tenet of many forms of liberalism is *volenti non fit injuria*: no harm is done a person when consent is given. This principle entails that at least some rights are alienable and waivable: by giving consent a person can – perhaps permanently – relinquish rights guaranteed to her in law. There are various liberal values fit to generate commitment to this principle. For example, it might be thought to be protective of persons' autonomy, their negative freedom, their opportunities to conduct 'experiments in living', or their privacy. In line with the political liberalism I espouse here, I take it that each of these defences can qualify as reasonable, and I will not adjudicate between them. *Prima facie*, commitment to the principle *volenti non fit injuria* keeps alive the question of whether FGM ought to be tolerated as a cultural practice when those on whom it is practised give their consent to it.

Ignoring the option of abandoning the principle altogether (which I take to be unacceptable from any liberal perspective), its application to the case of consensual FGM so as to place the practice outside the limits of liberal toleration could be blocked by reference to one of the following three claims.

1   All rights are inalienable (i.e. cannot be voluntarily relinquished). Thus, a woman's consent to FGM does not divest her of the right that FGM violates, and does not render the violation of that right tolerable. This strategy involves a sweeping claim about all rights that extends to rights that exist as such only in institutional contexts, and is thereby implausible for the reason that such rights can be made alienable or inalienable simply by making appropriate alterations to the institutional rules.[38] Furthermore, this sweeping strategy entails that no promisee has the right to release her promisor from a promise, which would (a) undermine the whole apparatus of contract law constructed upon this principle, and in any case (b) does not stand, in itself, as a feature of the institution of promising, which rather creates a relationship between the promisor and promisee that can be dissolved as a consequence of appropriate action on the part of the promisee.[39] A weaker claim along these lines is that all rights are non-waivable. This differs from the claim that all rights are inalienable because it is possible to waive a right – for example, the right to have a particular promise kept – without alienating that right altogether (i.e. the right to have kept any promise made).[40] However, the example of promising just

given again shows this sweeping claim to be false by standing as an exception to it. Such sweeping strategies are best avoided.

2   The principle *volenti non fit injuria* has restricted scope such that only non-fundamental or non-basic rights are alienable or waivable according to it; the right to have promises made kept, but not the right to freedom from physical assault, is non-basic; therefore the principle does not apply to the right to be free from physical assault and cannot be invoked in defence of the legalisation of consensual FGM.[41]

3   The principle *volenti non fit injuria* has wide scope and applies to all rights, but no woman could genuinely consent to FGM, in which case it cannot be appealed to in justification of permitting FGM in law; FGM, *qua* physical assault, violates the rights of women who undergo it, and these are rights that no woman could alienate or waive. (Legislation prohibiting FGM in Canada and in New South Wales makes explicit use of this strategy in stating that consent to FGM is 'not valid'.) There are, in fact, two ways in which the *a priori* claim on which this argument rests could be made. First, the modal claim that no woman *could* consent to FGM; and second, the empirical claim that no woman *does* consent to FGM. As we shall see, each of these claims is problematical.

The second and third strategies dominate the liberal response to FGM, and calls for FGM in immigrant communities, and abroad, to be banned remain the norm. However, there is reason to be cautious: commitment to freedom from physical assault as an inalienable or non-waivable right, and/or the *a priori* denial that consent could be, or ever is, given to the physical mutilations of FGM such that the right to be free from FGM is non-alienable or non-waivable, *prima facie* has implications for the limits of toleration in other real world cases in which many liberals have (rightly) jumped the other way. Consider, for example, the notorious 'Spanner case' in the UK.[42] In 1990 sixteen gay men were given prison sentences, or fines, for engaging in consensual sado-masochistic (SM) sexual activity. In 1987 the Obscene Publications Squad raided the home of a gay man and seized a videotape showing a number of men engaging in heavy beatings, genital abrasions, and lacerations as part of the sexual act. So extreme was the violence that police were convinced that men had been killed, and mounted a murder investigation. The investigation showed that no killings had occurred, and that the SM sex acts were consensual. That their consent had been given formed the men's defence, but Judge Rant ruled that they were guilty of assault (in most cases, causing actual bodily harm), and the ruling was upheld (although some sentences were reduced) by the Appeal Court. With reference to the case in 1993, the Law Lords judged that consent is no defence to charges of assault occasioning actual or grievous bodily harm.[43]

Many liberals are disturbed by the ruling in the Spanner case: it raises worrying questions about privacy, individual autonomy, and sexual freedom, and may set dangerous precedents for legal intrusion into areas of life that liberals have historically conceived of as beyond the reach of the state. With respect to the Spanner case, many liberals argued that consent should have been a defence, and that the judgements involved betrayed establishment homophobia and fear-generated prejudice against SM practitioners. However, if the prohibition of FGM for (putatively) consenting adult women is justified by liberals with reference to the claim that the rights it violates are inalienable or non-waivable, or that no-one could, or ever does, consent to such a procedure, then it is not clear that these liberal responses to the Spanner case can be defended. The physical damage of the assaults for which men in the Spanner case were prosecuted were as serious and damaging as much of the physical damage caused to women who undergo FGM, and consenting to beatings and genital laceration for sexual pleasure is as unthinkable to most people as giving consent to FGM is for most Western women (or as consensual castration is for most men). Liberals who opposed the prosecution of the Spanner defendants should oppose the prohibition of consensual FGM.

Let me be clear that the line I am arguing here is not that FGM is a laudable practice, nor that it ought not to be regulated in law. But there is a difference between regulation and prohibition. My argument is that the practice of FGM on adult women ought to be regulated (in part) according to the principle *volenti non fit injuria*, which makes consent a test of whether a woman has suffered a political harm by undergoing the procedure. Of course, even when consent is given there are harms that women can suffer in virtue of having been circumcised: a woman may come to deeply regret having been subject to this irreversible procedure, or may be traumatised by the procedure itself. However, if consent is given, and if it is informed, then the state ought not to legislate to protect people from these forms of harm (by analogy, the state ought not to prohibit sex change operations, or tattooing, on the grounds that a person may later come to regret her gender reassignment, or all-over body tattoo). Of course, giving an account of what constitutes consent, when it is informed, and devising workable tests for when it has been given, is fiendishly difficult. But this difficulty permeates all aspects of law in which the notion of consent figures and does not recommend abandoning consent as a normatively significant category relevant to establishing the presence of political harm at the level of principle. Now it may be that – in fact – most women (perhaps all women) who have undergone FGM would not pass the test of *volenti non fit injuria* (however conceived and applied), in which case the regulation of FGM would manifest as a prohibition 'on the ground'. But the fact that consensual FGM lies within the limits of reasonable pluralism means that blanket prohibition is an intolerant approach at the level of principle.[44]

Of course, there are differences between consensual FGM and the Spanner case. First, the men in the Spanner case were driven by sexual desire, whereas the aim of FGM is certainly not the enhancement of women's sexual pleasure. However, at a more general level, both sorts of activity are related to the definition of sexual identity (albeit in different directions), and so it is not clear how far this difference will take us in justifying different reactions to the cases.[45] Second, FGM is a traditional practice whereas SM sex is not. This fact could affect our thinking about consensual FGM in two ways. First, we might take more seriously the claim that, for some women, FGM is integral to their membership of a community of meaning, and search for medical procedures to lessen health risks and accommodate the practice (for adult, consenting women) within the bounds of liberal toleration.[46] Or second, reflection on the patriarchal power structures of traditional communities in which FGM is practised should raise suspicions about the claim that the consent of women who undergo FGM is sufficient to place its practice within the limits of toleration: the pervasive inequalities suffered by most women who agree to FGM procedures should raise the question of whether their agreement is evidence of genuine consent, or rather of submission.[47] However, to raise suspicions is not to have them confirmed: as Simmons notes, 'sufficiently unorthodox tastes [such as for FGM, or genital mutilation] should not be taken lightly as a sign of insanity', or as necessarily involving 'coercion or unfair bargaining'.[48]

In order to move forward on the question of whether to tolerate consensual FGM in immigrant groups, liberals need to beware of making the limits of their own cultural experience the limits of the thinkable: it will not do to prohibit consensual FGM on the grounds that no woman could, or ever does, possibly consent to such a procedure.[49] At the same time, liberals should demand a proper account of the significance of the practice to women who wish to practice it (as – indeed – they should of those who wish to engage in SM sex practices and other forms of bodily mutilation) to place in the context of a more general, philosophical account of the importance of membership of communities of meaning to the individual good. And, to have currency in a liberal account of toleration informed by rights that realises equal concern and respect, this account must do more than articulate attitudes of fearful submission on the part of women. Testimony from immigrant women who have undergone FGM does not tend to support a view of the practice as a free expression and confirmation of cultural identity, but the reasonableness defence does not contain the resources to rule out this possibility and place every case of consensual FGM outside the limits of toleration. This may strike many as a high price to pay for toleration. But the alternative – in which blanket prohibitions are applied at the level of principle on the grounds that no woman can alienate her rights to physical integrity, or could ever consent to FGM – imposes a burden of proof on its advocates to defend their claim to *a priori* knowledge of the limits of consent for all women which, I submit, is too heavy a burden,[50] and is anyway a morally unacceptable strategy given a commitment to political justification within the limits of reasonable pluralism.

'L'affaire du foulard'

On 10 February 2004 French MPs voted by 494 to 36 to ban the Islamic headscarf (the *hijab*), and other 'ostensible' religious symbols (for example, Jewish skullcaps, large Christian crosses, and Sikh turbans) from state schools. The bill was supported by 70 per cent of French people. Prior to the vote President Jacques Chirac voiced his support for it, stating that

It cannot be tolerated that under cover of religious freedom, the laws and principles of the republic are challenged. Secularism is one of the great achievements of the republic. It is a crucial element of social peace and national cohesion. We cannot allow it to be weakened. We have to work to consolidate it.[51]

There are an estimated 10 million Muslims living in France, and many of them disagreed with Chirac.[52] On 17 January 2004 tens of thousands of Muslims (mostly women) rallied in Paris and other French cities to protest against the proposed bill, claiming discrimination and intolerance on the part of the state. The secretary-general of the Union des Organisations Islamiques de France stated that 'Chirac's version of the secularist state . . . excludes religions and limits freedoms . . . the law is unfair'; and a spokesman for Collectif des Musulmans de France stated that the law created a climate 'more hostile towards us than it has ever been in France before'.[53]

The *hijab* is a head covering worn by Muslim women as a symbol of, and in order to protect, their modesty. Although not all Muslim women wear the *hijab*, it is an important religious practice mentioned in the Qur'an.[54] The roots of the recent French controversy over the *hijab* are in a chain of events which began in October 1989 in a state school in Creil, when three Muslim girls took to wearing the *hijab* to school.[55] The principal reacted by requiring that the girls drop their scarves to their shoulders during classes, but permitted them to wear the *hijab* on school grounds outside of class periods. The principal's justification for this prohibition was that permitting the girls to wear the *hijab* during class would open the floodgates to the demands of other children at the school (in a culturally mixed area) that exemptions from school requirements (on attendance, dress, etc.) be made for them on religious grounds. One of the girls refused to obey the prohibition and was excluded from the school; and Muslim girls across France wore the *hijab* to school in protest. In response, the national Minister of Education, Lionel Jospin, decreed that no girls should be excluded from school for wearing the *hijab*, and was consequently attacked by intellectuals on both the left and the right. His instruction was replaced in 1994 in a directive to all principals of public schools issued by a subsequent Minister of Education, François Bayrou, stating that conspicuous and provocative religious symbols should be prohibited in the classroom, and the controversy flared up again. President Jacques Chirac set up the Stasi commission to enquire into the question of secularism and religious symbolism in public spaces and, in the light of its findings, backed a bill banning ostensible religious symbols in public spaces.[56] The bill was passed on 15 March 2004, and on 20 October 2004 the legislation was used for the first time to expel two Muslim girls from a state school .[57]

What is at issue in the headscarves affair, given our concerns here, are the grounds on which the French state set the limits of toleration so as to place the wearing of the *hijab* in state schools outside of these limits. The wearing of the *hijab* is a practice central to Islam, which is an established religion giving meaning to the lives of Muslims. Muslim communities are prime examples of cultural groups in which membership realises an intrinsic good à la Kymlicka and Raz: if any community members have a claim to exemption from (some) rules governing the behaviour of non-members (in this case, a dress code) on a multiculturalist account of rights, then Muslims do. Furthermore, the wearing of the *hijab* does not, even on the French state's own account of the matter, directly violate the rights of non-Muslims: the *hijab* is just a headscarf. But wearing it is an integral part of being a Muslim for many Islamic women, and Islam unites people in paradigmatic communities of meaning. Surely it is obvious that the ban on headscarves is intolerant, given a commitment to liberal rights as embodying equal concern and respect, and the reasonableness defence of toleration? The costs of attending a state school for Muslim girls are, in virtue of this prohibition, far higher than the costs for non-Muslim girls. Given that wearing the *hijab prima facie* violates no-one's rights, surely a commitment to equal concern and respect requires that the state exempt Muslim girls from the dress code that applies to other students in its schools?[58]

There are three sets of considerations here which should make us pause for thought before dismissing the French state as intolerant in this way:

1   the ban might be justified as a necessary measure for the preservation of political stability in France (the 'stability' argument);
2   the opposition of the French state to the *hijab* might be justified by reference to a concern for the rights of the Muslim girls rather than non-Muslims (the 'anti-patriarchy' argument);
3   the prohibition of the *hijab* might be claimed to be necessary for the maintenance of a stable and just political society fit to secure all persons' rights; on this account, Muslims who claim that their rights are violated by the prohibition ask that the state act in a way that it cannot act if Muslims are to be in a position to press any rights at all (the 'republican' argument).

I shall consider these arguments in order of their plausibility, taking the least plausible 'stability' argument first.

The 'stability' argument could take two forms: (1) that worries about how the increased birth rate of Arabs in France might swamp a recognisable French culture justifies the ban; (2) that wearing the *hijab* is a potentially destabilising form of political protest by Muslim girls against the State. With respect to (1), it would have to be shown that banning the *hijab* is an effective way to limit the Arab birth rate in France. The tenuousness of this claim, in combination with its mistaken conflation of Arabs with Muslims, not to mention the incipient racism from which the argument as a whole issues,[59] means that it ought not to be taken seriously. Form (2) is more measured, and may well have serious currency given proper consideration of the history of the French state's discrimination against its Muslim citizens. However, to succeed in the terms in which it is made (i.e. in terms of stability), this argument would have to establish that girls wearing the *hijab* to school is potentially destabilising, and a threat to the French state; and this, I submit, stretches credulity.

Turning to the argument in (2), some French intellectuals have insisted that the *hijab* is an outward sign of patriarchy within Muslim communities, and as such ought not to be tolerated in a liberal society committed to equality for women.[60] Some considerations that were relevant to the toleration of consensual FGM are also relevant here. We might claim (a) that some rights are inalienable or non-waivable such that consent to actions fit to violate these rights does not render them non-existent, or place the violation outside the scope of justice. Or we might claim (b) to know *a priori* that no woman could genuinely consent to wearing the *hijab*, in which case all women who wear it are subject to coercion (in this case, by male co-members of their Muslim community) from which they have a right to be protected.

With respect to (a), what basic right does wearing a *hijab* violate? If rights protect important interests, then the claim that womens' basic rights are violated when they wear the *hijab* as part of an Islamic dress code depends on establishing that all people have an important interest in being free from dress codes. But there is no such important interest, and hence no such right. With respect to the second strategy (b) – and apart from the problems (encountered in the last section) involved in giving an account of how we come to know *a priori* what people could or could not possibly consent to – the testimony of many Muslim women who wear the *hijab* defeats it. Some claim that it is a genuine expression of their faith, others that it allows them to identify in a meaningful way with members of their cultural group, and some that it is a liberating practice which enables them to enter public spaces, places of work, and professions while being free from the unwelcome attention of men.[61] The point is not whether we agree with the justifications Muslim women give for wearing the *hijab*; rather, the point is whether we can dismiss them all *a priori* as symptoms of male hegemony. This would be a hard case to argue.[62]

Turning to the 'republican' argument, intolerance of the *hijab* in schools might be justified by reference to the realisation of an ideal of political community without which no person's rights are secure. On this view, rights are secure only in certain sorts of political contexts, and the exemption demanded by Muslims would degrade and endanger that context: the commitment to rights evinced in Muslim claims for multiculturalist exemptions itself voids such claims. This is a powerful argument with a venerable pedigree. The vision of political community with which this argument operates is built into French political life through a conception of citizenship in terms of *laïcité*.[63] *Laïcité* is often translated to mean 'secularism' (and, indeed, it is *laïcité* so understood that Chirac averred in his speech backing a ban on headscarves). This understanding of *laïcité* emerges from a commitment to the separation of church and state (which culminated, in France, in the disestablishment of the Catholic Church in 1905): in a secular state, religious practice is tolerated but only insofar as it remains in the private sphere. State schools – and other public arenas such as the workplace and civic spaces – must be kept free of religious practice, and its symbolism, if the state is to remain truly secular. And unless the state remains secular, freedom of religion for all is under threat: privatising religious belief ensures space for the practice of every religion. The significance of *laïcité*, so understood, is best grasped by placing it within the context of the republican tradition of thinking about politics from which it emerged in France, and in which civic loyalty and active participation in politics by citizens is stressed as essential for the stability and health of the just polity.[64]

The interpretation of *laïcité* as secularism is sometimes presented as a version of the doctrine of state neutrality: the *laïque* polity is either one in which no religious groups are given state support, or one in which all religious groups are given the same support.[65] These forms of neutrality pertain to the *consequences* of state action: whatever the state does, the interests of all affected parties ought to be affected in the same way. However, there is another version of neutrality according to which the *laïcité*-inspired ban on headscarves violates state neutrality. On this account, the *justification* of state action must not evince commitment to any particular way of life found among affected parties.[66] As we saw in chapter 5, this is the account of neutrality subscribed to by advocates of the reasonableness defence of toleration. In conditions of freedom the burdens of judgement make reasonable disagreement on the big questions inevitable and not to be regretted; justification of state action to reasonable people cannot, therefore, proceed by reference to any particular reasonable conception of the good. It is true that secularism as appealed to by Chirac is one reasonable conception of good. But unless we are prepared to say that Islam *per se* is unreasonable, neutrality in justification does not permit an appeal to secularism in justification of the ban on headscarves, and the French law qualifies as intolerant.

However, this is not the end of the matter, for there are (at least) two further ways of understanding *laïcité*.[67] First, *laïcité* can be understood in terms of individual autonomy: in the *laïque* polity, laws are made and policies enacted that encourage individuals to think and act free from the domination and influence of non-democratic groups within society. As with *laïcité*-as-neutrality, this justification for the ban on headscarves is not available on the reasonableness defence of toleration: the Enlightenment conception of the good life at its heart is just one among many reasonable conceptions of the good, of which Islam is another. In any case, an appeal to autonomy in support of the ban is not very plausible insofar as it provides at least as strong a reason to prevent schoolchildren from mindlessly following fashion – as they so often do – as it does for banning the *hijab*.[68]

Second, *laïcité* can be understood in terms of civic loyalty and active citizenship. As Laborde describes it,

> [*laïcité*] supplements the liberal emphasis on rights and procedures with a concern for the dispositions and attitudes of citizens and the content of the public culture. Abstract citizenship must be complemented with allegiance to a republican public culture, which provides the motivational anchorage essential to the legitimacy and stability of liberal society.[69]

This conception of *laïcité* is associated with the republican tradition of political thought which is, of course, central to French political history.[70] The maintenance of a just, rights- and freedom-respecting state is the responsibility of members of that state, and requires some degree of civic loyalty and active participation in politics on their part. However, membership of sub-political groups – such as religious groups – with their own hierarchical structures and particular sets of interests can undermine allegiance to the state.[71] Rather than requiring that people give up their membership of partial groups, advocates of *laïcité*-as-civic-loyalty require only that these allegiances be kept out of public and political life; and they insist that only by so privatising their partial allegiances can religious people secure freedom of religious practice through the stabilising influence delivered by their ultimate allegiance to the just state.[72]

This republican vision of civic loyalty is offered as an antidote to liberal complacency about the fragility of just states which, it is claimed, is built in to the liberal account of a person's rights as being *held against* the state, and other members of the political community. The thought is that making rights so understood the defining feature of the liberal citizen permits a state in which persons compete for power in order to further their own particular interests even at the expense of the health of the polity (from which they are alienated), and the good of their fellow citizens (with whom they do not identify). These problems with excessively individualistic versions of liberal theory are real: witness Margaret Thatcher's statement in the 'greed is good' era of 1980s Britain that 'There is no such thing as society.'[73] There are few liberal theorists who would now defend a vision of political life with so little room for thoughts about the common good, and how best to secure a state fit to deliver it. As we saw at the end of chapter 6, one response to excessively individualistic liberalism is communitarianism: deliver justice to communities, and thereby to their members. Another response is republicanism: insist on civic loyalty as a condition of citizenship, and thereby protect the just polity.

However, the realisation of this imperative in *laïcité*-as-civic-loyalty is not the only way to remedy the defects of excessively individualistic liberalism, and thus it is not clear that the prohibition on headscarves which issues from it is required by the legitimate concern that excessive individualism undermines the just state. For example, John Tomasi agrees with the republican contention that '[t]he criteria of good citizen conduct reside in those activities people must undertake if their society is to realize its ideal – that is, to flourish or succeed as a society of that type', but argues that,

> [If] liberal theorists take reasonable value pluralism as a basic social fact [then] their account of citizen virtue . . . must be importantly plural as well. Out of respect for the ideals of mutuality and reciprocity, these norms of good citizen conduct cannot be rigidly or universally identifiable from some external perspective, as substantive citizen norms might be identified within a civic humanist setting. . . . Any account of liberal virtues must be precisely as diverse as the society to which it is meant to be normatively applied.[74]

Tomasi's thought here is that if the just state is one in which reasonable pluralism is welcomed as a permanent fact, then good citizenship for the members of it must register the fact that people will differ in reasonable ways on the big questions.[75] Taking reasonable pluralism seriously means accepting that the 'motivational anchors' that tie people to the just state will be plural, and rightly so. In that case, it will not do to insist, as the strong *laïcité*-as-civic-loyalty account has it, that religious commitment can have no place in the public sphere. So long as this commitment does not undermine the political reasonability of those who exhibit it – and there is no *a priori* reason to think that it must, despite media depictions of those who wear traditional dress as fanatics and fundamentalists[76] – it is consistent with good liberal citizenship.[77] Furthermore, we might add, not only are religious (and other such) commitments consistent with good liberal citizenship, they are *the only* place in which motivational anchors of sufficient weight to secure the just state through the allegiance of its members can be found.[78] With respect to headscarves, there is no reason to think that wearing a headscarf to school disqualifies a girl from education into liberal citizenship by turning her into an unreasonable fundamentalist who refuses to accept the fact of reasonable pluralism. And given the significance of the *hijab* to the girls, prohibiting them from wearing it is likely to have the opposite effect from that intended on the *laïcité*-as-civic-loyalty account: rather than securing their co-operation as good French citizens, it is likely to turn them against the state.

Conclusion

The problems of toleration addressed by this chapter are just two multiculturalist cases that have appeared on the contemporary scene. However, the issues they raise for the liberal theory of rights and the reasonableness defence of toleration are fundamental, and have clarified further what is involved in cleaving to this account. As a result of the discussion of FGM, we saw that unless the liberal reluctance to allow the state between the sheets of consenting adults is to be abandoned, practices engaged in by adults – however inconceivable in their value to most people – must be permitted as possible categories of lawful activity in the name of toleration. And with respect to the discussion of 'l'Affaire du foulard', we saw that 'thick' conceptions of citizenship cannot be invoked so as to narrow the limits of toleration if the commitment to reasonable pluralism with which the reasonableness defence of toleration operates is genuine. These reflections about what citizenship means in pluralistic societies will be deepened in the next chapter, where I consider the limits of liberal toleration with respect to artistic expression through discussion of the 'Rushdie affair'.

Chapter 8

Artistic expression

'Free speech is a non-starter', says one of my Islamic extremist opponents. No, sir, it is not. Free speech is the whole thing, the whole ball game. Free speech is life itself.

Salman Rushdie[1]

Introduction

In September 1988 in the UK Viking/Penguin published the novel *The Satanic Verses* (hereafter referred to as *SV*) by Salman Rushdie. Rushdie was already a renowned (although not at this point, notorious) novelist: he had won the Booker Prize in 1981 for *Midnight's Children*, and was shortlisted for the same prize for his next novel, *Shame*. Rushdie was born in Bombay in 1947 to affluent Muslim parents, and completed his education in England at Rugby (an exclusive public school) and then Cambridge. While there Rushdie began an investigation of the historical roots of Islam which sowed the seeds for *SV*. Many of Rushdie's novels explore the themes of conflicts of identities, the search for belonging, finding a home, the need for faith (or something like it), intertwined with and overlaid onto accounts of Indian history and the Partition; the recurrence of these themes can in part be seen as reflecting Rushdie's own biography.

In *SV* Rushdie composed what he came to call 'a love song to our mongrel selves'.[2] In his own words, *SV* is

> the story of two painfully divided selves. In the case of one, Saladin Chamcha, the division is secular and societal: he is torn, to put it plainly, between Bombay and London, between East and West. For the other, Gibreel Farishta, the division is spiritual, a rift in the soul. He has lost his faith and is strung out between his immense need to believe and his new inability to do so. The novel is 'about' their quest for wholeness.[3]

Gibreel's loss of faith torments him through a series of dreams about the foundation of a religion (clearly very similar to Islam) in which the Prophet 'Mahound' (a European medieval corruption of 'Muhammad' meaning 'devil' or 'demon') is at times represented as a lewd, power-hungry womaniser who manipulates prospective converts with stories about his religious revelations, and in which prostitutes working in a brothel called *hijab* take the names of Muhammad's wives (the significance to Muslims of naming a brothel thus should be clear given the discussion of the last chapter).

British Muslims reacted to the publication of *SV* almost immediately. In December 1988 and January 1989 there were demonstrations in Bradford (a northern town heavily populated by Muslims) at which a small number of Muslims burned the book, and Muslim leaders called for it to be banned (as it was in Pakistan, Saudi Arabia, Egypt, Malaysia and many other countries). Seven people were killed in riots in Islamabad and Kashmir prompted by opposition to *SV*. On 14 February 1989 the Ayatollah Khomeini of Iran issued a *fatwa* against Rushdie, calling for all Muslims to attempt to kill him, with a promise of martyrdom in return. Riots in Bombay ten days later killed a further ten people. Rushdie and Viking/Penguin issued an apology to Muslims, but it was not accepted and the *fatwa* remained in place. Shortly thereafter Rushdie went into hiding under police protection, where he remains (although he does make rare public appearances). However, Iranian President Mohammed Khatami declared in June 2001 that the blasphemy case against Rushdie in Iran should be considered closed (whether this, and the death of the Ayatollah Khomenei, affects the *fatwa* remains a moot point).[4]

The topic of this chapter is whether Muslim demands for *SV* to be banned have any currency given the reasonableness defence of toleration supplemented with the liberal paradigm of harm as rights-violation. From here on I set aside the question of whether the *fatwa* is justified: there are no grounds on which a death sentence for expression of any form or content can be defended. Rather, our question is: does a novel such as *SV* lie outside the bounds of toleration in a society of equals committed to the protection of rights and political decision-making through public reason? Many liberals and intellectuals have thought that the answer to this question is obvious: in a just society no limits should be placed on freedom of expression beyond those required for the maintenance of public order and safety. In this connection, the famous prosecution of Penguin for the publication of D.H. Lawrence's *Lady Chatterley's Lover* in 1960 by the UK Home Office under the 1959 Obscene Publications Act is often cited. The prosecution – which reflected the defunct mores of a hypocritical Victorian society – failed, and few people now lament the fact. To take seriously any case for banning *SV*, most liberals think, is to risk a return to the dark days of paternalistic controls on art and expression in general: civilised societies have moved on.

It is certainly true that the liberal intelligentsia has moved on, but it is by no means clear that everyone else has moved with them: the issue of the censorship of art is still on the political agenda in Western democracies. Consider, for example, the public outcry in the UK over Marcus Harvey's painting, *Myra*.[5] Myra Hindley was a notorious murderer in the 1960s who, with her lover Ian Brady, brutally tortured and killed five children and buried their bodies on Saddleworth Moor. A photograph of Hindley taken at the time – a close-up of a peroxide blonde with staring eyes – subsequently became a hideously iconic image of cold-blooded evil which was instantly recognisable by all Britons. Harvey's painting shockingly reproduced this photographic image using children's hand prints. The painting was condemned by the British tabloid press, and was pelted with eggs and ink while on display at the Royal Academy of Arts. Or consider the reaction to the collection *Sensation* (in which *Myra* featured) when showed at the Brooklyn Museum in New York in 1999. The focus of complaint this time was a painting by Chris Ofili (winner of the Tate Museum's prestigious Turner Prize for modern art in 1998), *The Holy Virgin Mary*.[6] The painting depicts the Virgin surrounded by cuttings from pornographic magazines, and standing on a pile of elephant dung. When exhibited in Brooklyn the painting had to be protected by a sheet of plexiglass and two guards, for fear of defacement. Mayor Rudolph Giuliani condemned the exhibition: 'This is not art, it's disgusting. This should happen in a psychiatric hospital, not in a museum funded by the taxpayer.' Giuliani cut off the museum's city subsidy of $7.3 million (£4.4 million), a third of its budget, and attempted to evict the museum from its city-owned premises. The Brooklyn Museum then sued the City of New York for violation of their First Amendment rights (to freedom of expression) and won the case: Giuliani was ordered to restore the museum's city funding and cease the attempts to evict it from its premises. *Contra* the complacent pronouncements of liberal elites, we are not all agreed that an expressive act rightly becomes immune from legal prohibition when it acquires the status of a work of art.

The grounds on which objections to the *Sensation* pieces were made were various, and many of them can – and should – be discounted as grounds for legal prohibition in virtue of falling into one of the categories of offence identified by Feinberg (most probably 'fear, resentment, humiliation, and anger' or 'shock to moral, religious, or patriotic sensibilities', although possibly 'disgust and revulsion'). However, the grounds on which the most cogent objections to SV were made by Muslims are more clear, and – I shall argue – pose a challenge to the liberal paradigm which cannot be dismissed as easily as the objections to *Myra* and *The Holy Virgin Mary*. Although I shall conclude that these objections do not justify the censorship of SV, they nevertheless raise serious worries about the adequacy of the liberal paradigm which many liberals write off too glibly. However, before turning to analysis of Muslim objections to SV we need to be clear on the powerful liberal arguments for (almost) unrestricted freedom of expression.

Freedom of expression: the classic arguments

In this section I shall outline five classic liberal arguments for placing expressive acts of whatever form and content within the limits of toleration, subject to the constraint that such acts do not threaten public order or safety. This constraint is accepted by all defenders of freedom of expression: as Justice Holmes put it, '[t]he most stringent protection of free speech would not protect a man in falsely shouting fire in a theatre and causing a panic'.[7] Nor, as John Stuart Mill famously remarked, should 'an opinion that corn-dealers are starvers of the poor [remain unmolested] when delivered orally to an excited mob assembled before the house of a corn-dealer, or when handed about among the same mob in the form of a placard'.[8] The arguments I shall consider are: the argument from fallibility, the argument from truth, the argument from significant interests, the argument from democracy, and the 'second best' argument.

The 'argument from fallibility' is most famously associated with J.S. Mill, and serves as a counter to the argument that it is legitimate to place restrictions on the expression of opinions known to be false; in the case of SV, it serves as an answer to Muslims who claimed that the book should be banned because it presents a false account of history, Islam, and spiritual reality.[9] The argument is that restrictions on the expression of opinions on the grounds that these opinions are known to be false reveals an assumption of infallibility on the part of those who propose the restrictions; no such assumption can be justified; therefore, no such restrictions are legitimate. As Mill puts it, '[For a person to] refuse a hearing to an opinion, because they are sure that it is false, is to assume that their certainty is the same thing as absolute certainty. All silencing of discussion is an assumption of infallibility.'[10]

There are two ways in which to read this argument. First, that content-based silencing reveals certainty with respect to the particular opinion in question; and second, that it reveals a general assumption of infallibility with respect to all opinions. The second interpretation is indeed objectionable: no-one – with the possible exception of the Pope – can make this claim with a straight face. But no-one who calls for restrictions on freedom of expression – again, popes aside – actually makes this claim. If Mill's argument turns on imputing general assumptions of infallibility to people who call for restrictions on freedom of expression then it will have a very limited scope. In contrast, the first reading has a much wider scope: advocates of content-based restrictions on the expression of a particular opinion often do claim to know that that opinion is false; and making this claim does not entail a general assumption of infallibility. But the problem with this reading is that it is implausible to claim, as Mill seems to, that we are not entitled to certainty with respect to any opinion: on the contrary, we do know for certain that $2 + 2 = 4$, that the Earth is round, and that Tony Blair is the current British Prime Minister. Unless we are to subscribe to a hyperbolic form of Cartesian doubt – whereby we ought to doubt everything because, for example, it is logically possible that an evil demon is deceiving us with respect to everything we think we know except the fact that we exist[11] – then this version of Mill's argument leaves it unclear which restrictions on the expression of opinions are legitimate.[12] With respect to the specific case of Muslim content-based objections to SV we might claim that Muslims are not entitled to certainty with respect to the religious beliefs that underpin their objections (remember Barry's argument considered in chapter 3 that toleration is justified on the grounds that doubt with respect to our opinions is appropriate and required). However, as we saw in chapter 5, this strategy involves judgements on the part of the state about the truth of its members' beliefs that are not available on the reasonableness defence of toleration: the limits of toleration cannot trace the contours of truth given a commitment to political debate in public reason. In sum, the argument from fallibility either fails to address most calls for restrictions on expression, or objectionably requires the state to arbitrate on matters of the truth and falsity of its members' religious, moral and philosophical beliefs.

The second 'argument from truth' is more promising, and finds its classic statement in Mill's description of two advantages of permitting freedom of expression within limits set by a concern for public order and safety:

[a]   . . . though the silenced opinion be an error, it may, and very commonly does, contain a portion of the truth; and since the general or prevailing opinion on any subject is rarely or never the whole truth, it is only by the collision of adverse opinions that the remainder of the truth has any chance of being supplied.

[b]   . . . even if the received opinion be not only true, but the whole truth, unless it is suffered to be, and actually is, vigorously and earnestly contested, it will, by most of those who receive it, be held in the manner of a prejudice, with little comprehension or feeling of its rational grounds.[13]

Living at the height of the industrial revolution in Victorian Britain, all of Mill's writings are lit up by the conviction that human beings are capable of moral, intellectual, social, and political progress. For Mill, political principles and policies are justified to the extent that they tend to promote progress, and unjustified to the extent that they tend to impede it.[14] This conviction is evident in the defences of freedom of expression constitutive of his version of the argument from truth. Many opinions contain a 'portion of the truth' which will be lost if they are prevented from being expressed; and opinions that we know to be true risk being 'held as a dead dogma, not a living truth' unless they are disputed.[15] Thus, whether opinions are wholly true, partly true, or wholly false, their expression ought to be permitted in order that the human race can come closer to the truth.

The premises of this powerful argument cannot be denied: without free and open discussion there is no possibility of knowledge.[16] However, the argument assumes that the point of all acts of expression is the acquisition of knowledge, and this is its weakness. It is not the case that every instance of expression aims to deliver knowledge of truths to its audience, or to secure such knowledge for the expressive agent. Some forms of expression aim to stimulate a transcendent aesthetic experience (for example, Beethoven's late string quartets), or to provoke laughter; some aim to strengthen group bonds and identity (for example, football chants and songs); others express outrage or defiance (for example, the 1999 Seattle demonstrations against the World Trade Organisation, or the Million Man March on Washington for black rights in 1995); some aim at threatening their audience (for example, taunts of 'Scab!'

on the worst type of picket line, or the notorious neo-Nazi march through the Jewish town of Skokie, Illinois, in 1977); and others are a statement of identity or belonging (wearing gang colours to school in Los Angeles, or using a 'tag' to stake out territory with graffiti). It is not the case that the world is a seminar room in which each instance of expression is properly understood as a contribution to an ongoing conversation which will end in the acquisition of justified true belief by participants.[17]

With respect to Muslim complaints against SV in particular, it is anyway not true that what (most) Muslims objected to was critical discussion of the history and meaning of Islam: there is a thriving and long tradition of such disputation within Muslim scholarship itself, and Islam is not a cult of mindless followers. Rather, the grounds on which many Muslims objected to SV related to what they took to be a gratuitously bawdy portrayal of Muhammad as a lewd power-seeker, rather than to discussion of the content and accuracy of the eponymous 'satanic verses' (a subject which is debated by Muslim scholars themselves).[18] Whatever the exact details of the Muslim complaints, note for the moment that Mill himself seems to admit that objections to expression made on these grounds have some currency (albeit not hard enough to justify legal restrictions on expression): 'opinions contrary to those commonly received can only obtain a hearing by studied moderation of language, and the most cautious avoidance of unnecessary offence'.[19] For many Muslims of the opinion that Muhammad was not a lewd power-seeker, Rushdie's full blooded portrayal of him as such in SV did not exhibit a 'studied moderation of language'.

A descendant of the argument from truth which directly and unapologetically addresses this interpretation of Muslim complaints delivers Jeremy Waldron's claim that,

> Persons and people must leave one another free to address the deep questions of religion and philosophy the best way they can, with all the resources they have at their disposal. In the modern world, that may mean that the whole kaleidoscope of literary technique – fantasy, irony, poetry, word-play, and the speculative juggling of ideas – is unleashed on what many regard as the holy, the good, the immaculate, and the indubitable.[20]

Here we have the strongest form of the argument from truth: progress towards truth on the questions that matter to all of us – not just to the devout – requires complete freedom with respect to the content and the form of expression. Although question marks about the adequacy of the 'seminar room model' also hang over Waldron's defence of 'three-dimensional' toleration, the argument addresses directly the concerns of many Muslims who complained that SV constitutes a personal, grievous insult, and we will return to it shortly.

The third classic argument grounds the right to freedom of expression not in the attractive consequences of the establishment of a rule to protect these rights, but rather in how this right protects and promotes the significant interests of persons differentially situated with respect to the act of expression. This 'argument from significant interests' also has its roots in Mill,[21] and finds its most detailed contemporary expression in the work of T.M. Scanlon. Scanlon takes as his moral touchstone and starting point the claim that 'the powers of a state are limited to those that citizens could recognise while still regarding themselves as equal, autonomous, rational agents',[22] and states that,

> An autonomous person cannot accept without independent consideration the judgment of others as to what he should believe or what he should do. He may rely on the judgment of others, but when he does so he must be prepared to advance independent reasons for thinking their judgment to be correct, *and* to weigh the evidential value of their opinion against contrary evidence.[23]

With this autonomy-based limitation on the exercise of state power in place, Scanlon goes on to argue – in later papers[24] – that legal restrictions on freedom of expression can be justified if and only if they do not violate persons' rights to free expression as grounded in their significant interests in such expression. These interests are classified in terms of four ways in which persons can be affected by restrictions on freedom of expression.

(a) A *participant interest* is 'an interest in being able to call something to the attention of a wide audience . . . [for example] a speaker may be interested in increasing his reputation or in decreasing someone else's, in increasing the sales of his product, in promoting a way of life, in urging a change of government, or simply in amusing people or shocking them'.[25]

(b) *Audience interests* are similarly varied and relate to 'having a good environment for the formation of one's beliefs and desires',[26] and include 'interests in being informed, amused, stimulated in a variety of ways, and even provoked when this leads to reflection and growth'.[27]

(c) In contrast, *bystander interests* tend to be best served by restrictions on expression. These interests include 'avoiding the undesirable side effects of acts of expression themselves: traffic jams, the noise of crowds, the litter from leafleting . . . and more important . . . interests in the effect expression has on its audience . . . [for example] when expression promotes changes in the audience's subsequent behaviour'.[28]

(d) Finally, expression can affect persons' *citizen interests* as members of a political community through its effect on 'the value of having fair and effective democratic political institutions', where protection of this value requires the provision of 'an equal opportunity to participate . . . that is not necessarily in the interests of particular individuals'.[29]

A decision about whether to regulate an act of expression must assess the extent to which that act promotes or damages *significant* interests in each of these categories; and the significance of any such interest is assessed according to whether it is a condition for the exercise of autonomy. So, for example, Scanlon argues that subliminal advertising can be prohibited on the grounds that it aims to instil in its audience a desire for the product such that the audience's capacities to assess this desire as a good or bad reason for purchasing the product are diminished; a concern to protect the conditions of autonomy means that no participant (i.e. advertiser's) interest in creating this effect can override a ban on this form of expression.[30] Another example relates to 'judgmental regulation' – 'based on a judgment about what the correct opinions or attitudes are on a given question and . . . aimed at preventing expression that might mislead or degrade people'[31] – of the advertising of cigarettes and alcohol. Although participants in such expression have an interest in profits promoted by such advertising, the conditions of their autonomy will not be damaged by prohibiting such expression, and there is no audience interest in being targeted by such advertising. In general, Scanlon's view is that regulation of expression – including content-based regulation – is permissible unless it presents a threat to the interests outlined above, or to 'the equitable distribution of the means to their satisfaction'.[32] And the closer the interest is to serving as a condition for autonomy, the more significant it becomes in consideration of such regulation. Assessment of the case for the prohibition of SV, on this approach, turns on whether it damages the interests of Muslims in one or more of the categories Scanlon identified; I postpone this discussion until the next section.

Scanlon's fourth category of interests – those of persons *qua* citizens – forms the centrepiece of the fourth classic argument for freedom of expression, the 'argument from democracy'. I shall consider Ronald Dworkin's version of this argument, which he makes in the process of articulating what he calls 'the constitutional conception' of democracy. Dworkin argues that – in democratic decision-making and the theorising of it – the constitutional conception ought to trump the 'majoritarian premise', which states that 'political procedures should be designed so that, at least on important matters, the decision that is reached is the decision that a majority or plurality of citizens favors, or would favor if it had adequate information and enough time for reflection'.[33] In contrast, according to the constitutional conception, 'the defining aim of democracy . . . [is] that collective decisions be made by political institutions whose structure, composition, and practices treat all members of the community, as individuals, with equal concern and respect' (Dworkin calls these the 'democratic conditions' of government).[34] The test of a government's success *qua* democracy in the first instance is not whether it acts in ways that realise the majoritarian premise, but rather whether it treats its citizens with equal concern and respect. Of course, if it can meet both tests – that is, if 'majoritarian institutions provide and respect the democratic conditions'[35] – so much the better, from the point of view of stability; but in a genuine democracy the majoritarian premise is constrained by, and must give way to, the democratic conditions. On Dworkin's view, the American Constitution (or its equivalent) should be read (in large part) as an abstract articulation of these conditions to be interpreted by the Supreme Court (or its equivalent). This is his 'moral reading' of the Constitution.

The constitutional conception is accompanied by a particular understanding of the democratic collective – that is, 'the people' whom government is of, for, and by[36] – in what Dworkin calls 'communal' terms. What this means is that action by the people 'cannot be reduced just to some statistical function of individual action . . . [but rather] is a matter of individuals acting together in a way that merges their separate actions into a further, unified, act that is together *theirs*'.[37] This is not just a matter of psychological identification with the action of the collectivity to which one belongs (although such identification might sometimes contribute to the existence of a communal collective). Rather, it is a matter of a collection of individuals genuinely constituted as a group doing something that is more than the sum of each member's particular actions. Dworkin gives the example of an orchestra: no individual musician can play a symphony, although each has to do something which, combined with what all others do, constitutes the playing of a symphony by the orchestra.[38] This conception of political community accompanies the constitutional conception of democracy, because what the democratic conditions articulated in the Constitution (or its equivalent) aim at is preservation of the political community so understood through safeguarding the conditions for moral membership of this community for all (in particular, Dworkin thinks, by preventing state interference with the lives of those in the minority just so as to satisfy the preferences of those in the majority.) And it is only if such membership is protected for every person that democratic self-government – government of the people, by the people, for the people – is possible.

To make this concrete consider the famous 1954 US Supreme Court decision in *Brown v. Board of Education*[39] that racially segregated schools were unconstitutional given Section 1 of the Fourteenth Amendment to the Bill of Rights which states that,

> All persons born or naturalized in the United States, and subject to the jurisdiction thereof, are citizens of the United States and of the state wherein they reside. No state shall make or enforce any law which shall abridge the privileges or immunities of citizens of the United States; nor shall any state deprive any person of life, liberty, or property, without due process of law; nor deny to any person within its jurisdiction the equal protection of the laws.

On Dworkin's account, the decision in *Brown* provided an interpretation of the 'equal protection' clause of the Fourteenth Amendment which created (in part) the conditions for moral membership of the political community for blacks by ruling racial segregation to be unconstitutional. This landmark decision was thus a step towards genuine democratic community properly constituted wherein the preferences of the (racist) majority in Texas could not be taken as sufficient to justify legislation permitting segregation, given the commitment to equality written into the Constitution in the Fourteenth Amendment.

The connection between the constitutional conception of democracy and freedom of expression is in what Dworkin calls the 'relational conditions' for moral membership of the democratic community, which state 'how an individual must be treated by a genuine political community in order that he or she be a moral member of that community'.[40] He describes three such conditions: having a part in the collective decisions taken by the community, reciprocity with its members, and independence from the community. Dworkin mentions freedom of expression as essential only to the first of these conditions, but it is plausible to see it as central to all of them. Having a part in collective decision-making clearly requires freedom of speech: gag rules and censorship prevent participation in public discussion on key political questions. Reciprocity – being treated as a genuine member of the community by other members – shows the decision in Brown to be in the interests of democracy, but can also be read as requiring freedom of expression: if other members of my community prevent me in law from expressing opinions just in virtue of their perceived falsity or offensiveness then they do not take me seriously as a co-member because they deny me the opportunity to address them. Finally, independence from the community ensures protection of the conditions of individual self-respect by ensuring for a person 'control over his own life':[41] decisions about acceptable forms of sexuality, or required forms of religious practice would be placed outside the remit of collective decision-making, on this account. But so too, it is plausible to think, would be decisions about what to think, believe, and value, and how best to express these commitments. In sum, if the constitutional conception of democracy is adopted, then freedom of expression appears to be a key condition for membership of a political community fit to realise this ideal.[42] In that case, the preferences of Muslims that their religion not be treated as it is in SV are not sufficient to justify legislation to gag Rushdie (and others like him) and thereby exclude him from moral membership of the democratic community: such legislation would damage not only Rushdie, but democracy itself.

The final classic argument I shall consider proceeds not via consideration of the values promoted by freedom of expression, but rather via reasonable reluctance to arrogate to the state the job of regulating expression so as to ensure that it promotes these values. This 'second best' argument finds its most detailed expression in the work of Frederick Schauer, who makes it in terms of the First Amendment to the US Bill of Rights, which bluntly prohibits the state from 'abridging the freedom of speech, or of the press'.[43] Schauer claims that most justifications for this blanket protection of free speech – such as those contained in the four arguments already considered – are instrumental: free speech requires First Amendment protection because it promotes values x, y, and z. However, he argues, it is not the case that First Amendment free speech guarantees the realisation of the values in the name of which it is justified, and it may in fact impede the promotion of these values. Freedom of speech is under-inclusive with respect to its instrumental background justifications because many expressive acts will, for example, make no contribution to human progress (think of celebrity gossip magazines); and it is over-inclusive with respect to these justifications because many expressive acts will, for example, damage equality between the sexes serving as a prerequisite for a healthy democratic society (think of the recently published *The Surrendered Wife*,[44] which advertises itself on its jacket as follows: 'I was lonely and I was exhausted from trying to do everything myself. When I learned to stop controlling and criticising my husband and practised receiving graciously, something magical happened. The union I had always dreamed of appeared. The man who had wooed me was back.').[45] In other words, the set of actions protected by the First Amendment (or any equivalent) is not identical with the set of actions fit to promote the values appealed to in the background justifications for the First Amendment, in which case justification of the First Amendment must proceed by other means.

Schauer's suggestion is that the First Amendment is justified insofar as it disables representatives of the state from deciding when and whether particular expressive acts promote the values appealed to in the background justifications which putatively support the amendment. Such representatives are at best always and inevitably fallible with respect to these judgements, and often not fully aware of what motivates them in the making of such decisions; at worst they are blatantly self-interested and make policy through the lens of a political partisanship that extends their vision only as far as the next election. The First Amendment is justified, thinks Schauer, not because it will deliver the values that we as a political society hold dear, but because the alternative of allowing the state to regulate what gets said is even worse as a prospective way of achieving these values. The First Amendment is a second best.

> [T]he First Amendment is not the reflection of a society's highest aspirations, but rather of its fears, being simultaneously the pessimistic and necessary manifestation of the fact that, in practice, neither a population nor its authoritative decision makers can even approach their society's most ideal theoretical aspirations.[46]

Applied to *SV*, the argument is simple: even if it is true that *SV* presents a wholly false and epistemically trivial picture of Islam, that it inhibits human progress, that no-one's significant interests are damaged by its censorship, and that it excludes Muslims from moral membership of the democratic community, to permit the state to make these judgements with a view to legislation is the first step on a slippery slope the end of which is a nightmarish Orwellian polity.

This completes my survey of the main classic arguments for unlimited freedom of expression consistent with public order and safety considerations. These arguments will reappear at various points throughout the remaining chapters. In the next section I present two analyses of the Muslim objections to *SV* and relate them to the terms of some of these arguments.

Muslim objections: blasphemy and race relations

In this section I shall reconstruct Muslim objections to *SV* as sympathetically as possible so as to show how they might present a challenge to be taken seriously by liberals committed to the reasonableness defence of toleration.[47] This presentation will, I hope, serve as a counterbalance to some of the media coverage of Muslim responses to SV at the time of the controversy, much of which irresponsibly pandered to prejudices and stereotypes by selectively focusing only on the most extreme Muslim reactions to the book.[48]

The first, and most common, interpretation of Muslim calls for SV to be banned is in terms of the Feinbergian profound offence it caused them. This is, prima facie, a plausible interpretation: the offence taken by Muslims is non-trivial, it is often a consequence of bare knowledge of the contents of SV,[49] it is located at the level of their higher-order religious sensibilities, and it is a consequence of their belief that the portrayal of Islam in SV is wrong.[50] There are two responses to this interpretation. First, despite the fact that some Muslims objected to SV on the grounds of its profound offensiveness, there are other more powerful ways to mount the objection which make no appeal to profound offence, and which liberals are bound to take seriously. I shall consider these alternative interpretations shortly. However, for the moment – and second – I shall focus on the putative profound offensiveness of SV to Muslims, and how, as a consequence, their reactions to it can be seen as calls for an extension of the blasphemy law.

Blasphemy law in the UK categorises as a criminal offence any publication or act of expression which 'contains any contemptuous, reviling, scurrilous or ludicrous matter relating to God, Jesus Christ, or the Bible, or the formulas of the Church of England as by law established'.[51] However, 'it is not blasphemous to speak or publish opinions hostile to the Christian religion, or to deny the existence of God, if the publication is couched in decent and temperate language'.[52] Blasphemy law as it currently stands relates to the manner of expression rather than the matter or content:[53] Christian doctrine and religious belief may be questioned and attacked, but only in a 'decent and temperate' manner. Under this law, mockery, ridicule, and derision of Christian dogma and practice is a criminal offence. It is not clear whether blasphemy law aims at the protection of Christians from profound offence; certainly, at its origins in the seventeenth century, this was not the case.[54] Nevertheless, the law as it stands effectively provides Christians with such protection, and some Muslim complaints against SV can be read as calls for an extension of the blasphemy law to cover Islam as well as Christianity. The discrimination between Christianity and Islam embodied in the law is not consistent with setting the limits of toleration through the use of public reason to establish the rights persons have: only a partisan conception of public reason could deliver the special protection accorded to Christians by UK blasphemy law. And an extension of the law in this way would justify banning SV, just as the law was used to justify the 1977 prosecution of the periodical Gay News for the publication of a poem which included fantasies about homosexual sex with the crucified Christ (this was the last successful prosecution brought under this law).

There are four responses to the 'profound offence' interpretation. First, if blasphemy law were extended so as to cover Islam then the logic of the argument would require that it be extended to cover all religions. In order for this to occur the state would have to grant to certain groups the official status of 'religion'. But what criteria could be used to make such distinctions? And, more importantly, would we want to trust the state to devise these criteria and then apply them correctly? Given the worries aired by Schauer, serious doubts are in order here.

Second, even if the state could formulate such criteria and be trusted to apply them correctly, why should religious people be singled out as deserving of special protection in criminal law? Profound offence is not exclusive to such people: patriots, atheists, vegetarians, feminists – in fact, anyone possessed of any deep and heartfelt convictions (indeed, and *contra* the often repeated quip that a liberal is someone who can't take their own side in an argument, liberals included) – is in a position to suffer profound offence. A non-partisan account of public reason used to set the limits of toleration ought not to discriminate between religious and non-religious people, in which case the blasphemy legislation should be extended to cover all people of conviction (which, at least on some issues, is most of us).[55] This would make the law seriously unwieldy, and hugely increase the possibilities for criminal prosecution.

Third, even if these problems are tractable, it is not clear that an extension of the blasphemy law would provide Muslims with protection from the form of harm caused to them by SV, on this interpretation. Blasphemy law addresses the manner not the matter of an act of expression: it renders criminal any 'contemptuous, reviling, scurrilous or ludicrous' treatment of Christian belief and practice. But the profound offence (if such it was) taken by Muslims at SV related not only – and perhaps in some cases, not at all – to the manner of Rushdie's expression, but rather to its matter.[56] What many Muslims objected to in SV was the presentation of Muhammad as a lecherous, money-grabbing power-seeker, not Rushdie's mocking tone or the satirical tenor of his treatment of Islam: their objections would not have been mitigated had Rushdie used 'decent and temperate' language in presenting Muhammad as a lecherous, money-grabbing power-seeker. In that case, calls for the extension of blasphemy law miss the point of the harm caused to Muslims by SV.

Fourth, and finally, ignoring these problems it remains the case that profound offence, as painful and unpleasant as it is, is not a form of harm to be addressed through the criminal law on the liberal paradigm. As we saw in chapter 6, although this paradigm registers profound offence as a serious category of harm, such offence is nevertheless not sufficient to justify legislation to restrict material that causes it, under this paradigm, because profound offence is not something that persons have a right to be protected against, given an account of rights justified by appeal to public reason: rights do not extend to a person protection from her own unpleasant mental states.[57] On this account, rather than extending the law on blasphemy, it ought to be abolished altogether.[58]

For many liberals, that is the end of the matter with respect to the Muslim complaints: the profound offence they experienced in response to SV was undoubtedly real, and regrettable, but a just society cannot legislate to protect its members from this harm.[59] However, it is not the end of the matter, for there is another way in which to interpret the Muslim objections which makes no reference to the profound offence SV may (or may not) have caused, and which is clearly not as easy to dismiss from within the liberal paradigm as a whole, and given details of some of the classic defences of freedom of expression discussed in the previous section. In the remainder of this chapter I shall consider the argument that SV constitutes group libel or defamation and thereby impacts on race relations in a way damaging to the ideal of democratic community.

Doubts about the adequacy of blasphemy law as a tool for addressing the harm caused to Muslims by SV on the 'profound offence' interpretation arose because such offence was taken not only – and not primarily – at the manner of expression in the book, but at its matter; that is, at its treatment of Islam and its portrayal of Muhammad. However, there are further problems related to the 'profound offence' interpretation *per se*. Offence is something suffered by an individual person; it is constituted by a set of judgements (actual, or implied by the experience of the offence) which only an individual can make. However, an important dimension of the putative harm caused by SV is that it was suffered by Muslims *as a group*. When many Muslims objected to SV they did so not (or at least, not primarily) on the grounds that they as individuals had been harmed, but rather on the grounds that the book damaged the community of Muslims – and their shared faith – as a whole. Characterising Muslim complaints simply in terms of profound offence fails to register this significant aspect of the debate. One way to encompass this strand is to interpret the harm Muslims suffered in terms of group libel or defamation. Bhikhu Parekh describes libel *per se* as follows,

> [L]ibel . . . consists in making public, untruthful and damaging remarks about an individual that go beyond fair comment. Libel is an offence not so much because it causes pain to, or offends the feelings of, the individual concerned, for the damaging and untruthful remarks made in private do not constitute libel, as because they lower him in the eyes of *others*, damage his social *standing*, and harm his *reputation*.[60]

Libel relates to the content of what is said, and damages the status of the person who suffers it. This is reasonably intuitive: if another person publicly declares me to be a thief and liar when I am not, then my career may be damaged and my friends (actual and potential) may shun me. It is not so clear, however, how the concept of libel might apply to groups. What is the harm done to Muslims as a group by Rushdie's portrayal of Muhammad as a conniving and lustful opportunist?

Tariq Modood suggests that the aggressive expressive attacks in SV on the beliefs and practices of Muslims might be seen as a continuation of the historical persecution of Muslims by Christians in Western societies. When power relations in a society are unequal, and there is a history of persecution of the less powerful group by the more powerful group, then expressive attacks on the less powerful group will entrench prejudices and thereby continue a cold war of persecution. With respect to Muslims, Modood claims, [historical] vilification of the Prophet [as a lewd, dishonest, dissembling power seeker] and of [Islam] is central to how the West has expressed hatred for [Muslims] and . . . has led to violence and expulsion on a large scale.[61]

If this is the harm Muslims suffered, then what is the solution? On this interpretation, the legislative focus is the 1976 UK Race Relations Act. A person is criminally liable under this Act if by words, behaviour or public display,

(a) he intends thereby to stir up racial hatred (or arouse fear); or
(b) having regard to all the circumstances racial hatred is likely to be stirred up (or fear is likely to be aroused) thereby.[62]

As in the 'profound offence' interpretation, we can interpret Muslim demands on the 'group defamation' interpretation as a call for the extension of the Race Relations Act so as to cover religious as well as racial groups, on pain of discrimination.[63]

Does the 'group defamation' interpretation have any currency under the liberal paradigm? As we saw in chapter 7, a key methodological principle of this paradigm is that the ultimate focus of concern, from the point of view of political justification and of principles of justice, is the individual: harm to groups registers under this paradigm only insofar as harm is thereby done to members. In that case, the 'group defamation' interpretation must be made in terms of the significant interests had by individual Muslims in preventing the defamation of the group of Muslims as a whole. In a society in which Muslims as a group are relatively powerless, and in which they are related to more powerful Christian groups through a history of persecution, it is prima facie straightforward to translate the 'group defamation' interpretation into the language of liberal individualism. Continued persecution – albeit verbal and cold – damages the capacities of individual Muslims to resist the more common-or-garden forms of racist abuse (name calling, racist stereotyping, etc.) which, for many, are a daily reality. As Modood puts it,

> [I]n order to resist [the more usual defamation and discrimination] Muslims have to draw strength from the sources of their group pride, that is to say, from non-secular roots; and an attack upon those roots, even if it is not typical of the harassment Muslims currently experience, is the more devastating for it hits the group in a way that does most damage and undermines its strength as a group to resist attacks from any direction.[64]

In sum, we might interpret the harm caused to British Muslims by SV in terms of the continuation of their oppression as a group in a way that saps their individual capacities to resist the common forms of racism which, unfortunately, remain a reality for many relatively powerless minority groups (I shall refer to this as the 'damaged status' argument). As Bhikhu Parekh puts it,

Human beings feel ontologically insecure and fail to develop the vital qualities of self-respect, self-confidence and a sense of their own worth if they are constantly insulted, ridiculed, subjected to snide innuendoes, and made objects of crude jokes on the basis of their race, colour, gender, nationality, or social and economic background.[65]

Of course, this interpretation cannot be used to explain the reactions of Muslims to SV in Muslim countries, but I put this complication to one side.

Granting the connection between group defamation and damage to individual capacities to withstand racist abuse, is this a form of harm which registers – or ought to register – under the liberal paradigm? Or, to put things in the language of this paradigm: do persons have significant interests – which can be established as such in public reason, and with which rights ought to correlate – in being protected from defamatory expressive acts aimed at the group to which they belong that (are likely to) damage their individual capacities to resist racism as rooted in their self-esteem, self-respect, and sense of their own worth?

Bearing in mind Feinberg's claim that '[h]aving rights enables us to "stand up like men," to look others in the eye, and to feel in some fundamental way the equal of anyone',[66] this strategy of interpretation looks more promising than the 'profound offence' interpretation. The best place in which to locate this version of the Muslim objections is Scanlon's defence of freedom of expression in terms of significant interests. It is clear that Rushdie has a significant participant interest in publishing SV. By his own admission, his novel is not a trivial object the publication of which is to be permitted on the grounds that 'it is only a book'; rather, it attempts 'to see the world anew',[67] and to communicate this vision to its readers. Do Muslims have significant audience interests served by the book's publication which might trump the interest Rushdie has in publishing it? It is clear that *qua* members of the audience for SV, its questioning of Islam was unwanted by Muslims. But this is not sufficient to establish that Muslims do not have a significant audience interest in the publication of the book: persons are not always the best judges of what is in their interests, and – in Millean vein – Muslims may have a significant interest in being 'provoked when this leads to stimulation and growth'.[68] Without exposure to expression that questions their religious beliefs, Muslims are not in a position 'to weigh the evidential value of their opinion against contrary evidence',[69] and so are not in a position to exercise their capacities for autonomy.

Here we run up against the problem identified by Waldron in chapter 5: the external imposition on persons of standards for judging what constitutes a range of options in society adequate for pursuit of the goals central to their way of life is not available on an approach that takes seriously the resolution of political disagreements through the use of public reason. To insist, contrary to the explicit claims of actual Muslims made from 'the internal point of view of [their] religion',[70] that it is in their interests to be exposed to material that questions the fundamentals of their way of life and most dearly held values is to build a secular, humanist conception of the good into the account of public reason from which an account of these interests issues. As Joshua Cohen puts it,

> [Making] a commitment to freedom of expression [turn] on embracing the supreme value of autonomy as a human good . . . threatens to turn freedom of expression into a sectarian political position. Is a strong commitment to expressive liberties really available only to those who endorse the idea that autonomy is the fundamental human good, an idea about which there is much reasonable controversy?[71]

Moving on, perhaps there are significant citizen interests at stake – for both Rushdie and Muslims – in the debate about banning SV? According to Dworkin, remember, freedom of expression is a relational condition for moral membership of a genuinely democratic community: to exclude Rushdie from this community by banning his book would be a step away from, not towards, the ideal of democracy, and both Rushdie and his Muslim opponents have an interest in safeguarding democracy.

This is a powerful argument, but it has been criticised on the grounds that it does not take into account the reality of unequal power relations between different groups in society which means that freedom of expression for some is silencing for others: racial stereotyping creates an environment in which voices raised in protest by those stereotyped cannot be heard as such. This critique of Dworkin *prima facie* picks out exactly the aspect of the exercise of freedom of expression that the 'group defamation' interpretation of Muslim complaints focuses upon: that actual expressive acts do not occur in an egalitarian ideal vacuum, but rather are performed by real people in societies riddled with complex inequalities, especially of power (but also of economic goods). When expressive acts performed by those with power and advantage aim to entrench the position of those without power and advantage, the latter face a double whammy of existing inequality and an environment in which their complaints about it – or attempts to fight it – are ignored, or not even recognised. This might mean that commitment to democracy requires some restrictions on freedom of expression – such as those laid down in the Race Relations Act – as a remedial measure to combat inequalities with deep historical roots which stand as obstacles to the realisation of genuine democratic community. The philosophical argument here is specialised and detailed, and is made primarily in the context of debates about pornography and censorship; I therefore defer full discussion of this critique of Dworkin until the next chapter.

Conclusion

In this chapter I have attempted to present the Muslim objections to SV in a light fit to rebut pat dismissals of the objections as the rantings of fundamentalists bent on the destruction of democracy and the creation of an Islamic state in Britain. Of course, some Muslims did make these claims. But good argumentative hygiene dictates that we ignore the worst versions of an opponent's argument – even if in fact these are the only versions made – and instead address the best reconstruction. The reconstructions I have offered here appeal to the profound offence caused to Muslims by SV, and to the damage SV putatively caused to their status in society. Unless we are to abandon the liberal paradigm, the 'profound offence' interpretation has no force: it directs us to weed out from the body of law all legislation that addresses this form of harm, rather than extend such laws to achieve consistency. In contrast, the 'damaged status' argument is more promising. It appeals to values which are not obviously partisan and so inconsistent with public reason; indeed, they appear to lie at the heart of the liberal individualist paradigm. A full assessment of the force of the damaged status argument against the classic arguments for freedom of expression is deferred until the end of the next chapter, wherein a detailed version of the argument will be made.

Chapter 9

Pornography and censorship

I myself have never been able to find out precisely what feminism is: I only know that people call me a feminist whenever I express sentiments that differentiate me from a doormat or a prostitute.

(Rebecca West, novelist)[1]

Introduction

We saw at the end of chapter 5 that the question of pornography prima facie creates a possible problem of toleration even in a society of reasonable people: reasonable Muslims might object to the activities of reasonable pornographers even when the latter's activities are heavily regulated so as to shield Muslims from unexpected or unwelcome exposure to them. In chapter 6 I laid out the liberal rights-based account of harm according to which the Muslim's complaints against the pornographer do not qualify as reasonable, and so do not provide grounds for further legislation of his activities in the form of censorship.

However, objections to pornography on the grounds of the profound offence (bare knowledge or otherwise) it causes are not the only bases for potentially reasonable calls for its censorship. As I suggested at the end of the last chapter, rather than focusing on the offence caused by an expressive act, we might instead focus on the damage performance of that act by one person or group causes to the status of another group (the 'damaged status' argument). If the case can be made that pornography damages the status of women (and, perhaps, others) – and if it can be established in public reason that such harm ought to be addressed in law – then profound offence-based objections to pornography can be side-stepped in favour of objections drawing attention to inequalities of status caused by these acts. Given that the ideal of equal concern and respect is at the heart of the liberal rights-based paradigm of harm, these objections *prima facie* stand a better chance than profound offence-based objections of prompting serious reconsideration of whether a commitment to reasonableness justifies the wholesale avoidance of content-based censorship of expressive acts. The 'damaged status' argument has the potential to make the censorship of pornography a genuine and justified political option for a society of equals.

In this chapter I shall examine recent feminist objections to pornography that focus on the harm caused to women's status as speakers by pornography. If these arguments provide good grounds for reasonable objections to pornography then they might also be extended to incorporate the complaints of group defamation made by Muslims against SV.

The question of censoring pornography on the grounds of the specific harm it causes to women (as opposed to its undesirability *qua* obscene material) came to public prominence at a time when feminism was emerging as an important movement on the US political scene, and when many feminists were attempting to take on the pornography industry in the name of women's liberation;[2] feminist reactions to pornography in the UK have been somewhat more muted. However, in both countries – and, I suspect, in most liberal democracies – the zeitgeist with respect to pornography is that, so long as those who participate in its making are uncoerced adults, and so long as measures (such as watersheds, packaging to obscure front covers, zoning laws to limit retail outlets to certain areas, etc.) are taken to shield children and unsuspecting members of the public from exposure to it, the production and consumption of pornography ought to be allowed in the name of a commitment to freedom of expression.[3] However, it is not clear what is meant by this claim, because it is not clear exactly what considerations supporting freedom of expression are operative in this defence of non-censorship. Which of the five classic arguments for freedom of expression I laid out in the last chapter might be invoked to flesh out the zeitgeist?

The argument from fallibility and the argument from truth work best when the material in question has propositional content which it is the aim of the act of expression to communicate. Unless an expressive act has this character we cannot say that suppression of it through censorship reveals unwarranted assumptions of infallibility, for the material's lack of propositional content means that there is nothing that we can meaningfully be said to be assuming infallibility with respect to when we censor. Furthermore, without propositional content there is little sense to be made of the claim that the material might promote progress towards the truth: truths come to be known by us through the propositions that express them. As I mentioned briefly in the last chapter, not all expressive acts take the form, or have the function, of communicating propositions, and pornography – understood, for the moment, as sexually explicit material designed only to produce sexual arousal in its audience – seems to be a prime example. What truths does pornography purport to communicate? To which debates does it contribute? What sort of seminar room is that in which pornography is laid on the table as part of the group discussion?[4] In virtue of the nature of pornographic material, defences of the non-censorship of pornography in the name of freedom of expression do best to avoid these arguments.

The three remaining classic arguments are more promising. Using the argument from autonomy we could claim that the significance of the participant and audience interests we have in freedom of expression blocks the censorship of pornography: pornographers have important interests – financial and otherwise – in making and disseminating their material, and consumers of pornography have important interests in retaining access to material that enhances their sexual pleasure. Admittedly, we also have significant bystander interests in not being exposed to pornography in unexpected places, or to saturation point, but these interests can be protected by sensible regulation of the outlets for and distribution of pornography. Finally, we all have citizen interests in ensuring, as Ronald Dworkin insists, that all persons – pornographers included – count as members of the democratic community. If the argument from autonomy and the argument from democracy succeed then there is a powerful case for the regulation of pornography but not for any outright ban. The Muslim we encountered at the end of chapter 5 who takes bare knowledge offence at the activities of pornographers is required – in virtue of his commitment to live with fellow citizens on terms acceptable to all of them insofar as they are reasonable – to bear this cost, or to grow a thicker skin: his objections to pornography, given the pornographer's reasonable acceptance of various forms of regulation of his activities, are not reasonable.

The final classic argument is that the state cannot be trusted to frame legislation fit to promote reliably the background values according to which the principle of freedom of expression is justified. Applying this argument to pornography, the claim would be that judgements about what counts as pornographic material (that are required for any ban to be enforced) ought not to be arrogated to the state: the (admittedly, 'second best') option is to provide blanket protection for freedom of expression, even when this permits the production of pornographic material which damages the background values according to which such freedom itself is justified.

Thus, despite the failure of the Millean arguments to block censorship of pornography, liberals nevertheless have a powerful array of alternative arguments for permitting (within some regulatory limits) the production and distribution of pornography. In this chapter I will consider some important feminist objections to pornography that raise doubts about whether the liberal right to freedom of expression – understood classically so as to rule out all content-based restrictions apart from those that promote public order and safety – can be justified as a limit to reasonable toleration. If the feminist arguments I shall consider succeed then liberals are committed – according (specifically) to their own lights and (more generally) to a commitment to reasonableness as the way to settle political disagreements – to the censorship of pornography.

Before embarking it is important to note that there is a whole set of important arguments for the censorship of pornography which will not be addressed here: that pornography causes, or is an incitement to, sexual violence against women. If pornography could be shown to have causal powers such that consumption of it reliably drives men to rape women, or if it could be shown to be an unequivocal incitement to sexual violence against women in virtue of the character of male sexual psychology, then questions about the censorship of pornography get relocated to debates about public order and safety, not freedom of expression. No defender of freedom of expression would insist that the principle protects a person who shouts 'Fire!' in a crowded theatre, or who hands out pamphlets stating 'Death to the Corn Dealers!' to an angry mob outside a corn dealer's house; if pornography causes or incites sexual violence then it lies outside the scope of all of the classic arguments. Although much research has been done on these questions, and although the findings are often worrying and shocking, adequate discussion of these issues requires a proper assessment of the methods used in the relevant empirical studies, which would take us too far afield: henceforth the arguments I consider make no reference to, and do not rely upon, claims about the causal powers of pornography.[5]

Pornography and harm I: the social construction of inequality

Any case for the censorship of pornography to be made consistent with the reasonableness defence of liberal toleration must show that pornography causes a form of harm from which persons have a right to be protected in a society of reasonable persons, i.e. that pornography causes political harm. If – as we accepted in chapter 6 – persons do not have a right to be protected from unpleasant mental states produced by their bare knowledge of the offensive activities of others, then *prima facie* this case can only be made in terms of the wrongfulness of pornography in itself. And, indeed, the laws appealed to in debates about the regulation of pornography have had this character: the UK Obscene Publications Act of 1959 defined obscene material as that which has an effect 'such as to tend to deprave and corrupt persons who are likely . . . to read, see or hear . . . it',[6] and in the US obscene material has been defined as that which appeals to the 'prurient interests' of its consumers.[7] The clear appeal here is to the morally undesirable effects of obscene material on the character of those exposed to it. Arguments for the censorship of pornography that proceed in this way invoke a form of what Feinberg calls 'moralistic legal paternalism' (a variety of legal moralism), whereby 'It is always a good reason in support of a proposed prohibition that it is probably necessary to prevent moral harm . . . to the actor himself.'[8] This way of setting the limits of toleration is not available on the reasonableness defence because disagreement over the content of moral principles according to which the concept of moral harm is defined is reasonable, permanent, and not-to-be-regretted.

The best explication of the rejection of legal moralism with respect to the regulation of pornography is given by Ronald Dworkin. Dworkin argues that the requirement (which lies at the heart of the liberal conception of rights laid out in chapter 6, and is derived from a commitment to reasonableness) that the state treat all persons with equal concern and respect generates a right to pornography. This is because any argument for the censorship (or, even, the over-regulation) of pornography must draw on the value of using public policy so as to satisfy the 'external preferences' of the majority that 'their neighbors [be prevented from] read[ing] dirty books or look[ing] at dirty pictures', and that engagement with such material is 'demeaning or bestial or otherwise unsuitable to human beings of the best sort, even though this hypothesis may be true'.9 In Dworkin's view, although it can be legitimate to legislate so as to maximize the satisfaction of persons' preferences as regards their own situation, making the satisfaction of external preferences 'for the assignment of goods and opportunities to others'10 the aim of public policy is ruled out by a commitment to equal concern and respect, from which certain rights are derived which 'trump' utilitarian external preference-oriented policy making.11 He claims that one such right is the 'right to moral independence', which is

> a right [of persons] not to suffer disadvantage in the distribution of social goods and opportunities, including disadvantage in the liberties permitted to them by the criminal law, just on the ground that their officials or fellow-citizens think that their opinions about the right way for them to lead their own lives are ignoble or wrong.12

The legal moralism at the heart of the argument that pornography ought to be censored in virtue of its deleterious effects on the moral character of those who consume it conflicts with the right to moral independence, which can be seen as protecting – in large part – our citizen interests in the maintenance of a genuinely democratic community.13 Thus, reasonable persons committed to the rejection of legal moralism (as they should be, in virtue of their commitment to the equal concern and respect manifested in the classic liberal set of individual rights) cannot place pornography beyond the limits of toleration.

In response to the Dworkinian version of the anti-censorship argument I shall consider an account of pornography as part of the social construction of women's inequality. This response stands as a real challenge to Dworkin's argument because it purports both to avoid legal moralism, and to rely on precisely the egalitarian values that underpin the rights-based paradigm of harm, while establishing the diametrically opposed conclusion that pornography ought to be censored.14 If it can be shown that this interpretation of equality is reasonable, and if the claims made about the social construction of women's inequality are defensible, then liberal opposition to the censorship of pornography – at least insofar as it rests on the argument from democracy – must be rethought.

The best known advocate of this view, Catharine MacKinnon, presents it as follows:

> The harm of pornography, broadly speaking, is the harm of the civil inequality of the sexes made invisible as harm because it has become accepted as sex difference. Consider this analogy with race: if you see Black people as different, there is no harm to segregation; it is merely a recognition of that difference. . . . Similarly, if you see women as just different, even or especially if you don't know that you do, subordination will not look like subordination at all, much less like harm. It will merely look like an appropriate recognition of the sex difference.15

What does it mean to claim that pornography makes the harm of civil inequality invisible? In elucidating this claim MacKinnon draws on what she calls the 'dominance approach' to sexual discrimination, which is a version of the thesis that the social world is constructed. What this means is that the categories that constitute the social world, and the relations between people in it, are not natural features of the world given in advance of social relations, to which these forms of organisation then conform. Rather, these categories are a product of complex social relations between groupings of individuals with different interests and degrees of power over one another, and form part of the ideology of the society in question. So, for example, the categories 'mother', 'brother', 'white', 'employer', 'male', and 'female' are not natural, pre-social categories; rather, they reflect dynamic social relations between individuals who adopt these roles and engage in the relationships associated with them. MacKinnon's 'dominance' version of the social construction thesis relates specifically to gender and highlights the fact that men have more power – across all domains – than women. This fact of power inequality, she argues, means that men have ultimate control over the social construction of the gender category 'female', and use this control in order to retain and increase their power.[16] For MacKinnon, pornography is a key prop in this social construction, and violates civil equality between the sexes by perpetuating patriarchy:

> pornography institutionalizes the sexuality of male supremacy, which fuses the eroticization of dominance and submission with the social construction of male and female. Gender is sexual. Pornography constitutes the meaning of that sexuality. Men treat women as who they see women as being. Pornography constructs who that is. Men's power over women means that the way men see women defines who women can be. Pornography is that way.[17]

In what sense does pornography construct civil inequality between the sexes? Answering this question requires a more detailed definition of pornography than that given in the first section. In 1983 Catharine MacKinnon and Andrea Dworkin were asked by the legislators of the city of Minneapolis to write an ordinance to be used to protect citizens against the perceived civil rights violations caused by pornography. The definition of pornography in the 'Model Ordinance' – upon which the Minneapolis Ordinance, and ordinances in Indianapolis, Los Angeles County, and Massachusetts were modelled[18] – is as follows:

> [Pornography is] the graphic sexually explicit subordination of women through pictures and/or words that also includes one or more of the following: (a) women are presented dehumanized as sexual objects, things, or commodities; or (b) women are presented as sexual objects who enjoy humiliation or pain; or (c) women are presented as sexual objects experiencing sexual pleasure in rape, incest, or other sexual assault; or (d) women

are presented as sexual objects tied up or cut up or mutilated or bruised or physically hurt; or (e) women are presented in postures or positions of sexual submission, servility, or display; or (f) women's body parts – including but not limited to vaginas, breasts, or buttocks – are exhibited such that women are reduced to those parts; or (g) women are presented being penetrated by objects or animals; or (h) women are presented in scenarios of degradation, humiliation, injury, torture, shown as filthy or inferior, bleeding, bruised, or hurt in a context that makes these conditions sexual.[19]

As can be seen, the Model Ordinance definition of pornography isolates a specific set of sexually explicit materials united by their presentation of women as subordinate.[20] This means – importantly – that a distinction can be made between erotica and pornography, where the former set of sexually explicit materials does not present women as subordinate.[21] Thus, the Ordinance definition opens up the possibility of feminist 'pornography' (read: erotica).[22]

Using this definition in conjunction with the background thesis of the dominance approach, MacKinnon argues that pornography as protected by the First Amendment (or any other principle granting the same scope to freedom of expression) is 'on a collision course'[23] with the Fourteenth Amendment (or any other principle of civil equality). The subordination of women perpetuated by pornography – the images it peddles of women being beaten, raped, humiliated, etc., and enjoying it – translates as unequal freedom of speech for women: 'Pornography terrorizes women into silence';[24] it 'chills women's expression'[25] by making 'their speech impossible, and where possible, worthless. Pornography makes women into objects. Objects do not speak. When they do, they are by then regarded as objects, not as humans, which is what it means to have no credibility.'[26] A crude, though accurate, manifestation of the harm MacKinnon identifies is the view (which has on occasion been voiced by stupid judges in US and UK rape trials) that when a woman says 'no' to sexual intercourse she does not always mean 'no': in MacKinnon's view, pornography constructs the social reality of gender relations whereby this view gains currency.

MacKinnon's argument is egalitarian insofar as it presents pornography as perpetuating inequality of speech between men and women: free speech as exercised by pornographers under protection of the First Amendment denies equal speech to women as required by the Fourteenth Amendment.[27] The egalitarian character of MacKinnon's argument makes it *prima facie* promising as a reply to liberals such as Dworkin who reject arguments for the censorship of pornography as varieties of legal moralism, and insist that a commitment to equality delivers a right to pornography. However, for the argument to succeed we need to know more about how, exactly, to understand the claim that pornography denies equal speech to women in order to assess whether this is a form of harm that registers on the reasonableness defence of toleration. Before turning to that in the next section, however, it will be helpful to consider Dworkin's response to MacKinnon so as to get clear on the challenges that any anti-pornography argument invoking the value of equal speech for women must meet.

In common with most liberals, Dworkin condemns pornography as 'so comprehensively degrading that we are appalled and shamed by its existence'.[28] However, as is by now familiar, these judgements provide no grounds for the prohibition of pornography in a reasonable society of equals. Instead, Dworkin identifies two key non-moralistic versions of the speech-related argument for censorship made by MacKinnon.

The first, 'clash of rights', argument is that by protecting freedom of expression for pornographers, the First Amendment (or any similar principle of freedom of expression) denies freedom of expression to women. The thought here is that the First Amendment, or any similar principle, distributes an incompossible set of rights: the rights in question cannot be exercised by all those to whom they are distributed at the same time.[29] Dworkin accepts that pornography 'humiliates or frightens' women into not speaking, and can affect men in such a way that they fail to understand what women mean when they do speak.[30] However, the right to freedom of expression does not – and ought not to – extend to speakers protection from humiliation, fear, and failures of communication, in which case MacKinnon's reflections on how pornography 'chills women's expression',[31] although probably true, fail to establish a clash of rights to freedom of expression between pornographers and women. This version of MacKinnon's argument is, he claims, 'premised on an unacceptable proposition: that the right to free speech includes a right to circumstances that encourage one to speak, and a right that others grasp and respect what one means to say'.[32]

The second 'inequality' gloss Dworkin gives on MacKinnon's argument is in terms of a clash between liberty and equality: the domination of women by men means that pornography, which constructs this inequality, must be censored in the name of equality for women. The difference between this version of the argument and the first is that it focuses specifically on women as victims of unequal power relations, and proposes censorship as a way to address this inequality, whereas the first argument proceeds on the assumption that all persons – whatever their power relations with others in society – have a right to be heard as a consequence of the right to speak.

Dworkin makes two responses. First, he identifies a slippery slope from MacKinnon's view to a 'despotism of the thought-police',[33] which would prohibit,

> the graphic or visceral or emotionally charged expression of any opinion or conviction that might reasonably offend a disadvantaged group. It could outlaw performances of *The Merchant of Venice*, or films about professional women who neglect their children, or caricatures or parodies of homosexuals in nightclub routines.[34]

This approach is ruled out for liberals by their rejection of legal moralism.

Dworkin's second response is to deny that the principle of freedom of expression undermines equality on the grounds that, 'First Amendment liberty is not equality's enemy, but the other side of equality's coin.'[35] As we saw in chapter 8, Dworkin's 'argument from democracy' for freedom of expression relies on an ideal of democratic community wherein all persons have membership of this community (in part) through having an equal opportunity to express their views about how that community ought to be constituted. It is this ideal to which Dworkin appeals in his second response to this version of MacKinnon's argument. Because '[h]ow others treat me – and my own sense of identity and self-respect – are determined in part by the mix of social conventions, opinions, tastes, convictions, prejudices, life styles, and cultures that flourish in the community in which I live',[36] showing equal concern and respect for all requires securing protection for each to attempt to influence this 'moral environment' through (non-coercive) means; one important opportunity for such influence is speech and expression, in which case, equal rights to freedom of expression for all are required by a commitment to equality. This response amplifies Dworkin's idea of the right to moral independence laid out at the start of this section: not only do we, *qua* equals, have a right to be free from limits on our liberty justified by reference to the preferences of others that our liberty be limited, we also, *qua* equals, have a right to attempt to influence the environment in which these preferences are formed. In which case, the only tool available to women committed to combating the degradation visited upon them by pornography is more speech.[37]

Dworkin's responses create the following challenges for egalitarian speech-related feminist arguments for the censorship of pornography. Either it must be shown (1) that the proposition on which the 'clash of rights' argument rests – namely that the right to freedom of expression includes or entails a right to have the contexts of meaningful expression and communication protected – is not, *pace* Dworkin, unacceptable. Or it must be shown (2) that pornography comprehensively denies to women the speech required for them to shape their moral environment. And if the censorship of pornography is to be justified in the name of reasonable toleration using either or both of these arguments, then the arguments must be acceptable to reasonable people. In the next section I consider the most sophisticated argument for (2) which, if successful, indicates a way in which to argue for (1).

Pornography and harm II: silencing

In the first section of this chapter I claimed that the Millean arguments for freedom of expression fail to supply a defence of non-censorship because pornography lacks propositional content, and so does not qualify as speech in the sense relevant to these arguments. The speech acts to which the Millean arguments apply are *locutions* – that is, utterances that have a certain meaning in virtue of their propositional content – and pornography is not such an act. However – and drawing on the work of the Oxford philosopher of language J.L. Austin[38] – there are at least two other ways in which an act of expression (even one lacking propositional content) can qualify as a speech act.

1 An act of expression can be a *perlocutionary* speech act: here, an action is performed *by* expressing something, which is usually explained in terms of how the act affects an audience. For example, a barrister in court not only attempts to communicate a particular meaning to the jury, she also attempts

to *persuade* them with her arguments; or, in writing a piece of music a composer might aim to *move* her audience, without reliance on locution at all, given the non-propositional content of her act of expression.

2   An act of expression can be an *illocutionary* speech act: here, the act of expression itself *constitutes the doing of something*, in virtue of satisfying the relevant 'felicity conditions' given by the linguistic and social conventions which delineate when an expressive act can succeed as an illocution. For example, in saying 'I do' in response to the question 'Do you take this man to be your lawful wedded husband?', when that question is posed by a priest or registrar, in the presence of witnesses, with banns having been posted, and all other legal conditions met, I perform the act of marrying: to say 'I do', with the relevant felicity conditions met, is to do something, i.e. get married. Or, in placing the sign in Figure 9.1 at the entrance to a road, traffic authorities perform the act of denying entry to vehicles, even though this expressive act lacks propositional content.

The categories 'locution', 'perlocution', and 'illocution' are not, of course, mutually exclusive: many expressive acts qualify as more than one type of speech act. In what follows I shall focus on an interpretation of pornography as an illocutionary speech act which denies to women the felicity conditions whereby they can perform certain illocutionary speech acts. If this argument succeeds then the right to freedom of expression as exercised by pornographers is not compossible with the same right as exercised by women, in which case the 'clash of rights' argument for the censorship of pornography may not be as easy to dismiss as Dworkin thinks. Furthermore, the success of the argument would also establish that pornography denies to women the power of speech required to shape their moral environment, in which case a commitment to equal concern and respect as evinced in the argument for freedom of expression from democracy requires the censorship of pornography.

Rae Langton argues that, in a quite literal sense, pornography silences women.[39] Pornography does this not only by humiliating and frightening women (and thereby succeeding in terms of these perlocutionary effects, as

Figure 9.1 No entry sign

Dworkin admits), but furthermore in terms of its illocutionary force. It does this in virtue of the fact that the felicity conditions it sets for certain illocutionary speech acts make it impossible for women to perform those acts: pornography causes illocutionary disablement in women. As Langton puts it,

> Some speech acts build a space, as it were, for other speech acts, making it possible for some people to marry, vote, and divorce. Some speech acts, in contrast, set limits to that space, making it impossible for other people to marry, vote, divorce. Some speech determines the kind of speech there can be. This shows that it is indeed possible to silence someone, not just by ordering or threatening them into simple silence, not just by frustrating their perlocutionary goals, but by making their speech acts unspeakable. . . . *The felicity conditions for women's speech acts are set by the speech acts of pornography.* The words of the pornographer, like the words of the legislator, are 'words that set conditions'. They are words that constrain, that make certain actions – refusal, protest – unspeakable for women in some contexts. This is speech that determines the kind of speech there can be.[40]

Consider an analogy. Current UK law specifies various felicity conditions for persons to succeed in performing the act of marrying by performing the speech act of saying 'I do'. These conditions mean that it is impossible for same sex couples, people who are already married, close blood relations, and minors to perform the act of marrying by saying 'I do'. It is not that such people who try to perform this speech act fail because they do not secure others' understanding of their utterances (the case is not analogous to people on a beach who fail to see that a gesturing woman is 'not waving, but drowning'[41]). Rather, the conventions that govern the utterance of the words 'I do' in the context of marriage mean that, however often such people repeat these words in surroundings that resemble those in which genuine marriages are performed (registry office, flowers, tearful mothers, etc.), and however well they are understood *qua* locutions by others, they will never succeed in marrying by uttering them.[42]

As with marriage, so with sex, and the illocutions through which much of it is performed, according to Langton. In the domain of sex and sexuality, pornography sets the felicity conditions for illocutionary speech acts of consent and refusal, acceptance and protest, encouragement and rejection, abandonment and withdrawal: by depicting women in the ways described by the Model Ordinance, pornography limits what it is possible for women to say in sexual contexts, and causes illocutionary disablement for women with respect to speaking the acts in the second set of conjuncts just listed. This is particularly worrying with respect to rape: the conventional force of pornography with respect to 'the language games of sex [is] such that saying "no" can fail to count as making a refusal move, and telling the story of one's own subordination can fail to count as a move of protest'.[43]

If Langton's analysis is convincing then it will not do, à la Dworkin, to claim that women ought to protest against pornography with more speech rather than with prohibitive legislation, because the class of illocutionary speech acts constitutive of protest are made impossible for women by pornography. If Langton is correct then there is a genuine clash of rights contained in the First Amendment, and the argument that in a society of equals this clash would be resolved by means of the censorship of pornography looks more promising: only one class of people – women – suffer illocutionary disablement through pornography, so banning it would make women better off, and pornographers no worse off, with respect to their capabilities for performing the illocutionary acts in question.[44] And if commitment to an egalitarian ideal of democracy requires securing for each person the opportunity to shape the moral environment of their society, and illocutionary speech acts are an important way of doing this, then realisation of the ideal of democracy also requires the censorship of pornography.[45]

Are things this straightforward? In what follows I shall focus on problems in Langton's analysis related to the fact that the illocutionary disablement of one group by another requires that the former have authority in the domain in which the disablement is caused. With respect to pornography and women's speech, this can be seen in Langton's claim that the type of illocutions performed by pornographers so as to silence women are *exercitive*, that is, speech acts that 'confer powers and rights on people, or deprive people of powers and rights':[46] pornography is an exercitive speech act because it deprives women of the powers to refuse, reject, and withdraw from sex, and to protest against pornography.[47] For a speaker to perform exercitive speech acts requires that that speaker have authority with respect to the domain in which she does things with her words. Langton's argument is that pornographers silence women by performing such speech acts in the domain of sex, in which case she must be committed to the claim that pornographers have authority in that domain.[48]

What does it mean for a person or group to have authority in a domain? Langton gives the following examples: a legislator exercises authority so as to deprive certain citizens of political powers (as in the denial of the right to vote to blacks in apartheid South Africa); a slave is deprived by his master of the power of issuing orders to his master; a parent prohibits a child from walking barefoot in the snow; and a patient prohibits a doctor from performing a treatment on her body.[49] However, only in the first two cases does the authority figure effect illocutionary disablement on others (the parent does not make it impossible for the child to go out in the snow simply by issuing a verbal prohibition, and the patient's prohibition does not make the doctor's prescription disappear; Langton's use of these misplaced examples is strange and unfortunate for her argument). With respect to the two genuine examples of illocutionary disablement she offers, Langton does not theorise the authority of the legislator and the slave-master. However, if there are strong family resemblances between the authority of the legislator and the slave-master in their domains, and the authority of the pornographer in the domain of sex, then perhaps we have enough to make plausible Langton's analysis of pornography as silencing women.

The question is, then: do pornographers occupy a position in the domain of sex similar to that occupied by the legislator in the domain of the polity, and the slave-master in the domain of, say, the plantation? An important dissimilarity is that the legislator and the slave-master have the power of coercion over members of their domain, in a very literal sense: legislators have the executive and judicial branches of the state to enforce their edicts (the police will prosecute those who do not obey the law, courts will try them, and the prison system will enforce punishment if they are found guilty), and slave-masters have shackles, the lynch mob and, historically, the coercive power of the law. Of course, there are all sorts of complicated questions about how legislators and slave-masters acquire and control such powers, and all sorts of excellent arguments to show that slave-masters ought to be deprived of the power of coercion, and legislators granted it only when certain conditions are met. But these are not to the point. Empirically, the authority of the legislator and the slave-master is – in large part – comprised of their possession of, or control over, powers of coercion with respect to members of their domain, and Langton makes it clear that the authority of pornographers is, similarly, an empirical question.[50] However, pornographers *qua* pornographers lack similar powers of coercion in the domain of sex, which is vast and includes all sexually active men and women. Admittedly, pornography is a huge and profitable industry and as such confers serious economic clout on those who produce it; and it is true that the abuse visited on the women and children involved in making pornography is real, widespread, and terrifying. However, the focus of Langton's analysis is not these negative effects of pornography; rather, the focus is on the harm (of illocutionary disablement) caused to women – all women – by pornography. The domain in which the pornographer has authority must therefore extend to all women. But if pornographers lack powers of coercion à la the legislator and the slave-master with respect to all women, then in virtue of what do they have authority sufficient to cause this harm?

One possibility is to focus not on the authority of pornographers *qua* pornographers, but on their authority *qua* men. This raises the question of the sense in which men have authority in the domain of sex. If, again, we take family resemblances between authorities to be the key to understanding them, then we need to show that – like legislators and slave-masters in their domains – men have the power of coercion over women in the domain of sex; in other words, that men have the power to rape women. In the sense required for the analysis, this is true. To claim that men have the power to rape women is not to claim that all men would exercise this power if they thought they could get away with it, and nor is it to claim that every man could rape a woman if he tried: legislators and slave-masters have powers of coercion with respect to all members of their domain even when these powers are not exercised, and/or the legislator or slave-master in question abhors force, and/or the legislator or slave master would in fact not succeed in any attempt to use coercion to force others to bend to his will. However – and here we trespass on heated debates between some separatist feminists and their critics – what legislators and slave-masters must do in order to possess the power of coercion is to present a *credible threat* of coercion. Making the analogous argument: if pornographers have authority with respect to sex in virtue of being men, and if authority is in large part comprised of the power of coercion which is in large part possessed in virtue of presenting a credible threat of coercion to members of the relevant domain, then men have authority with respect to sex if and only if they present a credible threat of rape to women. This is, I think, why debates about pornography and censorship sometimes turn into debates about the nature of male sexual desire: if it is true that all men are potential rapists insofar as they not only (by and large) have the physical capacity to rape women, but also the latent (or not so latent) desire to do so, then the threat of sexual coercion men present to women is very credible.[51]

We have come a long way from Langton's Austinian analysis of pornography. Happily, however, we need not pass judgement on the debate about male sexuality in order to reach a provisional conclusion. Analysing the authority of pornographers in terms of their authority as men stymies the argument for censorship in which it might be used. This is because, on this analysis, illocutionary disablement is caused to women by men – actual, real men, considered as a sex – in virtue of how they set the felicity conditions for illocutions in the domain of sex. Pornography here appears as a reminder – albeit a powerful one – of the threat men pose to women. However, it is not the cause of illocutionary disablement, which is instead a product of the threat of coercion that actual, real men pose to women, in virtue of the power they wield over them. What we get on this analysis instead are arguments for political measures to remove the threat that men pose to women by redressing the power inequalities between them. These are important issues, but they are not issues of toleration in the sense that we are interested in: I take it that no reasonable person could accept forms of social and political organisation in which women are under constant threat of rape by men. In that case, what is required is an explanation of why pornographers *qua* pornographers have authority in the domain of sex, whether or not they are men, and we are back to our original problem. Perhaps an analysis of pornographers' authority could be produced so as to supply this explanation. However, given the reflections about pornographers' limited powers of coercion with respect to women, and the low social status attached to the role of pornographer (would we encourage our children to become pornographers? or be proud of their successes in this area?), we are entitled to a large dose of scepticism here.

Conclusion

Setting to one side problems related to pornographers' authority, Langton's analysis provides a *prima facie* promising answer to the challenges posed by Dworkin's rejection of MacKinnon's pro-censorship argument. These were: (1) that a pro-censorship argument would have to make it plausible that protection of the right to freedom of expression entails or requires protection of the conditions in which others understand what the speaker intends to communicate or do through the expressive act; and (2) that protection of the right to freedom of expression for pornographers damages women's capacities to shape their moral environment. If persuasive, Langton's argument meets the challenge of (2) by showing how pornography stunts women's capacities to do things with words so as to shape the environment in which men's conceptions of women's sexuality are formed. And it meets the challenge of (1) by showing that sometimes a concern for freedom of expression does require legislation to shape the contexts in which it occurs, because these contexts set the felicity conditions whereby certain forms of speech – illocutions – become possible. This response to (1) might be met with a denial that illocution is a significant form of expressive act. But such a denial is tantamount to abandoning the idea that free speech matters because it creates a community in which people can communicate with one another, rather than just making sounds at one another. If we think that the possibility of communication is at the centre of the value of free expression, and if illocution is a key vehicle of communication, then the argument for the censorship of pornography so as to protect women from illocutionary disablement cannot so easily be dismissed.[52]

Meeting these challenges depends on making the analysis watertight, and as we saw in the last section there are serious omissions with respect to the question of pornographers' authority. However, the framework of analysis might fare better when applied to cases in which the authority of the group whose speech is claimed to cause illocutionary disablement to others is more clear. In particular, the authority of Rushdie and his publishers – when understood as representatives of Western intelligentsia – might be such as to contribute to the illocutionary disablement of Muslims by making their voices of protest appear as fundamentalist rantings (witness the ubiquity at the time of the controversy of images of Muslims burning books). Applying Austinian speech act theory to this problem of toleration might be more productive in rendering voices of protest reasonable because – as Tariq Modood highlights – SV was written by a citizen of a country with a history of persecution towards Muslims, and in which Muslims form a minority still subjected to attacks and abuse motivated by religious hatred.[53] If Muslim objectors to SV could establish that Rushdie and his publishers had the authority necessary to visit illocutionary disablement on Muslims in the domain of the polity, then the argument that SV ought to be censored on the grounds of the defamation it causes to Muslims as a group might gain strength.

I leave the questions of whether – and how – to apply speech act theory to the SV controversy to the reader's judgement. However, whatever conclusion we reach here there remains one further challenge that arguments for censorship – of artistic works, or pornography – premised on speech act theory must meet. This is to show that Austinian speech act theory is not, *qua* theory, subject to reasonable dispute. And it is here, I believe, that anyone committed both to the reasonableness defence of toleration, and to Austinian analyses of the harm that the speech of some can cause to the speech of others, will face a *prima facie* insurmountable problem. Austinian speech act theory is not universally accepted by philosophers of language, who know the terrain if anyone does. If reasonable disagreement exists about the virtues of Austinian speech act theory among those who are paid to think about the specific questions Austin addressed, then we cannot expect the invocation of this theory in the political arena to be free from reasonable dispute, even if the problems related to the definition of authority are solved, and the case for censorship made on the back of this theory is watertight. Of course, one option at this point is to abandon commitment to the reasonableness defence of toleration in favour of a perfectionist approach to policy making in which the truth of a theory can be asserted as sufficient grounds for its invocation in policy making, even in the face of unanimous reasonable disagreement with it. For all the reasons laid out in chapter 5, I think this option is undesirable, and the reasonableness defence provides the best bet for justifying toleration in contemporary conditions of permanent pluralism. Perhaps a way could be found to reach the insights of Austinian analyses without relying on premises about which reasonable disagreement is inevitable: on this question, the jury is out, but that is no reason for despair. In the face of the powerful classic liberal arguments for freedom of expression we have isolated an intellectually serious way forward for pro-censorship arguments which does not collapse into legal moralism, and with which liberals committed to the resolution of problems of toleration in terms of a set of rights defined as such in public reason must engage. The debate progresses.

Chapter 10

Holocaust denial[1]

> Our language lacks the words to express this offence, the demolition of a man.[2]
> (Primo Levi, on a year spent in Auschwitz)

Introduction

Holocaust denial (HD) is the activity of denying the occurrence of key events and processes which constitute the Holocaust. HD brings into particularly sharp focus many of the difficult questions faced by advocates of the reasonableness defence of toleration (and, indeed, defenders of toleration everywhere) insofar as it is predictably motivated and accompanied by anti-semitism, causes profound offence and upset to Jews (and many others), and yet (in its most pernicious forms) imitates legitimate academic history. Because the most sophisticated HD takes this form it is unclear what grounds there can be, given the reasonableness defence, for its prohibition in law; indeed, in this chapter I shall argue that there are no such grounds, and that HD must be tolerated in law. However, the most sophisticated deniers hunt bigger game: not only do they demand legal permission to deny the Holocaust, they also insist – often, they claim, as a consequence of their legal right to propagate HD – that they be granted equal access to the institutions constitutive of the Academy. It is on this terrain that the most interesting debates are located.

The division of theoretical labour involved here reflects J.S. Mill's identification of the two arenas in which individual liberty – including freedom of expression – ought to be protected to provide a bulwark against a possible 'tyranny of the majority' with respect to norms regarding the best way to live and the right things to think and say.[3] These arenas are law, and the institutions of civil society. In line with this division the two questions to be addressed in this chapter are: (1) given the reasonableness defence of toleration, ought HD to be placed outside the limits of toleration in law?; and (2) in the Academy? These questions are discussed in the third and fourth sections respectively. I shall conclude that although the reasonableness defence does not support the legal prohibition of HD, the exclusion and, if necessary, expulsion of Holocaust deniers from the Academy is permitted and (further) required by the reasonableness defence of toleration.

Before assessing any of the arguments, however, it is important to get straight about the facts of the Holocaust and the nature of HD: the following section contains a brief account.

The Holocaust, and its denial

By the end of the Second World War in Europe in May 1945, about 12,000,000 non-combatants had died at the hands of the Nazis and their collaborators.[4] Victims included Catholics, Poles, homosexuals, Jehovah's Witnesses, communists, prisoners of war (POWs), mentally and physically handicapped people, the Sinti and Roma (colloquially often known as 'gypsies'), and Jews; however, only the latter three groups were attacked systematically, and of these the greatest number who perished were Jews. The deaths were caused by starvation and disease (in labour, extermination, and POW camps, and in the ghettos), medical experimentation and euthanasia (by which means an estimated 275,000 people were killed), shooting (by murder squads, the *Einsatzgruppen*, who killed over a million people after the invasion of the Soviet Union in 1941) and, finally, by poison gas (carbon monoxide or Zyklon-B hydrogen cyanide) in vans run by the *Einsatzgruppen*, and in chambers located in industrialised extermination camps at locations including Chelmno, Belzec, Sobibor, Treblinka, Auschwitz-Birkenau and Majdanek (at the height of its activity up to 8,000 Jews were gassed every day at Auschwitz-Birkenau). The bodies were burned in giant crematoria.

The suffering caused by the Nazis and their collaborators, and the numbers involved, are bewildering and horrifying in their magnitude, and in the details. No death should be discounted, and every death is to be mourned. However, for the purposes of discussion here I shall focus on the persecution and attempted annihilation of the European Jews, as it is this aspect of the Nazi atrocities to which Holocaust deniers devote most attention. I shall understand the Holocaust as follows: 'the systematic and bureaucratically administered destruction by the Nazis and their collaborators during the Second World War of an estimated six million Jews based primarily on racial ideology.[5]

The Holocaust, so understood, eliminated nearly two in three Jews in Europe in the name of preserving the purity of the Aryan race. Until the advent of the Final Solution, the persecution of Jews had not involved explicit plans for their extermination, and had instead taken the following forms: segregation (encoded in 1935 in the Nuremberg Laws which deprived Jews of German citizenship and made marriage or sexual relations between Jews and non-Jews illegal); the 1937 'aryanisation' of Jewish businesses (whereby Jews were forced to liquidise their businesses, or sell them at bargain prices to German 'Aryans'); the pogrom on *Kristallnacht* ('Night of the Broken Glass', 9–10 November 1938) when SS officers destroyed Jewish shops, synagogues and businesses, and desecrated Jewish cemeteries; and the subsequent (1939) and increased segregation of Jews who were marked as such by identity cards, and by the required addition of 'Israel' or 'Sara' to their given names. After Germany's invasion of Poland in September

1939, and the start of the war, the Nazis created ghettos – closed off, highly populated, unsanitary areas of cities – into which Jews were herded (the most notorious of these was the Warsaw ghetto, in which half a million people were crowded into 1.3 square miles).[6]

After the invasion of the Soviet Union in 1941 Nazi persecution of the Jews took an even darker form. On 31 July 1941, Reichsmarschall Hermann Göering (Hitler's second-in-command) issued an order to Reinhard Heydrich (Chief of the Reich Main Security Office) to plan in organisational, functional, and material terms the Endöslung der Judenfrage: the Final Solution of the Jewish question.[7] Around the same time the Einsatzgruppen began their murderous work (massacring over 1 million people in batches by rounding them up and shooting them on the edges of mass graves, or by gassing them in mobile vans); and shortly thereafter construction work began on the first extermination camps at Belzec and Chelmno. On 20 January 1942 Heydrich convened the 'Wannsee Conference' in Berlin, where fourteen high-ranking Nazis met for an hour and a half over lunch to discuss the practicalities of implementing the Final Solution, and to assign responsibility for different tasks.[8] The total number of Jews killed in all the camps was more than 3 million.[9] As the war drew to an end the Nazis evacuated the camps, and attempted to destroy the crematoria and other cogs in their industrialised killing machine, so as to remove evidence of their mass murders. Up until the end of the war in Europe on 8 May 1945, SS camp guards forced prisoners to undertake 'death marches' to various locations in Germany, again in an attempt to cover their tracks: many were shot, or died of starvation and disease. Although Allied troops liberated hundreds of thousands of emaciated prisoners, they also found open graves filled with the starved bodies of men, women, and children, and epidemics of typhus and other diseases claimed the lives of many. After the conclusion of the War and International Military Tribunal was established to prosecute Nazis involved in 'War Crimes', 'Crimes against Peace', and 'Crimes against Humanity'. The 'Nuremberg Trials' sentenced twelve leading Nazis to death, imprisoned three for life, and issued shorter prison sentences for others.[10] Subsequent trials conducted by national authorities continued into the 1980s, and various organisations remain dedicated to seeking out any remaining Nazi war criminals.[11]

The outline just given states some of the facts about the Holocaust. We know these are facts in virtue of the abundance of evidence in the form of documents (the Nazis were meticulous record-keepers) and photographs, eyewitness testimony (of perpetrators, victims, and liberators), demographic analysis of Jewish and other populations pre- and post-Holocaust, and scientific analysis of the remains of crematoria and gas chambers at various camps, all of which converge to support the same conclusions that:

1   A *highly technical*, well-organized extermination programme, using gas chambers and crematoria, among other instruments and methods, was implemented to kill millions of Jews.

2   An estimated *six million* Jews were killed.
3   There was an *intention* to commit genocide of Jews based primarily on racial ideology.[12]

These three historical facts form the focus of HD. Deniers do not argue that the Nazis did not kill large numbers of Jews and others. Rather, they claim that the gas chambers and crematoria did not, or could not have, existed; that the number of Jews killed was far less than 6 million; and that there was no intention – as expressed in a formal plan or order issuing from Hitler – to persecute the Jews on the grounds of racial ideology. I take it that these three facts about the murder of the Jews constitute the Holocaust, and that those who deny them are Holocaust deniers.[13]

   It is important to mark a distinction between Holocaust *denial* and Holocaust *revisionism*. Revisionism in academic history can be a legitimate exercise in challenging accepted analyses and interpretations of historical events, thereby bestowing on those events a new meaning, or providing new explanations of subsequent events. To take Deborah Lipstadt's example, a group of American historians in the 1920s argued that, contrary to received opinion as informed by Allied propaganda, Germany had not wanted the Second World War and made great efforts to avoid it.[14] A more recent example is Daniel Goldhagen's *Hitler's Willing Executioners*, in which it is argued that the German people willingly colluded with the Nazis in perpetrating the Holocaust in virtue of their deep-seated anti-semitism.[15] Revisionist contributions to the history of the Second World War and the Holocaust are important both for the sake of history *per se*, and for the sake of the political identity and self-understanding of existing and future Germans.[16] And even historians who are not revisionists nevertheless engage in reflection on how best to understand the Holocaust, and the various forms of evidence for it.[17] Deniers claim that they are revisionists, and as such deserve a place in the Academy alongside less controversial historians. Their academic opponents claim that their methods justify their exclusion and expulsion. I shall return to this debate in the next section. For the moment – and to get a sense of what we are dealing with – I shall outline two prominent cases of HD and the public controversy surrounding them by way of illustrating what deniers claim.[18]

   First, consider the case of Robert Faurisson who published a pamphlet in 1979 entitled 'The Problem of the Gas Chambers' in which he claimed that:

1   The Hitler 'gas chambers' never existed.
2   The 'genocide' (or 'attempted genocide') of the Jews never took place. In other words: Hitler never gave an order nor permission that anyone should be killed because of his race or religion.
3   The alleged 'gas chambers' and the alleged 'genocide' are one and the same lie.
4   This lie, which is largely of Zionist origin, has made an enormous political and financial fraud possible, whose principal beneficiary is the state of Israel.

5 The principal victims of this fraud are the German people (but not the German rulers) and the entire Palestinian people.
6 The enormous power of the official information services has, thus far, had the effect of ensuring the success of the lie and of censoring the freedom of expression of those who have denounced the lie.
7 The participants in this lie know that its days are numbered. They distort the purpose and nature of the Revisionist research. They label as 'resurgence of Nazism' or as 'falsification of history' what is only a thoughtful and justified concern for historical truth.[19]

Faurisson's denial of the existence of the gas chambers in (1) and (3), his denial of the fact of genocide in (2) and (3), and his denial of the racially motivated Nazi policy of eliminating the European Jews in (2) qualifies him as a Holocaust denier according to my definition.[20] However, his 'conclusions' in 4–7 reveal a further feature of his HD: that the 'facts' revealed by deniers' 'research' have been covered up by 'official information services' (6) for the political and economic benefit of Israel. The idea that such a cover-up exists often has its roots in the belief that there exists an international Zionist conspiracy bent on manipulating political and economic forces in order to benefit the Jewish people and the state of Israel.[21] *Prima facie*, assertion of the existence of such a Zionist conspiracy is not essential to denial activity: denial of the three propositions on pp. 155–6 appears to be conceptually possible in the absence of such an assertion. Further, and *prima facie*, HD need not be anti-semitic. The accuracy of these *prima facie* features of HD will be assessed in due course. For the moment suffice it to note that, as a matter of fact, assertions about Zionist conspiracies and anti-semitism almost always monotonously accompany HD.

When Faurisson published his pamphlet he was a Professor of Literature at the University of Lyon 2. The physical threats and harassment he received from students outraged at the publication led the university to suspend him from teaching on the grounds that they could not guarantee his safety. In response, a petition was got up by French left-libertarian intellectuals calling for the protection of Faurisson's 'safety and the free exercise of his legal rights', including his right to 'freedom of speech and expression'.[22] The most prominent signature on this petition was that of Noam Chomsky, a highly respected philosopher of language and globally influential left-wing political commentator and activist. Chomsky's signature was taken as an endorsement of what the petition referred to as Faurisson's 'extensive independent historical research' – and of the idea that the 'research' generated 'findings' about the Holocaust – and Chomsky was attacked by various intellectuals as having given credence to Faurisson's HD as a legitimate, alternative version of history.[23] In response, Chomsky published 'Some Elementary Comments on the Rights of Freedom of Expression',[24] in which he revived Voltaire's famous dictum 'I detest what you write, but I would give my life to make it possible for you to continue to write', with the aim of defending Faurisson's rights to freedom of expression without endorsing the content of his claims. Chomsky granted permission for this piece to be used by

Faurisson and his publishers however they wished; they took him at his word and used it as a preface to a longer work of HD by Faurisson.[25] Chomsky subsequently requested that the piece not be used in this way, but the request was denied. Chomsky's description of Faurisson as 'a relatively apolitical liberal of some sort', and his attacks on the French intelligentsia who criticised his support for the petition as exhibiting 'fanaticism' and 'deep-seated totalitarian strains',[26] heightened criticism of him in the French press and elsewhere.[27]

In September 1990 Faurisson was interviewed by the magazine *Le Choc du Mois*, wherein he stated:

> No one will have me believe that two plus two make five, that the earth is flat, or that the Nuremberg Tribunal was infallible. I have excellent reasons not to believe in this policy of extermination of Jews or in the magic gas chamber. . . . I would wish to see that 100 per cent of all French citizens realize that the myth of the gas chambers is a dishonest fabrication endorsed by the victorious powers of Nuremberg in 1945–6 and officialized on 14 July 1990 by the current French Government, with the approval of the 'court historians'.[28]

The 'officialisation' to which Faurisson referred is the 'Gayssot Act' passed by the French legislature on 13 July 1990. This act amends the 1881 law on the Freedom of the Press by making it an offence to contest the existence of the category of crimes against humanity as defined in the London Charter of 8 August 1945, on the basis of which Nazi leaders were tried and convicted in the Nuremberg trials. Upon publication of the interview associations of French Resistance fighters, and deportees to German concentration camps, brought a successful private criminal action against Faurisson and the publisher of *Le Choc du Mois*, as a result of which Faurisson *et al.* had fines and costs imposed on them of FRF326,832 (£33,373). Faurisson subsequently challenged this ruling through the United Nations Human Rights Committee on the grounds that the act under which he was prosecuted curtailed his right to freedom of expression and academic freedom as laid out in the International Covenant on Civil and Political Rights.[29] His case was dismissed by the committee, who found that the Gayssot Act does not violate the covenant.

The second case I shall consider is that of David Irving. Although he lacks a formal education or training in history, Irving has written over thirty books on the Third Reich, its major figures, and the German perspective on the Second World War. His earliest books – in the 1960s and 1970s – were published by major, respectable presses. However, most of his work since the 1980s has been published by his own vanity press, Focal Point, and has been increasingly concerned with HD. His 'research' – especially in books such as the revised edition of *Hitler's War* – purports to establish (among other things) that the three facts about the Holocaust listed on pp. 155–6 are disproved by historical documents over which Irving claims to have a mastery unmatched by other historians of the period.[30] However, Irving came to the attention of the general public as a result of the publication of a book not authored by him. In 1993 Penguin Books published Deborah Lipstadt's *Denying the Holocaust: The Growing Assault on Truth and Memory*. In this book she addressed in great detail the historical antecedents and current manifestations of HD, with a primary focus on America, and with the aim of undermining their claims by revealing the flaws in their methodologies, their deliberate manipulations and distortions of various forms of evidence for the Holocaust, and their far-right, anti-semitic political affiliations and agendas. In the book David Irving is described – although not discussed at length – as 'discredited',[31] and as

> one of the most dangerous spokespersons for Holocaust denial. Familiar with historical evidence, he bends it until it conforms with his ideological leanings and political agenda. A man who is convinced that Britain's great decline was accelerated by its decision to go to war with Germany, he is most facile at taking accurate information and shaping it to conform to his conclusions.[32]

Irving reacted by writing to Penguin Books to demand that the book be withdrawn on the grounds that Lipstadt's remarks defamed his reputation as a historian. Penguin refused Irving's demands and he issued a defamation writ in September 1996. The strategy of the defendants in the case was not to claim that Irving had misunderstood what Lipstadt had written, nor to deny that her words were defamatory. Instead, their strategy was that of justification; that is, to establish that what Lipstadt said about Irving in her book was true, in which case there could be no libel.[33] This did *not* mean that the Holocaust was put on trial; rather – and apposite to our concerns here – what the case put on trial were Irving's methods *qua* those of a reputable historian. The public hearing began at the High Court on 11 January 2000, and the court adjourned on 15 March 2000. Irving acted as his own counsel, and the prosecution failed.

In issuing his judgement Justice Gray stated that 'Irving treated the historical evidence in a manner which fell far short of the standard to be expected of a conscientious historian', that he 'misrepresented and distorted the evidence which was available to him', that his denial of the existence of gas chambers and the systematic nature of the murders of the Jews was 'contrary to evidence',[34] and that 'the Defendants have established that Irving has a [right-wing, pro-Nazi] political agenda. It is one which, it is legitimate to infer, disposes him, where he deems it necessary, to manipulate the historical record in order to make it conform with his political beliefs'.[35] Commenting on Irving's methods, expert witness Richard Evans – Professor of Modern History at Cambridge and an expert on modern German history, and its basis in documentary evidence – stated that Irving

> relied on material that turned out directly to contradict his arguments when it was checked. He quoted from sources in a manner that distorted their authors' meaning and purposes. He misrepresented data and skewed

documents. He used insignificant and sometimes implausible pieces of evidence to dismiss more substantial evidence that did not support his thesis. He ignored or deliberately suppressed material when it ran counter to his arguments. When he was unable to do this he expressed implausible doubts about its reliability.[36]

As a result of the trial, Irving was ordered to pay the legal fees incurred by the defence (approximately £2 million). After paying a fraction of this amount, Irving was declared bankrupt. He appealed the judgement but his request for a new trial was rejected by the appeals court on 20 July 2001. He continues in his activities as a denier.[37]

So much for HD and the fate of these prominent advocates of it. The question to be addressed in the rest of this chapter is whether we have a right to engage in HD in a society of reasonable people: if so, then HD must be tolerated; if not, then it can be made illegal. However, this general question must be broken down into two further questions. Another way of asking whether people have a right to engage in HD is to ask whether we have a right to stop them; assuming that the set of rights is compossible,[38] if we have a right to stop them then they do not have a right to propagate HD. There are two arenas in which we might have a right to prevent HD, which generate the two further questions just mentioned: (1) do we have a right to prohibit HD in law?; and (2) do we have a right to exclude and expel from the Academy those who engage in HD? Because a negative answer to (1) does not entail a negative answer to (2), the two questions must be addressed separately. In the context of (2) Faurisson and Irving are particularly interesting because they both purport to be serious historians, and crave the approval of those they take to be such: Faurisson and Irving want access to the Academy. However, because a positive answer to (1) entails a positive answer to (2), and because there are plenty of deniers who eschew academic ambitions (for example, Ernst Zündel, one of whose claims is that the Nazis possessed secret weapons that are still being launched from a hole in the ice in Antarctica, and that we see these objects as flying saucers),[39] we should first address (1).

Holocaust denial and the law

It is currently illegal to deny the Holocaust in Austria, Belgium, France, Germany, Israel, Spain, and Switzerland.[40] What is taken to constitute HD, and the severity of the punishment for it, varies from law to law. For example, the laws in Austria, Belgium, Germany, Israel, and Switzerland include trivialisation of the Holocaust as a punishable offence, whereas no mention is made of trivialisation in the French and Spanish laws; HD in Austria can be punished by twenty years in prison, and can attract a custodial sentence of five years in Israel and Germany, whereas in Belgium and France the maximum sentence is one year. Successful prosecutions under these laws are rare, and the total number of such prosecutions is small.[41] However, the fact that all the laws have been

introduced since 1985, and that a Private Member's Bill was tabled in the
House of Commons in February 1997 (by Mike Gapes, Labour MP for Ilford)
which would have made HD an offence,[42] shows that the question of whether
to prohibit HD in law is live.

Prima facie most of the classic arguments for the right to freedom of expression laid out in chapter 8 do not lend support to the legal prohibition of HD; in
fact, HD is a paradigm of the sort of speech that these liberal arguments aim to
defend as a matter of right. I shall consider them briefly in turn.

Unlike pornography, HD has propositional content: it aims to establish the
truth of knowable propositions about how the Nazis treated the Jews in the
Second World War. To that extent (and unlike the case of pornography), the
arguments from fallibility and from truth have direct application with respect to
HD. The argument from fallibility is that any claim to certainty with respect to
a proposition reveals an unwarranted assumption of infallibility; thus, no such
claim can be used to justify restrictions on the expression of propositions
contrary to that about which certainty is claimed. We saw in chapter 8,
however, that we can be certain of the truth of a proposition without assuming
infallibility: that I am certain that $2 + 2 = 4$ does not show that I assume myself
to be incapable of error in the formation of my other beliefs. I submit that the
same holds for certainty with respect to the proposition 'The Holocaust
happened', in which case this argument from fallibility does not rule out the
prohibition of HD in law.

The argument from truth is more powerful: permitting the expression of even
wholly false propositions encourages us to revisit the grounds of our belief in the
true propositions contested by such expression, thus strengthening this belief.
Applied to HD, the argument is that – insofar as we are concerned with
promoting progress towards the truth – HD ought to be permitted in law
because confrontation with it forces us to re-examine and reaffirm the value of
the evidence supporting our belief that the Holocaust happened.

One worry about this argument relates to the status in 'the web of belief' of
the propositions expression of which it protects as a matter of right.[43] For
example, we know that $2 + 2 = 4$, but what is the value in having our belief that
$2 + 2 = 4$ constantly challenged by mathematically incompetent people who
believe that $2 + 2 = 5$? Although it is logically possible that I am mistaken in
my belief that $2 + 2 = 4$ (and there is no logical contradiction contained in the
proposition '$2 + 2 = 5$'), this belief rightly lies at the heart of my system of
belief: revising it would involve revision of a vast number of other beliefs in this
system. Given how well the belief functions in its role in this system – and
given the welter of good mathematical reasons for believing it to be true – there
is little to be gained by countenancing such a revision. We are as sure as we can
be of the fact that $2 + 2 = 4$, and of our grounds for believing this, in which case
constant engagement with the mathematically incompetent will not promote
progress towards mathematical truth; rather, it will impede such progress by
occupying time that could have been spent exploring the cutting edge of mathematics so as to establish new truths.

Does the belief that the Holocaust happened have a status in the web of belief similar to that of propositions such as '2 + 2 = 4'? The fact that it is possible to do revisionist history with respect to some of the details of the Holocaust might seem to suggest not: for example, the claim that human remains were used in the extermination camps to make soap on a large scale is now rarely made by historians.[44] In contrast, mathematicians do not debate the truth of '2 + 2 = 4'. However, given that our question here is whether the Holocaust *as defined in terms of the three propositions listed on pp. 155–6* has a status in the web of belief similar to that of '2 + 2 = 4', the existence of revisionist approaches to the details of the Holocaust *not* related to these propositions fails to establish that our belief that the Holocaust happened lacks such a status in the web of belief. One way in which to make this case is by examining the status of this belief in the web of *moral* belief; for example, it could be argued that the belief that the Holocaust happened is fundamental to our understanding of evil.[45] And a further counter-argument would rely on making disanalogies between historical and mathematical truths; for example, that the former rely on empirical evidence for the establishment of their truth, whereas the latter do not.

Regardless of the plausibility of these strategies of argument, however, a more fundamental point is that making it legally permissible to challenge statements such as '2 + 2 = 4' and 'the Holocaust happened' does not impose a legal duty on anyone to engage with people who make such challenges; mathematicians and historians who have better things to do with their time can simply ignore them. To that extent, permitting HD in law need not impede, and might promote, progress towards truth, in which case the argument from truth counsels against the legal prohibition of HD.

Turning to the argument from significant interests, it is clear that deniers have significant participant interests in propagating their denial. Despite the inevitable anti-semitism that motivates HD, the almost universal self-image of deniers is as courageous firebrands who have uncovered truths that political, economic, and intellectual elites are trying to keep covered up: legally preventing deniers from 'spreading the word', as they see it, would impact on the conditions of their autonomy, given their self-image. Of course, this does not show that such prohibitions are unjustified. But it does mean that, using this argument, audience, bystander and citizen interests in being protected from exposure to HD by means of the law would have to be very weighty.

I shall return to the question of how HD affects our audience and bystander interests shortly. For the moment, let me note that the citizen interests we have in protecting the conditions for democratic community – forming the centre-piece of the argument from democracy – support permitting HD in law: deniers must be granted the right to express themselves in order that a genuinely communal conception of 'the people' whom government is of, for, and by be realised. To exclude deniers by withholding this right on the grounds that we hate what they say would be either to prioritise the majoritarian conception of democracy, or revert to legal moralism in lawmaking, neither of which is a strategy open to liberal democrats committed to treating people with equal concern and respect in setting the limits of toleration.

The final 'second best' argument is perhaps at its most powerful when applied to HD: despite the fact that we know the Holocaust happened, putting lawmakers and judges in a position whereby they must decide what constitutes historical truth – as is required by any law prohibiting HD – places society at the top of a slippery slope to an Orwellian polity in which the state defines what is true. Many journalists misinterpreted the Irving trial along these lines; although their analyses were flawed, their objections to the idea that historical truth can be, and ought to be, established in a court of law were well-placed.[46]

Of course, if the anti-semitism so often embedded in HD constitutes an incitement to violence, a threat to Jews, or a disturbance of the peace, then the expressive act in question ought to be prohibited. However, these grounds for legal prohibition are consistent with all the classic arguments for the right to freedom of expression (remember J.S. Mill on the angry mob outside the corn dealer's house): what is legislated here is incitement to violence, which can coincide with – but is not essential to – HD. The proposal under consideration is that denial of the Holocaust – even when not accompanied or motivated by the expression of anti-semitic sentiments fit to incite violence against Jews – ought to be prohibited in law. This would require that the lawmakers pass judgement on what counts as truth; but if we care about all the values that inform our commitment to the right to freedom of expression – truth, progress, autonomy, democracy – then we had better not permit the state to arrogate the task of deciding on the content of what can get said.

The arguments against the legal prohibition of HD seem conclusive. However, there are three features of HD which might give us pause for thought before moving on. First, HD is without a doubt profoundly offensive to Jews. That deniers should dismiss the testimony of Holocaust survivors at best as fictions of their imagination, and at worst as lies motivated by a desire for pecuniary gain and hatred of Gentiles, reveals a revolting arrogance and an incomprehensible lack of basic human empathy. One way in which to make this argument more powerful is to couch it in terms of the significant interests that figure in Scanlon's approach to content-regulation, whereby the effect of the prohibition of HD on the significant participant interests of deniers must be weighed against its effect on the audience interests of Jews (and, indeed, all of us). If it could be argued that the profound offence caused to Jews (and all of us) by HD damages the conditions of our autonomy such that our audience interests in being protected from HD are of a greater significance than deniers' participant interests in engaging in HD, then perhaps the argument from significant interests supports the legal prohibition of HD.

There are two reasons to doubt that this strategy could succeed. First, as we have seen in earlier chapters, the profound offence caused by an act of HD may provide (at most) grounds for the regulation of such acts – for example, to prevent the distribution of HD pamphlets in Jewish neighbourhoods – but it provides no grounds for a total ban on such activities. If regulated well, expressive acts of HD are reasonably avoidable, in which case – given the overall social value of free expression – the more far-reaching measure of a ban is not justified. And second, the sense in which profound offence damages the conditions of autonomy for an offended party is seriously obscure. From the fact that I suffer a shock to my moral, religious or patriotic sensibilities by being in the audience for an expressive act the content of which I believe to be non-trivially wrong, it does not follow that my capacities to be self-directing are damaged; indeed, we might argue, suffering such profound offence will encourage me to cleave more closely to the values and projects I care about in defence of them, thereby increasing my capacities for autonomy.

The second reason for pause for thought is that even if we decide that profound offence ought never to be used in justification of a ban on any expressive act, we might nevertheless make a case for banning HD on the grounds that the harm it causes to Jews is not that of, or goes beyond, profound offence, and is a harm from which people have the right to be protected in a society of reasonable people. The question of how best to understand this case has appeared as a theme throughout the last two chapters. In chapter 8 I considered the possibility that Muslim complaints against Rushdie and his publishers might be understood in terms of group defamation; that is, an attack on a group that continues their historical persecution, and damages the status and reputation of the group thereby diluting its potential as a source of strength for individual group members attempting to resist discrimination.[47] The claim that HD defames Jews as a group is tantamount to denial of the conceptual distinction between HD and anti-semitism claimed to be *prima facie* plausible on p. 157. On this approach, given the significance of the Holocaust to Jewish group identity, and given the importance of this group identity to particular individuals under threat of anti-semitic discrimination, to deny the Holocaust *is* to be anti-semitic. This argument, like the argument from profound offence, could also be made in Scanlonian terms. First, in terms of how such defamation damages the audience interests of Jews (and others); the challenge here is to establish how HD *qua* defamation erodes the conditions of autonomy such that the significance of the audience interests it damages justifies a ban. Or second, HD *qua* group defamation could be presented as damaging the significant bystander interests of Jews even when it does not affect their audience interests (or in addition to the damage it causes to these interests). For example, it might be claimed that HD encourages and perpetuates anti-semitism among those it addresses, thereby promoting 'changes in [their] subsequent behaviour'[48] which increase the likelihood of anti-semitic attacks on individual Jews; and living in fear of such attacks is damaging to autonomy.

However, before either of these elaborations of the group defamation argument can be pursued, the mechanics of the harm of defamation itself requires analysis. One intriguing possibility for such analysis is in terms of illocutionary disablement. In chapter 9 I analysed the uses to which feminists have put speech act theory to justify calls for the censorship of pornography, and suggested at the end of the chapter that using speech act theory to analyse the sense in which the capacity of individual Muslims to resist discrimination is damaged by group defamation might be more productive than using it to justify the censorship of pornography. The reason for this is that the illocutionary disablement of one party by another requires that the latter have authority in the domain in which disablement occurs. One of the problems with the feminist argument is that is it not clear to what extent pornographers – *qua* men, or *qua* pornographers – have authority in the domain of sex. However, the claim that Rushdie and his publishers have authority in the domain of Western civil societies in which Muslims have historically been persecuted, and in which they still suffer from discrimination, is more plausible: Penguin Books is one of the most successful presses in the world, and Rushdie remains the darling of the liberal intelligentsia. If fleshed out properly the public status, and/or connections with cultural elites, of Rushdie and his publishers might provide an interpretation of the authority required to visit illocutionary disablement on less powerful groups that would keep afloat the 'group defamation' approach to the harm SV causes to Muslims.

Does speech act theory as applied to the effect of HD on Jews hold similar promise? The thought here is that the bystander interests we all have 'in the effect expression has on its audience ... [for example] when expression promotes changes in the audience's subsequent behaviour' are of significance sufficient to warrant the prohibition of HD.[49] This is because the illocutionary disablement HD causes for Jews means that their continued persecution by antisemites – who find confirmation of their prejudices in the details of HD – fails to register as such. Every reasonable person – whether Jewish or Gentile – has a significant interest in preventing these social conditions.

There are at least two problems with this analysis (in addition to the more generic problem with the approach mentioned at the end of chapter 9, namely that speech act theory is a philosophical approach about which there is much reasonable disagreement, in which case it cannot be invoked in political justification conducted in public reason). First, it is not the case that all HD is overtly anti-semitic; in fact, deniers such as Irving and Faurisson – at least in their published work – make great efforts to disguise their anti-semitism, knowing that revelation of it would marginalise them even further. Furthermore, existing European and Israeli legislation outlawing HD – with the possible exception of the German law – make no mention of anti-semitism, which is dealt with (if at all) under separate legislation.

Second – and echoing a problem that besets the feminist version of speech act theory – the success of the argument that deniers are agents of illocutionary disablement for Jews depends on showing that deniers have authority with respect to the domain in which Jews experience disablement, that is, civil society. But this seems even less plausible with respect to deniers than it does with respect to pornographers, who at least achieve a huge circulation for their material, and whose publications often form part of an otherwise respectable stable. In contrast, deniers themselves claim that they are sidelined by establishment institutions (witness Faurisson's complaint, in his appeal to the UN Human Rights

Committee, that 'his opinions have been rejected in numerous academic journals and ridiculed in the daily press'),[50] and circulation of their material – even given their presence on the World Wide Web – is, according to the best estimations of it, tiny.[51] The proposed argument aims to establish that HD causes Jews to suffer illocutionary disablement in civil society, but its success depends on showing that deniers have authority in this domain sufficient to construct the possibilities for illocution by Jews. If most people are never exposed to HD – and HD remains marginalised, and excluded from the Academy – then it is hard to see how deniers have the authority to achieve this social construction.

This takes us neatly to discussion of the second arena in which deniers demand that they be tolerated: the Academy.[52] However, before moving on to this question, let me register the third reason for pause for thought with respect to the powerful liberal arguments for permitting HD in law. With respect to profound offence, and group defamation, might it be the case that the national context in which HD occurs makes a difference as to whether these forms of harm, when caused by HD, are appropriately addressed in law through prohibition? Laws against HD in Germany and Israel lay down particularly severe penalties, and indeed the law in Germany makes explicit reference to the 'insult' caused to German Jews by HD. Should the significance of speech acts in different contexts be considered in the light of the history of power relations between opposed groups in those contexts? How should such consideration affect our judgements of the significance of these acts with respect to the law? For example, could we interpret the prohibition of HD in Germany as part of a package of legal measures to secure reparative justice for victims of the Holocaust; that is, as a public acknowledgement on the part of the state, as representative of the people, that *this happened?*[53] Reflections such as these traverse deep waters in which lurk difficult questions about the scope of liberal political justifications, and the limits of ideal theory in a non-ideal world. I leave them for the reader to ponder.

Turning now to the second question of toleration with respect to HD, deniers sometimes argue that they ought to have a right of access to the Academy in virtue of having the right to freedom of expression *per se*. However, this argument rests on a mistaken inference: that the right to freedom of expression entails the right to access to all fora in which acts of expression can be performed.[54] If this inference held then every would-be writer would have the right to be published, and every aspiring artist the right to be exhibited, regardless of the quality of their work. That deniers such as Faurisson and Irving conceive of themselves as academics does not impose a duty on members of the Academy to take them seriously as such. In the next section I discuss the conception of the Academy that underlies this claim, how it blocks deniers' calls for access to the Academy, and how the non-toleration of HD in the Academy serves all our significant audience interests.

Holocaust denial in the Academy

Many instances of HD are presented as serious pieces of academic research; these are the most sophisticated, and hence most dangerous, tokens of the type. The innocuously named Institute for Historical Review (IHR) disseminates much of this material through its publication *The Journal of Historical Review* (JHR).[55] The statement of purpose for this publication claims that it 'upholds and continues the tradition of historical revisionism [by] scholars . . . ',[56] and it is put together according to the conventions of style that govern genuine academic journals. And a similar statement for the IHR as a whole claims that it is 'a public interest research, educational and publishing center dedicated to promoting greater public awareness of key chapters of history, especially twentieth century history, that have social-political relevance today. The IHR is non-ideological, non-political, and non-sectarian'.[57] To the uninitiated, or the unwary browser, the IHR can appear to be an independent think tank, and the *JHR* to be a legitimate scholarly journal. It is this that makes these outlets for HD particularly dangerous: it is easy for the layman to laugh off claims about 'Nazi secret weapons' made by cranks such as Zündel, but less easy for non-historians to dismiss pieces in the *JHR*, which are peppered with seemingly respectable bibliographical and archival references. However, there is no doubt that both outlets are Trojan horses for HD: the *JHR* is devoted to publishing HD, and the IHR is the major force behind HD in America. The IHR's founder, Willis Carto, has been an activist in ultra-right politics;[58] before becoming director of the IHR in 1978, David McCalden led a racist breakaway from the (far-right) UK political group the National Front;[59] and its current director, Mark Weber, has established links to neo-Nazi groups in the US.[60] Furthermore, content analysis of the *JHR* shows that 51.9 per cent of all pieces it has published deal with 'revisionism' and the Holocaust,[61] and that none of these pieces has been critical of the Nazis' anti-Jewish policies.[62]

Those associated with the IHR – and those, such as Faurisson and Irving, who publish in the *JHR* – clearly conceive of themselves as talented historians whose political views are used to justify their exclusion from the Academy. Ought they to be so excluded? I shall argue that HD – however well its form apes that of legitimate history – ought to be kept out of universities by the refusal to employ (or a commitment to suspend) academics who advocate it in their courses; by the rejection of applications by postgraduate students who wish to engage in such 'research'; by the principled refusal of funding to the agents of HD by bodies committed to funding legitimate academic research; and by the outright and principled rejection by academic journals and presses of manuscripts and papers engaging in HD.

The best way to reach this conclusion is by countering the most common arguments *for* the inclusion of HD and its agents in the Academy. These are (1) that all truth and knowledge is relative, and thus that HD is as legitimate as other, admittedly more standard, versions of history; (2) that the academic historians and administrators who keep deniers out of the Academy are elitist gatekeepers for the establishment, who serve only their own interests; and (3) that the therapeutic purpose of a university education is to enable students to navigate an epistemologically uncertain world in a self-directed way, and that exposure to HD – as part of this world – would help them acquire the skills necessary to do this. I shall deal with (1) and (2) reasonably quickly.

As we saw in chapter 3, relativism is a form of scepticism that, in this case, is constituted by the denial that there is one set of historical truths, and denial that when historical statements conflict, only one statement at most can be true.[63] If relativism is true with respect to history, so the argument goes, then the exclusion of HD from the Academy cannot be justified, as it presents truths and increases knowledge to the same extent as other historical narratives with which it competes. I shall not rehearse the arguments against relativism *per se* laid out in chapter 3. Instead, I will make two reflections. First, if relativism is true with respect to history – and perhaps all other academic disciplines – then the correct course of action is not to expand universities so as to include deniers, but rather to abolish history departments (and perhaps universities) altogether.[64] If those in the Academy have no special claim to knowledge, then why pay them to pursue it? A likely response here is that academics do have such a claim: they are better placed to further knowledge with respect to their subject than the man on the street. However, *within* academe, relativism holds, and HD is a form of history that falls within these boundaries. Apart from the dubiousness of asserting that relativism is true with respect to academic history, this response begs the question by assuming that HD is history. This is precisely what legitimate historians deny, and takes us to the second argument.

The second argument for admitting deniers to the Academy is political, and issues from the mouths of deniers themselves. The central claim here is that the exclusion of deniers by academic historians is motivated by their desire to protect the monopoly they have on research funding, access to (in England) HEFCE-funded students, entry into fora for exchange and debate about research findings, and influence over future directions of research through the education of postgraduates and in their capacities as advisors to the relevant policy makers. In short, academic historians are an elite who entrench their privileges by excluding people such as deniers, whose 'research' threatens to expose their own weaknesses as historians.

This argument can be dealt with swiftly. Deniers such as Irving and Faurisson have time and again been shown by historians – sometimes under oath – to distort, exaggerate and falsify documentary evidence, and to ignore material that does not support, or directly contradicts, the conclusions they want to establish. We do not need to assess whether deniers correctly characterise historians as gatekeepers for a corrupt establishment in order to assess whether historians have good reasons to keep deniers out of the Academy. Even if the accusation of elitism levelled against academic historians holds, they are still justified in keeping deniers out of the Academy, because deniers are not historians. Note that the claim here is not that deniers are *bad* historians, and so ought to be excluded from the Academy. This claim would enable the dangerous precedent of excluding and expelling academics whose research is not up to scratch. Rather, the claim is that deniers are not historians at all, and so have no – even *prima facie* – claim to be included in the Academy. Vidal-Naquet makes the point thus: 'Could one conceive of an astrophysicist entering into dialogue with a "researcher" claiming that the moon is made of Roquefort cheese?'[65]

The final argument for inclusion is more interesting insofar as it trades, not on the merits of HD as history, but rather on a consumerist conception of a university education much in vogue – at least in the UK – in these days of a fee-paying student body. This argument issues from the mouths of students. Ronald Barnett argues that

> Amid globalisation, changing state–higher education relationships, the e-revolution, the proliferation of knowledges in the new knowledge society and the arrival of markets (plural), the idea of universities playing an unequivocal role in uncovering and disseminating 'the truth' has to be jettisoned.[66]

In an age of what Barnett calls 'supercomplexity' – in which we are faced with a proliferation of different choices informed by different frameworks of analysis and understanding – universities ought to equip students to live with uncertainty, rather than attempt to deliver to them knowledge of truths.[67] The point of a university education, on this view, is the delivery of transferable skills which will enable graduates to navigate a supercomplex world. However as James Panton notes 'the transformation of the university from a seat of knowledge and higher learning into a provider of education as a "service" to be consumed entails a radical transformation of the relationship between students and the academy'.[68] This vision marks the end of what Dennis Hayes (following A.H. Halsey) calls 'Donnish Dominion':[69] the authority of academics in the university is undermined because the knowledge they possess (if it is allowed that they do) is irrelevant to what students (on this view, legitimately) expect *qua* consumers of a university education.[70] On this view, a university education is a form of therapy for students directed by academics who ought to seek only to facilitate students' understanding of their own subjectivity.

This picture will be depressingly familiar to academics working in the UK higher education sector. However, this changed vision matters for our purposes insofar as it can be invoked in defence of including HD and its agents in the curriculum of a university education. The argument is that in order for students to acquire the skills they will need in order to exercise their judgement effectively in the supercomplex world they will inhabit as graduates, they should be exposed to as wide a range as possible of different approaches to given topics, even when the approaches in question are as deeply methodologically flawed as HD: it is only by being trusted to exercise their judgement on matters such as these that students will learn to do so efficiently. The academic who denounces HD oversteps the mark: university academics ought to present their wares to students as market stallholders, and allow students to develop their judgement as they will in choosing between them. This argument does not issue from the mouth of an imaginary interlocutor: it has been put to me by a number of first-year students in classes in which I have discussed the question of HD in the

Academy, who unequivocally conceive of themselves as consumers, have a clear conception of what they are entitled to as such, and characterise the end of 'Donnish Dominion' as a welcome beginning of democratisation in the Academy.

What are we to say in response? Ignoring the many excellent arguments to show that something of irreplaceable value is lost by moving to a consumerist student-centred pedagogy, the most powerful argument against this model invokes the audience interests we all have (that is, not just academics and students, but everyone), in 'having a good environment for the formation of [our] beliefs and desires', such that we are in a position to be 'informed, amused [and] stimulated in a variety of ways, and even provoked when this leads to reflection and growth'.[71] Part of what makes our environment good in these ways is, I submit, the presence of public intellectuals. The role of the public intellectual has of course changed over time,[72] and academic status and/or a university education are neither necessary nor sufficient for adoption of this role.[73] However, there is no other institution in contemporary developed societies so well suited to nurturing nascent intellectuals, both in the academic staff, and in the student body.[74]

What the public intellectual brings to debate across the board is knowledge, and the ability to communicate that knowledge in non-specialised ways. The traditional model of the university to which the consumerist vision reacts has precisely these features at its heart by operating with a characterisation of the lecturer–student relationship as one of the joint pursuit of knowledge through communication between the lecturer and student on an increasingly level footing as the student progresses through her studies. In the traditional model, the relationship between lecturer and student is one of apprenticeship, and apprenticeships only work if (a) the apprentice acknowledges the authority of the master, and (b) the master communicates clearly with the novice apprentice. The first feature of the master–apprentice relationship stands opposed to the 'market stall' model of a university education intrinsic to the consumerist model: the possibility of apprenticeship requires that the apprentice acknowledge that the master knows better than she does with respect to the question of what she ought to know. And the second feature explains why the traditional model of the university provides a particularly fertile environment for the cultivation of public intellectuals: an apprentice learns, in part, through emulation of her master, and a master – *qua* master – must communicate clearly with a novice apprentice. This clarity of communication is one of the key skills that the public intellectual brings to her activity in society as a whole. It means that the public intellectual can function as a conduit for the transmission of knowledge between the Academy – in which such knowledge is acquired by means of highly specialised research – and society, where the technicalities of academic research delivering such knowledge need not be elaborated.[75]

In sum, the relationship of apprentice and master is not a relationship of consumption, and serves all our audience interests in having a good environment for the formation of our beliefs by providing an excellent breeding ground for public intellectuals. If the argument for including deniers in the Academy requires the radical overhaul of our idea of a university such that it can no longer function as such a breeding ground, then concern for our significant audience interests in maintaining an environment in which we can form our beliefs responsibly militates against such inclusion by standing opposed to this vision of the university. And – as I argued in chapter 5 – part of what it is for a person to be in a position to practise toleration of whatever form is for her to take responsibility for her beliefs. If conditions conducive to such belief formation are lost, the practice of toleration *per se* is in danger of becoming a sham.

Conclusion

In summary, I have argued here that HD – albeit *qua* one of the most pernicious forms of expression on the contemporary scene – ought not to be prohibited in law. Facts about the profound offence it causes, and/or the damage that participation inflicts on the moral character of its advocates, are not sufficient to rebut the powerful cases for permitting it in law that are founded on the classic liberal arguments for freedom of expression. However, it does not follow that deniers have a right to access the Academy. Indeed, given the value to all of us of a culture containing public intellectuals who are in a position to present their knowledge to us in a clear-sighted way fit to prompt us to reflect on our own beliefs, and given that most public intellectuals find a home – at some point, and in some way – within universities, we have not only the right, but also a duty, to exclude and expel deniers from our institutions of higher education. If universities are protected in this way we can hope that the public intellectuals they continue to produce, support, and shield will contribute to a public culture in which the audience for HD diminishes to the extent that the use of the right to freedom of expression so as to propagate HD becomes a curiosity of the late twentieth century, a thing of the past. As we move further away from the Holocaust, and as its survivors disappear altogether, this hope must become ever more urgent.

Chapter 11

Conclusion
New challenges for liberal toleration

The aim of this book has been to connect the best contemporary theory of toleration with some of the hardest current real world cases by showing how sympathetic reconstructions of arguments opposed to liberal practices of toleration go straight to the heart of the theory of toleration that holds the most promise with respect to the justification of these practices. In other words, the reasonableness defence of toleration, and the account of political harm in terms of liberal rights that accompanies it and sets the limits of toleration, is problematised by consideration of the objections of groups and persons whose practices either lie outside the limits of toleration, on this account, or who bring complaints of political harm against those whose practices lie inside these limits.

In review, I argued in chapter 2 that the possibility of toleration in the face of various putative 'paradoxes' generated by accounts of the opposition providing one of its circumstances is best secured by analysing this opposition in terms of responsible belief formation. This stipulation avoids doing violence to our commonsense conception of toleration, according to which mindless thugs, rabid racists, and hate-filled homophobes who exercise principled self-restraint with respect to action directed by their prejudices do not thereby qualify as tolerant. Of course, there is no logical contradiction in an account of toleration that permits the possibility that a society of people filled with irrational fear and searing loathing of one another, but who restrain themselves on principled grounds when it comes to action on these feelings, qualifies as a tolerant society. However, if we want to use principles of toleration as catalysts for political progress towards a better world in which the character of conflict is tempered and lessened, then we do best to rule out this possibility. The 'wide interpretation' of opposition also opens up room for the practice of toleration by allowing that a person can have genuine, significant, and heartfelt oppositions to others (in the sense that she takes the commitments from which the oppositions issue to be justified by having responsibly formed the beliefs constitutive of these commitments), and yet not treat these oppositions as overriding practical imperatives that squeeze out principles of toleration in practical reasoning. The challenge in that case is to explain why it is that oppositions can have this character, and as a consequence, indicate which oppositions are candidates to be reined in by any principle setting the limits of toleration.

To this end, in chapters 3, 4 and 5 I surveyed the three dominant contemporary theories of toleration according to which its practice is possible and required. The account that holds most promise is associated with political liberalism, and makes toleration a requirement of reasonableness, understood (primarily, for our purposes) in terms of a person's acceptance of the permanence of reasonable pluralism, and her exercise of the capacity for a sense of justice. Although this account takes us quite some way with respect to understanding which oppositions ought not to be acted upon in the name of toleration, it has its limits – as illustrated by the dispute between Waldron's reasonable pornographer and reasonable Muslim – and these have serious consequences for the realisation of the reasonableness defence in principles to inform policies of toleration to govern real world hard cases. I suggested in chapter 6 that the way forward is to start with the classic liberal account of the limits of toleration in terms of individual rights: here, the violation of rights constitutes a political harm that *ipso facto* registers on the liberal account of the limits of toleration, and whereby the practice that causes the violation is placed outside these limits. Taking the reasonableness defence of toleration and an account of its limits in terms of rights, then, the way forward with respect to hard cases is to consider whether the complaints of parties in opposition against one another could be made in terms of the violation of their rights, where any such complaint must be justified as such consistent with a commitment to the permanence of reasonable pluralism, and the exercise of a sense of justice. This was the strategy I adopted in reconstructing objections to liberal policies of toleration in Part II.

Consideration of the Muslim complaints in the 'Rushdie affair', the justification of legislation governing FGM and Muslim head wear, feminist objections to pornography, and the meat of the Irving trial has shown that drawing the limits of toleration with a harm principle that makes the violation of individual rights intolerable does not – given the reasonableness defence – straightforwardly or obviously recommend the legislative solutions to these problems that liberals very often take for granted. Reflections on how political equality might be damaged by defamatory expressive acts, and on how the umbrella of reasonable pluralism might extend further than the reach of a secular, humanist imagination, have – while problematising the reasonableness defence of toleration, and in part in virtue of this problematisation – shown that this defence offers rich and promising ways forward for the theory and practice of toleration. In a world of conflict in which the need for toleration is increasingly urgent, the approach I have outlined and developed in this book counsels that greater efforts be directed towards the catholic education of people as they form and revise their beliefs, so as to ensure that the commitments informing their inevitable oppositions are responsibly held, thereby positioning them as potential tolerators. And it mandates a framework for deliberation about the resolution of such oppositions whereby the content of the rights used to set the limits of toleration can be expanded to deliver protection to those who can make a case for it consistent with acceptance of the fact of reasonable pluralism while exercising their capacities for a sense of justice. In a world in which pluralism is reasonable, permanent, and not-to-be-regretted, and in which the conflicts to be mediated by principles of toleration will not disappear, there are no other politically feasible options fit to provide a baseline of fair stability through toleration on which all further visions of justice depend.

Notes

1 Toleration: a call to arms

1 John Major, Interview with the *Mail on Sunday*, 21 February 1993.
2 'I feel terribly guilty', *The Guardian*, 4 November 2004. Available on-line: http://www.guardian.co.uk/g2/story/0,1342743,00.html. Accessed 3 December 2004.
3 'UK "most racist" in Europe on refugees', *The Guardian*, 3 April 2001. Available on-line: http://society.guardian.co.uk/asylumseekers/story/0,467684,00.html. Accessed 4 December 2004.
4 'Criminal Justice in England and Wales', Commission for Racial Equality Fact Sheet, 1999. Available on-line. http://www.cre.gov.uk/publs/cat_facts.html. Accessed 14 December 2004.
5 'Education and Training in Britain', Commission for Racial Equality Fact Sheet, 1998. Available on-line: http://www.cre.gov.uk/publs/cat_facts.html. Accessed 14 December 2004.
6 'Schools "failing to fight racism"', *The Observer*, 14 September 2003.
7 'Employment and Unemployment', Commission for Racial Equality Fact Sheet, 1997. Available on-line: http://www.cre.gov.uk/publs/cat_facts.html. Accessed 14 December 2004.
8 'Racial Attacks and Harassment', Commission for Racial Equality Fact Sheet, 1999. Available on-line: http://www.cre.gov.uk/publs/cat_facts.html. Accessed 14 December 2004.
9 'Criminal Justice in England and Wales', Commission for Racial Equality Fact Sheet, 1999. Available on-line: http://www.cre.gov.uk/publs/cat_facts.html. Accessed 14 December 2004.
10 'Racial Attacks and Harassment', Commission for Racial Equality Fact Sheet, 1999. Available on-line: http://www.cre.gov.uk/publs/cat_facts.html. Accessed 14 December 2004.
11 *Bowers v. Hardwick* 478 U.S. 186 (1986). This case actually related to the state of Georgia's law banning oral and anal sex for all persons, whatever their sexual preferences.
12 *Lawrence* et al. *v. Texas* 000 U.S. 02–102 (2003).
13 *Goodridge* et al. *v. MA Dept of Public Health* 440 Mass. 309 (2003).
14 'Bush vows no compromise on gay marriage', *The Washington Times*, 31 July 2003.
15 Available on-line: http://www.allianceformarriage.org/site/PageServer?JServSession Idr010=6luryxxvm2.app8b. Accessed 14 December 2004.
16 *Brown v. Board of Education* 347 U.S. 483 (1954).
17 For extended discussion see my *Liberalism and the Defence of Political Constructivism* (New York: Palgrave MacMillan, 2002), pp. 9–14.
18 The latter oppression refers, of course, to Oscar Wilde's conviction for 'gross indecency with other male persons' and his subsequent incarceration.

19 J. Locke, *A Letter Concerning Toleration*, J.H. Tully (ed.), Indianapolis: Hackett Publishing Co., 1983. The *Letter* was originally published in Latin as *Epistola de Tolerantia*.
20 For more on the politics of seventeenth-century England, and the historical context of Locke's writings, see R. Ashcraft, *Revolutionary Politics and Locke's 'Two Treatises of Government'*, Princeton, N.J.: Princeton University Press, 1986; I. Harris, *The Mind of John Locke*, Cambridge: Cambridge University Press, 1994; R. Kroll, R. Ashcraft, and P. Zagorin (eds), *Philosophy, Science, and Religion in England 1640–1700*, Cambridge: Cambridge University Press, 1992; J. Marshall, *John Locke: Resistance, Religion and Responsibility*, Cambridge: Cambridge University Press, 1994; G.A.J. Rogers (ed.), *Locke's Philosophy: Content and Context*, Oxford: Clarendon Press, 1994; and J. Tully, *An Approach to Political Philosophy: Locke in Contexts*, Cambridge: Cambridge University Press, 1993.
21 See Locke, *ibid.*, p. 28ff.
22 See Locke, *ibid.*, pp. 26–8.
23 I should note at this point that my approach to the *Letter* is entirely analytical; that is, I am concerned only to analyse the arguments of the *Letter* independent of the context in which they were made. An alternative approach is to treat the *Letter* primarily as a political act, in which case it cannot be properly understood outside of its historical context.
24 See Locke, *ibid.*, p. 36.
25 See Locke, *ibid.*, p. 51.
26 Locke, *ibid.*, p. 52.
27 Locke, *ibid.*, p. 27.
28 Locke also makes the further, and different, argument that coercive force cannot be used to secure men's salvation, which depends instead on using 'the Light of their own Reason' to discern the 'way to Heaven' (Locke, *ibid.*, p. 27). I shall not address this version of the argument.
29 See S. Mendus, 'Locke: Toleration, Morality and Rationality' in J. Horton and S. Mendus (eds), *John Locke: A Letter Concerning Toleration In Focus*, London and New York: Routledge, 1991, p. 149; J. Waldron, 'Locke: Toleration and the Rationality of Persecution' in J. Horton and S. Mendus (eds), *John Locke: A Letter Concerning Toleration In Focus*, p. 111, p. 113.
30 See Waldron, *ibid.*, p. 116.
31 See A.J. Simmons, *On The Edge of Anarchy: Locke, Consent, and the Limits of Society*, Princeton, N.J.: Princeton University Press, 1993, p. 133; S. Mendus, 'Locke: Toleration, Morality and Rationality' in J. Horton and S. Mendus (eds), *John Locke: A Letter Concerning Toleration In Focus*, pp. 152–3.
32 See Waldron, *ibid.*, pp. 117–18.
33 See, for example, Waldron, *ibid.*, p. 120; Mendus, *ibid.*, pp. 149–50.
34 See J.S. Mill, *On Liberty* in *Utilitarianism*, M. Warnock (ed.), London: Fontana Press, 1962; *The Subjection of Women*, Massachusetts: MIT Press, 1970; *Considerations on Representative Government*, Buffalo, NY: Prometheus Books, 1991.
35 Mill, *On Liberty*, p. 129.
36 Mill, *ibid.*, p. 135.
37 Mill, *ibid.*, p. 138; chapter 2 of *On Liberty* develops these arguments.
38 Mill, *ibid.*, p. 138; chapter 3 of *On Liberty* develops these arguments.
39 Mill, *ibid.*, p. 138.
40 Mill, *ibid.*, p. 136.
41 Mill, *Utilitarianism*, p. 258. Hence his famous remark that, 'It is better to be a human being dissatisfied than a pig satisfied; better to be a Socrates dissatisfied than a fool satisfied' (*ibid.*, p. 260).
42 Mill, *On Liberty*, p. 136. This explains Mill's insistence that the LP does not apply to children, madmen and 'barbarians'; such people are not in a position to be improved by free and equal discussion (*ibid.*, pp. 135–6).
43 Mill, *ibid.*, p. 185.

44 Mill, *ibid.*, p. 137.
45 Mill, *ibid.*, p. 184.
46 See H.L.A. Hart, *Law, Liberty and Morality*, London: Oxford University Press, 1963. In contrast to rule-utilitarianism, act-utilitarianism is the view that each particular act is to be judged according to the principle of utility. For criticism of Hart on Mill see C.L. Ten, *Mill On Liberty*, Oxford: Clarendon Press, 1980.
47 Mill, *ibid.*, pp. 210–11. For development of the objection see R.P. Anschutz, *The Philosophy of J.S. Mill*, Oxford: Clarendon Press, 1953; P. Devlin, *The Enforcement of Morals*, London: Oxford University Press, 1965.
48 J.C. Rees, *John Stuart Mill's 'On Liberty'*, Oxford: Clarendon Press, 1985, p. 142.
49 For more on Mill, *On Liberty*, and his utilitarianism, see G. Dworkin (ed.), *Mill's On Liberty: Critical Essays*, Lanham, Maryland: Rowman and Littlefield, 1997; J. Gray, *Mill on Liberty: A Defence*, London: Routledge, 1996; G. Himmelfarb, *On Liberty and Liberalism: The Case of John Stuart Mill*, New York: Knopf, 1974; H.J. McClosky, *John Stuart Mill: A Critical Study*, London: Macmillan, 1971; J. Plamenatz, *The English Utilitarians*, Oxford: Blackwell, 1958; J. M. Robson, *The Improvement of Mankind: The Social and Political Thought of John Stuart Mill*, Toronto: University of Toronto Press, 1968; J.B. Schneewind (ed.), *Mill: A Collection of Critical Essays*, London: Macmillan, 1969.
50 The key exceptions here are the collections produced by the *Morrell Studies in Toleration Programme* hosted by the University of York (see the introduction to the bibliography for details).
51 Here I adapt material from P. Nicholson, 'Toleration as a moral ideal' in J. Horton and S. Mendus (eds), *Aspects of Toleration: Philosophical Studies*, London and N.Y. Methuen, 1985, pp. 158–75.

2 Opposition and restraint

1 M. Warnock, 'The Limits of Toleration' in S. Mendus and D. Edwards (eds), *On Toleration*, Oxford: Clarendon Press, 1987, p. 125.
2 John Horton was the first theorist to note this consequence of the weak interpretation. See J. Horton, 'Three (Apparent) Paradoxes of Toleration', *Synthesis Philosophica*, vol. 9, fasc. 1, 1994: 7–20. See also J. Horton, 'Toleration as a Virtue' in D. Heyd (ed.), *Toleration: An Elusive Virtue*, Princeton, N.J.: Princeton University Press, 1996, p. 31.
3 A 'Grand Wizard' is an authority figure in the Ku Klux Klan.
4 See Horton, 'Toleration as a Virtue', p. 35. The assumption here is that becoming tolerant of more people is tantamount to becoming more tolerant. Of course, this assumption could be questioned.
5 P. Nicholson, 'Toleration as a Moral Ideal' in J. Horton and S. Mendus (eds), *Aspects of Toleration: Philosophical Studies*, London and New York: Methuen, 1985, p. 166.
6 *Ibid.*, p. 162.
7 Warnock, *ibid.*, p. 126.
8 For an interesting, more general discussion of the nature of evaluative disapproval see R. Dworkin, 'Liberty and Moralism' in *Taking Rights Seriously*, London: Duckworth, 1977.
9 Note that this is not to say that evaluative disagreements about matters of taste are not possible; to the contrary, we engage meaningfully in such disputes – about food, music, fashion, neighbourhoods, etc. – all the time. Rather, the point is that disagreements with respect to *first-person judgements* about matters of taste are not possible.
10 See also the discussion of Holocaust denial in chapter 10.
11 R.J. Herrnstein and C. Murray, *The Bell Curve: Intelligence and Class Structure in American Life*, New York: Simon and Schuster, 1996.

12 For critical discussion see J. Dupré, 'Normal People', *Social Research*, vol. 65, no. 2, 1998: 221–48.
13 Louis Farrakhan is the leader of the US black separatist organisation, The Nation of Islam.
14 D.D. Raphael, 'The Intolerable' in S. Mendus (ed.), *Justifying Toleration: Conceptual and Historical Perspectives*, Cambridge: Cambridge University Press, 1988, pp. 142–3.
15 Note, however, that any number of alternative accounts of what it takes for an evaluative judgement to be justified are possible here, and would generate the paradox as stated: the paradox is not simply a paradox for Kantian accounts of toleration.
16 The problem here is analogous to a problem with the idea of mercy: to be a candidate for mercy (as opposed to forgiveness, or punishment) a person must be a genuine wrongdoer, but genuine wrongdoers are *ipso facto* not deserving of mercy. Thanks to Bob Fogelin for this observation.
17 See Horton, 'Toleration as a Virtue', p. 33.
18 If you do not share this intuition then my remarks here ought to be read as an argument to show that you ought to share it.
19 See S. Mendus, 'Locke: Toleration, Morality and Rationality' in J. Horton and S. Mendus (eds), *John Locke: A Letter Concerning Toleration In Focus*, London and New York: Routledge, 1991, esp. p. 153ff. For an argument that the limits of toleration ought to be set by reference to consideration of whether one's opponent holds their beliefs responsibly – such that those who do not 'discuss and publish their theories as rational proposals' ought not to be tolerated – see K. Popper, 'Toleration and Intellectual Responsibility' in S. Mendus and D. Edwards (eds), *On Toleration*, p. 19.
20 Laurence Sterne is claimed to have said that, 'There is a balance . . . of good and bad every where; and nothing but the knowing it is so can emancipate one half of the world from the prepossessions which it holds against the other – that [was] the advantage of travel . . . it taught us mutual toleration; and mutual toleration . . . taught us mutual love.'
21 Jeremy Waldron discusses a similar quality valued by Mill, which Waldron calls 'open-mindedness', in J. Waldron, 'Mill and the Value of Moral Distress' in *Liberal Rights*, Cambridge: Cambridge University Press, 1993.
22 See Nicholson, 'Toleration as a Moral Ideal', p. 166.
23 Thus, the wide interpretation answers John Horton's call that theories of toleration be sensitive to the details of the contexts in which putative cases of toleration arise. See Horton, 'Three (Apparent) Paradoxes of Toleration'.
24 B. Williams, 'Tolerating the Intolerable' in S. Mendus (ed.), *The Politics of Toleration*, Edinburgh: Edinburgh University Press, 1999, pp. 66–7.
25 Of course, this will not be the case with respect to all commitments; some commitments ought to be acted upon, whereas others ought to prompt toleration. These are substantive questions about the limits of toleration, and will be addressed in Part II.
26 Horton, 'Toleration as a Virtue', p. 33.

3 Toleration from scepticism

1 Attributed, in A. Jay (ed.), *The Oxford Dictionary of Political Quotations*, Oxford: Oxford University Press, 2001, p. 311.
2 For a good survey of such positions see J. Rachels, 'Subjectivism' in P. Singer (ed.), *A Companion to Ethics*, Oxford: Basil Blackwell, 1991.
3 An argument is valid when it could not be the case that all the premises of the argument are true and yet the conclusion is false. Thus, an argument is invalid when all its premises could be true and yet its conclusion false. Crudely put, an argument is invalid when the conclusion does not follow from the premises. Precisely put, 'Any argument is valid if and only if the set consisting of its premises and the negation of

its conclusion is inconsistent' (T. Honderich (ed.), *The Oxford Companion to Philosophy*, Oxford: Oxford University Press, 1995, p. 894).

4 For a good survey see M. Baghramian, *Relativism*, London: Routledge, 1994, chapter 9.

5 D. Wong, *Moral Relativity*, Berkeley: University of California Press, 1984, p. 1.

6 See, for example, G. Harman, 'Moral Relativism Defended', *The Philosophical Review*, vol. 84, 1975: 3–22.

7 See American Anthropological Association Executive Board, 'Statement on Human Rights' (submitted to the UN Commission on Human Rights), *American Anthropologist*, vol. 49, no. 4: 539–43.

8 See, for example, E. Hatch, 'The Good Side of Relativism', *Journal of Anthropological Research*, vol. 53: 371–81.

9 R.A. Shweder, 'The Astonishment of Anthropology' in C.W. Gowans (ed.), *Moral Disagreements: Classic and Contemporary Readings*, London: Routledge, 2000, p. 107.

10 Shweder, 'The Astonishment of Anthropology', p. 111.

11 B. Williams, *Morality: An Introduction to Ethics*, Harmondsworth: Penguin Books, 1972, p. 34.

12 Williams, *Morality*, p. 39. On this point see also G. Harrison, 'Relativism and Tolerance', *Ethics*, vol. 86, 1976: 122–35.

13 J.L. Mackie, *Ethics: Inventing Right and Wrong*, London: Penguin Books, 1977, p. 36.

14 Wong, *Moral Relativity*, p. 180.

15 *Ibid.*, p. 181.

16 *Ibid.*, p. 181. There is an ambiguity in the final sentence of this passage in virtue of the phrase 'according to his moral beliefs', which could refer to the moral beliefs of either A or B. I shall read this sentence as referring to A's moral beliefs.

17 This problem also arises implicit in Wong's work. See D. Wong, 'Coping with Moral Conflict and Ambiguity' in L. Foster and P. Herzog (eds), *Defending Diversity: Contemporary Philosophical Perspectives on Pluralism and Multiculturalism*, Amherst, Mass.: University of Massachusetts Press, 1994, esp. p. 23.

18 Wong, *Moral Relativity*, p. 187.

19 The deliberate reference here is to Michael Sandel's attack on Rawls' liberalism for operating with – so he claims – a conception of the self as 'unencumbered'. See M. Sandel, *Liberalism and the Limits of Justice*, Cambridge: Cambridge University Press, 1982.

20 Wong, *Moral Relativity*, p. 181.

21 See R. Rorty, 'Postmodern Bourgeois Liberalism' and 'The Priority of Democracy to Philosophy' in his *Objectivity, Relativism, and Truth*, Cambridge: Cambridge University Press, 1991; and 'Private Irony and Liberal Hope', 'The Contingency of a Liberal Community' and 'Solidarity' in his *Contingency, Irony, Solidarity*, Cambridge: Cambridge University Press, 1989.

22 See Rorty, 'The Priority of Democracy to Philosophy', p. 176.

23 On the strong poet see Rorty, 'The Contingency of a Liberal Community'. On culture critics see R. Rorty, 'Private Irony and Liberal Hope' and 'Professionalized Philosophy and Transcendentalist Culture' in his *Contingency, Irony, Solidarity*. For discussion of George Orwell as one such contributor to 'postmodern' political justification see Rorty's 'The Last Intellectual in Europe: Orwell on Cruelty' in the same volume.

24 R. Rorty, 'Private Irony and Liberal Hope', p. 78.

25 For a scathing attack on this picture of solidarity see T. Eagleton, 'Defending the Free World', *The Socialist Register*, 1990: 85–95. For a systematic critique of Rorty's assertions about how his version of solidarity explains and spurs people to political action see N. Geras, *Solidarity in the Conversation of Humankind: The Ungroundable Liberalism of Richard Rorty*, London: Verso, 1995.

26 Rorty, 'Private Irony and Liberal Hope', p. 78.

27 Rorty, 'Postmodern Bourgeois Liberalism', p. 200.

28 *Ibid.*, p. 202.
29 Friedrich Nietzsche was a nineteenth-century philosopher who critiqued what he called the 'slave-morality' of his age on the grounds that it generates self-oppression by those who endorse it; it is sometimes claimed that the antidote to slave-morality recommended by Nietzsche was the development of 'will-to-power' by Übermensche ('Over-men'), who are superior to the masses. St Ignatius of Loyola was the founder of the Catholic order of priests, the Society of Jesus (or the Jesuits), who was committed to the conversion of 'the infidel' in the Holy Land. He wrote the Jesuit Constitutions which recommended absolute self-abnegation and obedience to the Pope and superiors.
30 Rorty, 'The Priority of Democracy to Philosophy', p. 190.
31 In fact, Rorty is signally pessimistic about the prospects for liberal societies.

> If I were a wagering Olympian, I might well bet my fellow divinities that pragmatism, utilitarianism and liberalism would, among mortals, be only faint memories in a hundred years time. For very few unexpurgated libraries may then exist, and very few people may ever have heard of Mill, Nietzsche, James and Dewey, any more of free trade unions, a free press, and democratic elections.
>
> (R. Rorty, 'Afterword: Pragmatism, Pluralism, and Postmodernism' in *Philosophy and Social Hope*, London: Penguin Books, 1999, p. 274)

A recent dystopian novel that makes this point well is P. Roth, *The Plot Against America*, London: Jonathan Cape, 2004.
32 Rorty, 'Private Irony and Liberal Hope', p. 73.
33 *Ibid.*, p. 87. On the tensions between private, Romantic ironism and public, liberal pragmatism in Rorty's work see N. Fraser, 'Solidarity or Singularity? Richard Rorty between Romanticism and Technocracy' in A. Malachowski (ed.), *Reading Rorty*, Oxford: Basil Blackwell, 1990.
34 See J.S. Mill, *On Liberty*, London: Fontana Press, 1962, chapter 2.
35 See B. Barry, *Justice as Impartiality*, Oxford: Clarendon Press, 1995, chapter 7.
36 *Ibid.*, p. 169.
37 *Ibid.*, p. 168. Assuming the presence of this desire is justified, thinks Barry, given the assumption that all persons 'desire to live in a society whose members all freely accept its rules of justice and its major institutions' (*ibid.*, p. 164). In Barry's view, given that *something* has to be assumed of persons to whom political justification is addressed, this is unobjectionable. For criticism see J. Horton, 'Liberalism and Multiculturalism: Once more unto the breach' in B. Haddock and P. Sutch (eds), *Multiculturalism, Identity and Rights*, London: Routledge, 2003.
38 See Barry, *Justice as Impartiality*, pp. 169–70.
39 *Ibid.*, p. 179.
40 *Ibid.*, pp. 170–1.
41 *Ibid.*, p. 172.
42 M. Matravers and S. Mendus, 'The Reasonableness of Pluralism' in C. McKinnon and D. Castiglione (eds), *The Culture of Toleration in Diverse Societies: Reasonable Toleration*, Manchester: Manchester University Press, 2003.
43 *Ibid.*, p. 44.
44 *Ibid.*, pp. 45–7.
45 For discussion see J. Horton, 'The Good, the Bad, and the Impartial', *Utilitas*, vol. 8 no. 3, 1996, pp. 325–7.
46 As John Horton has argued, this fact means that the agreement motive in Barry's argument carries a lot of weight, because without it the urgency of the practical imperatives of such evaluative beliefs may override political accommodation through toleration. See Horton, *ibid.*, pp. 315–20.

4 Toleration from value pluralism

1 Parts of this chapter are adapted from my 'Toleration and the Character of Pluralism' in C. McKinnon and D. Castiglione (eds), *The Culture of Toleration in Diverse Societies*, Manchester: Manchester University Press, 2003.

2 M. de Montaigne, *Essays*. Available on-line: http://www.quotations.co.uk. Accessed 13 January 2005.

3 However, note that not all incommensurabilists assert all of these theses. For example, John Broome denies T1 and T2, and instead explains the truth of T2*, T3 and T4 in terms of an ineliminable vagueness in our comparative judgements of values. See John Broome, 'Is Incommensurability Vagueness?', in R. Chang (ed.), *Incommensurability, Incomparability and Practical Reason*, Cambridge, Mass.: Harvard University Press, 1997. Another example is Charles Larmore, who accepts T1 but denies T2 and T2*: he argues that ranking comparisons can be made between values in the absence of a master-value, on other grounds. See C. Larmore, *The Morals of Modernity*, Cambridge: Cambridge University Press, 1996.

4 See J. Bentham, *An Introduction to the Principles of Morals and Legislation*, London: Methuen, 1996.

5 See P. Singer, *Practical Ethics*, Cambridge: Cambridge University Press, 1993.

6 Thanks are due to John Horton for pressing this point with me.

7 Ruth Chang argues that the incomparability of values stated in T2 and T2* can be escaped by denying what she calls the 'trichotomy' thesis; that is, that if values cannot be ranked as 'better than', 'worse than', or 'equally good', then they must be incomparable. She claims that the trichotomy thesis fails to acknowledge a further, and separate, relation between values – that of 'on a par with' – which allows for an explanation of the sense in which values are not better than, worse than, or equivalent in value which does not entail the theses of evaluative incomparability. See Chang (ed.), *Incommensurability, Incomparability and Practical Reason*, pp. 4–7.

8 J. Raz, *The Morality of Freedom*, Oxford: Clarendon Press, 1986, p. 352. See also J. Gray, 'Where Pluralists and Liberals Part Company' in M. Baghramian and A. Ingram (eds), *Pluralism: The Philosophy and Politics of Diversity*, London and New York: Routledge, 2000, p. 92.

9 Ruth Chang notes that the example may need a little refinement in order to fully convince: 'Suppose I am faced with a choice between a friendship and a dollar. If I judge that the friendship is worth more than a dollar, have I thereby lost all my friends?' (Chang (ed.), *Incommensurability, Incomparability and Practical Reason*, p. 19). The point is taken, but if we substitute 'wealth' for 'money' in the example, it remains convincing.

10 The 'and' in this sentence is important. What makes T3 a thesis of incommensurability is that it takes T1 and T2 (or T2*) to give an explanation of its putative truth. Without this qualification, T3 would state an important, but bland, truth about human life.

11 The Poor Clares are an order of Roman Catholic nuns whose vows include poverty, chastity, and silence.

12 Note: the claim is *not* that all sets of values, principles, and practices standing as alternatives to liberal democracy are (incommensurably) valuable. There was nothing valuable in Hitler's fascist state, or in the Taliban regime in Afghanistan.

13 Shoguns were the practical rulers of Japan until the beginning of the Meiji era in 1868.

14 Bushido demands of its practitioners that they look backward at the present from the moment of their own death, as if they were already, in effect, dead, and it requires seven virtues of its practitioners: rectitude, courage, benevolence, respect, honesty, honour and loyalty.

15 See I. Berlin, 'The Decline of Utopian Ideas in the West' in his *The Crooked Timber of Humanity*, H. Hardy (ed.), London: John Murray, 1990, esp. p. 40.

16 For a sustained attack on Berlin on these grounds see G. Crowder, 'Pluralism and Liberalism', *Political Studies*, vol. XLII, no. 2, 1994: 293–305. See also I. Berlin and B. Williams, 'Pluralism and Liberalism: A Reply', *Political Studies*, vol. XLII, no. 2, 1994: 306–9.

17 See Berlin, 'The Decline of Utopian Ideas in the West'.

18 I. Berlin, 'The Pursuit of the Ideal' in his *The Crooked Timber of Humanity*, p. 13. See also I. Berlin, 'Introduction' in his *Four Essays on Liberty*, Oxford: Oxford University Press, 1969, p. li; I. Berlin, 'Two Concepts of Liberty', *ibid.*, pp.167–72.

19 See, for example, L. Strauss, 'Relativism' in his *The Rebirth of Classical Political Rationalism*, Chicago: University of Chicago Press, 1989, pp. 13–19.

20 See Berlin, 'The Pursuit of the Ideal', pp. 10–12.

21 However, for an objection to Berlin's incommensurabilism that does not take this form – and that argues instead that it is overstated and too quick – see R. Dworkin, 'Do Liberal Values Conflict?' in M. Lilla, R. Dworkin and R. Silvers (eds), *The Legacy of Isaiah Berlin*, New York: New York Review of Books, 2001.

22 See J. Gray, *Isaiah Berlin*, London: HarperCollins, 1995, chapter 6. See also Gray, 'Where Pluralists and Liberals Part Company'.

23 See Berlin and Williams, 'Pluralism and Liberalism: A Reply'.

24 Berlin, 'Two Concepts of Liberty', p. 168.

25 See *ibid.*, pp. 121–2.

26 *Ibid.*, p. 169.

27 *Ibid.*, p. 148.

28 Given Berlin's conception of negative liberty as damageable by acts, omissions, unintended consequences of acts, and (as he sometimes claims) the operation of nature, it cannot be the case that toleration is limited by a harm principle requiring the avoidance of all incursions on negative freedom, because it is impossible to achieve this. Of course, it is a fine and difficult question what constitutes an avoidable depletion of negative liberty; but the difficulty of answering this question does not undermine the general principle giving rise to it.

29 In response to this criticism Berlin and Williams claim that, 'it is irrelevant . . . that liberal institutions may be understood as the correct expression of outlooks other than pluralism. No doubt they can be and have been, but this only shows that a good cause can have more than one friend'. Berlin and Williams, 'Pluralism and Liberalism: A Reply', p. 308. Similarly, John Gray claims that the incommensurability theses *cohere* with liberalism (Gray, *Isaiah Berlin*, p. 13). As true as both these claims may be, they do not answer the criticism: the claim is not that the incommensurability theses are *inconsistent* with liberal toleration but, rather, that they do not entail it.

30 Transitivity is a relational property: 'A binary, i.e. two-term, relation is transitive when if anything x has it to anything y, and y to anything z, then x has it to z' (T. Honderich (ed.), *The Oxford Companion to Philosophy*, Oxford: Oxford University Press, 1995, p. 879).

31 Raz, *The Morality of Freedom*, p. 325.

32 *Ibid.*, p. 369.

33 *Ibid.*, p. 415.

34 *Ibid.*, p. 372f.

35 *Ibid.*, p. 380.

36 However, Raz's view of the nature of political authority is not so straightforward. See *ibid.*, chapters 2–4.

37 *Ibid.*, p. 404.

38 *Ibid.*, p. 405.

39 J. Raz, 'Multiculturalism: A Liberal Perspective' in his *Ethics in the Public Domain*, Oxford: Clarendon Press, 1994, p. 165.

40 *Ibid.*, *passim*.

41 *Ibid.*, p. 165.

5 Toleration from reasonableness

1 Portions of this chapter are adapted from my *Liberalism and the Defence of Political Constructivism*, New York: Palgrave MacMillan, 2002.
2 G. Orwell, 'The Prevention of Literature', *Polemic*, January 1946.
3 The qualifier 'at least some of' in this sentence indicates that toleration has limits: some commitments ought to be imposed on others because they are commitments to the prevention of harm (however conceived). For stylistic reasons I shall henceforth suppress this qualifier.
4 See, for example, G. Sher, *Beyond Neutrality: Perfectionism in Politics*, Cambridge: Cambridge University Press, 1997.
5 This kind of approach finds its most famous historical precedent in the political writings of Immanuel Kant. See, for example, Immanuel Kant, *The Metaphysics of Morals*, M. Gregor (ed.), Cambridge: Cambridge University Press, 1996. For detailed discussion of this 'constructivist' feature of political justification in the work of John Rawls see my *Liberalism and the Defence of Political Constructivism*. See also Onora O'Neill, *Towards Justice and Virtue: A Constructive Account of Practical Reasoning*, Cambridge: Cambridge University Press, 1996.
6 Justifying reasons are to be contrasted with motivating reasons: the former justify a course of action and the latter motivate a person to undertake that course of action. Ideally, persons in a just state will have justifying and motivating reasons to practise toleration (although their justifying reasons may not, and need not, be identical to their motivating reasons). However, the work of political justification is done once justifying reasons for the practice of toleration are provided.
7 Another version of political liberalism is in C. Larmore, *Patterns of Moral Complexity*, Cambridge: Cambridge University Press, 1987; and C. Larmore, *The Morals of Modernity*, Cambridge: Cambridge University Press, 1996, esp. pp. 121–51.
8 J. Rawls, 'Justice as Fairness: Political not Metaphysical' in *John Rawls: Collected Papers*, Cambridge, Mass.: Harvard University Press, 1999, p. 395. For a probing critique of Rawls' 'epistemic abstinence' see Joseph Raz, 'Facing Diversity: The Case of Epistemic Abstinence', *Philosophy and Public Affairs*, vol. 19, no. 1, 1990: 3–46.
9 See, for example, J. Rawls, *Political Liberalism*, New York: Columbia University Press, 1993, pp. 150–4.
10 *Ibid.*, p. xxiv.
11 See J. Cohen, 'Moral Pluralism and Political Consensus' in D. Copp, J. Hampton and J.E. Roemer (eds), *The Idea of Democracy*, Cambridge: Cambridge University Press, 1993, p. 272.
12 J. Rawls, *Justice as Fairness: A Restatement*, Cambridge, Mass.: Harvard University Press, 2001, p. 189. See also Rawls, *Political Liberalism*, p. xviii.
13 Rawls, *Political Liberalism*, p. 147. See also p. 127.
14 See *ibid.*, pp. 12, 144–5.
15 Rawls thinks that an overlapping consensus can emerge from a *modus vivendi* via constitutional consensus. See *ibid.*, pp. 164–8.
16 Rawls also thinks that participation in an overlapping consensus stimulates important changes in citizens' attitudes towards one another which broadens and deepens the principles of toleration they support. See *ibid.*, pp. 133–72. See also J. Cohen, 'A More Democratic Liberalism', *Michigan Law Review*, vol. 92, 1994: 1503–46; C. McKinnon, 'Civil Citizens' in C. McKinnon and I. Hampsher-Monk (eds), *The Demands of Citizenship*, London and New York: Continuum, 2000.
17 Rawls characterises these assumptions as ideas of practical reason as it addresses questions of justice; that is, they are assumptions about persons and their circumstances that we have to make if we are to conceive of them as addressing problems of justice through the use of their shared practical reason at all. See Rawls, *Political Liberalism*, Lecture III, pp. 89–129. For commentary see C. McKinnon, *Liberalism*

and the Defence of Political Constructivism, pp. 29–56. See also Cohen, 'Moral Pluralism and Political Consensus'.

18 Again, it is important to stress that this is a methodological assumption, not an assertion about the way the world is. See Rawls, *Political Liberalism*, p. 108.

19 See *ibid.*, p. 94.

20 *Ibid.*, p. 19.

21 *Ibid.*, p. 16.

22 See *ibid.*, pp. 137, 217.

23 *Ibid.*, p. 243.

24 J. Rawls, 'The Idea of Public Reason Revisited' in his *John Rawls: Collected Papers*, p. 594.

25 Larmore, *The Morals of Modernity* and Rawls, *Political Liberalism*, p. 241.

26 Rawls, *Justice as Fairness: A Restatement*, pp. 35–6.

27 Rawls, *Justice as Fairness: A Restatement*, p. 36. See also Larmore, *The Morals of Modernity*, pp. 152–76.

28 Rawls, *Political Liberalism*, p. 61.

29 See *ibid.*, pp. 60–1.

30 For an excellent interpretation of Rawls' later work, and survey of criticisms, see J. Mandle, *What's Left of Liberalism?*, Lanham, Maryland: Lexington Books, 2000.

31 See Rawls, *Political Liberalism*, pp. 62–3, 150–4; *Justice as Fairness*, pp. 36–7.

32 Brian Barry attributes this view to Rawls. See B. Barry, *Justice as Impartiality*, Oxford: Clarendon Press, 1995, chapter 7.

33 In virtue of his claim that the pluralism in which overlapping consensus delivers principles of justice must be conceived of as reasonable, Rawls' position is also distinct from the pragmatism found in Rorty, despite Rorty's claims to the contrary. See Richard Rorty, 'The Contingency of a Liberal Community' in *Contingency, Irony, Solidarity*, Cambridge: Cambridge University Press, 1989, esp. p. 57; 'The Priority of Democracy to Philosophy', *Objectivity, Relativism and Truth*, Cambridge: Cambridge University Press, 1991, *passim*. For more on why this reading of the burdens thesis is to be rejected see Larmore, *The Morals of Modernity*, pp. 171–4.

34 See Rawls, *Political Liberalism*, pp. xxiv–xxv, 36–7, 144; Rawls, *Justice as Fairness*, pp. 3, 34.

35 D. Estlund, 'Making Truth Safe for Democracy' in D. Copp, J. Hampton and J. E. Roemer (eds), *The Idea of Democracy*, p. 90.

36 See Rawls, *Political Liberalism*, p. 63.

37 See Rawls, 'Justice as Fairness: Political not Metaphysical' in *John Rawls: Collected Papers*, pp. 390, 408, 411–13.

38 Just one mention of incommensurability remains towards the end of Rawls, *Political Liberalism* (p. 370).

39 Rawls, 'Justice as Fairness: Political not Metaphysical', p. 395. See also pp. 127, 150.

40 These claims about the nature of practical reason take us into deep philosophical waters that cannot be traversed here. For discussion of the role of practical reason in Rawls' political thinking see Cohen, 'Moral Pluralism and Political Consensus'. For critique of Rawls on this issue see O. O'Neill, 'Review of Political Liberalism', *The Philosophical Review*, vol. 106, no. 3, 1997: 411–28. For more general discussion of the role and operation of practical reason in thinking about questions of value see G. Cullity and B. Gaut, *Ethics and Practical Reason*, Oxford: Clarendon Press, 1997.

41 See also Larmore, *The Morals of Modernity*, pp. 153–5.

42 L. Wenar, '*Political Liberalism*: An Internal Critique', *Ethics* vol. 106, 1995: 61.

43 *Ibid.*, p. 45.

44 *Dogmatic Constitution on Divine Revelation*, article 6, cited in *ibid.*, p. 44, n. 20.

45 'A doctrine is fully comprehensive when it covers all recognized values and virtues within one rather precisely articulated scheme of thought; whereas a doctrine is only

partially comprehensive when it comprises certain (but not all) nonpolitical values and virtues and is rather loosely articulated' (Rawls, *Political Liberalism*, p. 175).

46 For a more philosophical statement of this point as it applies to the interpretation of Rawls' *Political Liberalism* see T.E. Hill Jnr., 'The Stability Problem in Political Liberalism', *Pacific Philosophical Quarterly*, vol. 75, 1994: 333–52.

47 See J. Waldron, 'Toleration and Reasonableness' in C. McKinnon and D. Castiglione (eds), *The Culture of Toleration in Diverse Societies*, Manchester: Manchester University Press, 2003.

48 See Waldron, 'Toleration and Reasonableness', p. 22.

49 This is a version of the criticism that Rawls only justifies liberalism for, and to, liberals. For a specific attack on Rawls' justification of toleration along these lines see S. Meckled-Garcia, 'Toleration and Neutrality: Incompatible Ideals?' in C. McKinnon and D. Castiglione (eds), *Toleration: Moral and Political*, Special Issue of *Res Publica*, vol. 7, no. 3, 2001: 293–313.

50 These questions will be given detailed consideration in chapter 8 and chapter 9.

51 See Waldron, 'Toleration and Reasonableness', pp. 28–31.

52 See *ibid.*, pp. 31–3.

53 See *ibid.*, p. 23.

54 *Ibid.*, p. 23.

55 For a full account of the distinction between philosophical and political reasonableness upon which this modified response relies see E. Kelly and L. MacPherson, 'On Tolerating the Unreasonable', *The Journal of Political Philosophy*, vol. 9, no. 1, 2001: 38–55.

6 Political harm: the liberal paradigm

1 Available online: http://www.quotations.co.uk. Accessed 13 January 2005.

2 For example, Locke, Kant and Mill all make the protection of individual rights the key reason for which the state may legitimately interfere with the lives of individuals and groups.

3 See http://www.allianceformarriage.org (accessed 27 December 2004), http://www.aclu.org/LesbianGayRights.cfm?ID=14470&c=101 (accessed 27 December 2004), and http://www.hrw.org/press/2003/09/us090403.htm (accessed 27 December 2004). See also the first section of chapter 1 in this book for discussion.

4 All subsequent references to harm should be taken to incorporate the threat of harm, unless otherwise indicated.

5 J. Horton, 'Liberalism and Multiculturalism: Once more unto the breach' in B. Haddock and P. Sutch (eds), *Multiculturalism, Identity and Rights*, London: Routledge, 2003, p. 39.

6 See J. Feinberg's four-volume *The Moral Limits of the Criminal Law*, in particular, *Harm to Others* (Vol. 1), Oxford: Oxford University Press, 1984, and *Offense to Others* (Vol. 2), Oxford: Oxford University Press, 1985. See also *Harm to Self* (Vol. 3), Oxford: Oxford University Press, 1986, and *Harmless Wrongdoing* (Vol. 4), Oxford: Oxford University Press, 1988.

7 Feinberg, *Offense to Others*, pp. 10–13.

8 Feinberg, *ibid.*, p. 11.

9 Feinberg, *ibid.*, p. 13.

10 Such as happened – notoriously – in Skokie, Illinois, in 1977. See Feinberg, *ibid.*, pp. 86–93.

11 Feinberg, *ibid.*, pp. 51–7.

12 Most, but not all. For example, the offence a person takes at the performance of public sex acts may relate to moral principles she holds dear, and ground her judgement that such acts would be wrong even if she never witnessed them, in which case

it qualifies as profound offence. Or, the offence caused by Body Count's tune 'Cop Killer' played loudly on the bus may be profound in the same way. The chorus runs:

> I'm a COP KILLER, better you than me.
> COP KILLER, fuck police brutality!
> COP KILLER, I know your family's grieving,
> (FUCK 'EM!)
> COP KILLER, but tonight we get even, ha ha
> > For the full lyrics see http://www.purelyrics.com/index.php?lyrics = jbmrvfqa
> > (accessed 11 January 2005)

13 Feinberg, *ibid.*, p. 26.
14 See Feinberg, *ibid.*, p. 35.
15 Following J.S. Mill, Feinberg claims that 'no amount of offensiveness in an expressed opinion can counterbalance the vital social value of allowing unfettered personal expression'. Feinberg, *ibid.*, p. 39.
16 See Feinberg, *ibid.*, p. 44.
17 Feinberg, *ibid.*, p. 11.
18 Whether Feinberg is right to accord free expression this trumping role in his balancing tests – and whether his interpretation registers the damage that the free speech of some can do to the conditions for free speech for others – will be discussed in the chapters in Part II.
19 See Feinberg, *ibid.*, pp. 64–5, 33–4.
20 Feinberg, *ibid.*, pp. 65–6.
21 Feinberg, *ibid.*, p. 69.
22 Feinberg, *ibid.*, p. xiii.
23 Feinberg, *ibid.*, p. 68.
24 Feinberg rules out these responses by making claims about the incommensurability of harm and offence: 'It is a misconception to think of offenses as occupying the lower part of the same scale as harms; rather offenses are a different sort of thing altogether, with a scale all of their own' (Feinberg, *ibid.*, p. 3). However, we need not follow Feinberg on this point and, indeed, should not if we are to maximise the plausibility of the reasonable Muslim's case rather than ruling out from the start the possibility that the profound offence suffered by the Muslim is a form of harm which ought to be addressed by the liberal state.
25 Some material in this section is adapted from my, 'Rights: Their Basis and Limits', in R. Bellamy and A. Mason (eds), *Political Concepts*, Manchester: Manchester University Press, 2003.
26 For something approaching such a survey see J. Waldron, 'Rights' in R.E. Goodin and P. Pettit (eds), *A Companion to Contemporary Political Philosophy*, Oxford: Blackwell, 1995.
27 See J. Waldron, 'Liberal Rights: Two Sides of the Coin' and 'Rights in Conflict' in his *Liberal Rights: Collected Papers 1981–1991*, Cambridge: Cambridge University Press, 1993; J. Waldron, 'Introduction' in J. Waldron (ed.), *Theories of Rights*, Oxford: Oxford University Press, 1984; J. Raz, 'On the Nature of Rights', *Mind*, vol. XCIII, 1984, pp. 194–214.
28 The Patriot Act (The USA Patriot Act, Public Law 107–56, 26 October 2001) was passed (with next to no debate) eleven days after the attack on the World Trade Center in 2001, in the name of enhancing US security. The act expanded the US terrorism laws to cover 'domestic terrorism'; greatly increased the powers of surveillance available to law enforcement agencies; curtailed the right to due process guaranteed to citizens and non-citizens under the Fourteenth Amendment to the Bill of Rights; and granted to Federal Bureau of Investigation agents the power to investigate US citizens without probable cause of crime if the investigation is claimed to serve 'intelligence purposes'.
29 See Waldron, 'Rights in Conflict', pp. 212–13.

30 Raz, 'On The Nature of Rights', pp. 201–4.

31 Waldron, 'Introduction', *Theories of Rights*, p. 10.

32 For criticism of the IB approach see my 'Rights: Their Basis and Limits'.

33 R. Dworkin, 'What Rights Do We Have?' in his *Taking Rights Seriously*, London: Duckworth, 1977, pp. 272–3.

34 Dworkin, 'Introduction' in *Taking Rights Seriously*, p. xi.

35 See Dworkin, 'What Rights Do We Have?', pp. 275–6.

36 I. Kant, *The Moral Law: Kant's Groundwork of the Metaphysic of Morals*, tr. H.J. Paton, London: Unwin Hyman, 1989, p. 96.

37 A good introductory overview of Kant's moral and political thought is C. Korsgaard, 'Introduction' in her *Creating the Kingdom of Ends*, Cambridge: Cambridge University Press, 1996.

38 See T.E. Hill, 'Servility and Self-Respect' in his *Autonomy and Self-Respect*, Cambridge: Cambridge University Press, 1991; J. Feinberg, 'The Nature and Value of Rights', *Journal of Value Inquiry*, vol. 4, 1970. This aspect of the liberal conception of rights is evident in Article 1 of the UN Universal Declaration of Human Rights (1948): 'All human beings are born free and equal in dignity and rights. They are endowed with reason and conscience and should act towards one another in a spirit of brotherhood.'

39 J. Rawls, *Justice as Fairness: A Restatement*, Cambridge, Mass.: Harvard University Press, 2001, p. 44.

40 See Dworkin, *ibid*. The denial that persons have a fundamental right to liberty distinguishes liberal egalitarian theories of rights from libertarian theories of rights. For a classic example of the latter, see R. Nozick, *Anarchy, State and Utopia*, Oxford: Blackwell, 1974, esp. pp. 26–53.

41 See for example, the UN Universal Declaration of Human Rights, Articles 22 (the right to social security), 23 (the right to work etc.), 24 (the right to rest and leisure), 25 (the right to food, housing, health care), 26 (the right to education).

42 See H. Steiner, *An Essay on Rights*, Oxford: Blackwell, 1994.

43 J. Rawls, *Political Liberalism*, New York: Columbia University Press, 1993, p. 298.

44 See Nozick, *Anarchy, State and Utopia*, pp. 160–4.

45 For example, Rawls does not think that commitment to the basic right to hold personal property entails commitment to a capitalist economic structure, or to unlimited rights of acquisition and behest. See Rawls, *ibid.*, p. 328.

46 Cf. J. Horton, 'The Good, The Bad, and The Impartial', *Utilitas*, vol. 8, no. 3, 1996, pp. 320–4.

47 The most important texts on the communitarian side of this debate are: M. Sandel, *Liberalism and the Limits of Justice*, Cambridge: Cambridge University Press, 1982; A. MacIntyre, *After Virtue*, London: Duckworth, 1981; M. Walzer, *Spheres of Justice: A Defence of Pluralism and Equality*, Oxford: Blackwell, 1983; and C. Taylor, *Philosophy and the Human Sciences: Philosophical Papers* Vol. II, Cambridge: Cambridge University Press, 1985. For a good surveys of the debate see S. Mulhall and A. Swift, *Liberals and Communitarians*, Oxford: Blackwell, 1996; W. Kymlicka, *Contemporary Political Philosophy*, 2nd edition, Oxford: Oxford University Press, 2002.

48 This criticism is associated with C. Taylor, 'Atomism' in his *Philosophy and the Human Sciences*.

49 Interview with Margaret Thatcher, 'Aids, Education, and the Year 2000', *Woman's Own*, 31 October 1987, pp. 8–10. Available on-line: http://www.margaretthatcher.org/speeches/displaydocument.asp?docid=106689. Accessed 27 December 2004.

50 This line of attack is associated with Sandel, *Liberalism and the Limits of Justice*.

51 The 'dominance', power-oriented approach to sexual inequality is associated with C. MacKinnon, *Feminism Unmodified*, Cambridge, Mass.: Harvard University Press, 1987.

52 For criticism of liberal theory on the grounds that it fails to address the inequalities of power created by and in the family see V. Munoz-Darde, 'Should the Family be

Abolished, then?', *Proceedings of the Aristotelian Society*, vol. XCXIX, part 1, 1999; S. Moller Okin, *Justice, Gender and the Family*, New York: Basic Books, 1989.

53 As O. O'Neill puts it, 'Nothing shows why indifference or self-centredness should not be life-projects for liberals, providing, of course, that others' rights are respected' (*Towards Justice and Virtue: A Constructive Account of Practical Reasoning*, Cambridge: Cambridge University Press, 1996, p. 144).

54 Kant argued that all moral obligations are derived from one supreme moral principle, the Categorical Imperative, which asks each of us to 'Act as if the maxim of your action were to become through your will a universal law of nature' (a maxim is a subjective principle of action, or the purpose of an action).

55 J. Waldron, 'A Right to do Wrong' in his *Liberal Rights*, p. 85.

7 Culture and citizenship: headscarves and circumcision

1 N. Tebbit, interview in *Los Angeles Times*, reported in *The Daily Telegraph*, 20 April 1990.

2 I borrow this term from S.L. Carter, *The Dissent of the Governed*, Cambridge, Mass.: Harvard University Press, 1998, p. 27.

3 I shall not attempt to survey the vast literature of this debate here. An excellent overview is W. Kymlicka, *Contemporary Political Philosophy*, 2nd edition, Oxford: Oxford University Press, 2002, chapter 8. The best collection addressing questions of multiculturalism and toleration is J. Horton and S. Mendus (eds), *Toleration, Identity and Difference*, Basingstoke: Macmillan, 1999.

4 See The Motor Cycle Crash Helmet (Religious Exemption) Act (1976).

5 See The Slaughter of Poultry Act (1967) and The Slaughterhouses Act (1974).

6 *Wisconsin v. Yoder*, 406 U.S. 205 (1972).

7 Kymlicka identifies five categories of religious and cultural groups with which multiculturalists are concerned: national minorities, immigrant groups, isolationist ethnoreligious groups, metics, and African-Americans. See Kymlicka, *ibid.*, pp. 348–65. Each type of group faces quite different problems of justice, not all of which are related to toleration. For example, national minorities often demand devolution or secession, whereas most metics desire acceptance by and integration into their host state.

8 For example, few of us have direct experience of members of ethnoreligious isolationist groups such as the Amish (and having watched the film *Witness* doesn't count!).

9 Kymlicka, *ibid.*, p. 353.

10 An alternative is the claim that membership is an instrumental good for members. This is weaker than the 'intrinsic good' claim because it does not support a distinction between cultural and non-cultural groups, and will mandate – at most – principles to protect and encourage pluralism in general rather than multiculturalism in particular. See my 'Exclusion Rules and Self-Respect', *Journal of Value Inquiry*, vol. 34, no. 4, 2000; N. Rosenblum, *Membership and Morals: The Personal Uses of Pluralism in America*, Princeton, N.J.: Princeton University Press, 1998.

11 W. Kymlicka, *Liberalism, Community and Culture*, Oxford: Clarendon Press, 1989, pp. 192–3.

12 For more on self-respect see my *Liberalism and the Defence of Political Constructivism*, New York: Palgrave Macmillan, 2002, chapter 3; T.E. Hill Jnr., *Autonomy and Self-Respect*, Cambridge: Cambridge University Press, 1991.

13 See C. Taylor, 'What is Human Agency?' in his *Human Agency and Language: Philosophical Papers* Vol. 1, Cambridge: Cambridge University Press, 1985.

14 This view of the intrinsic good of cultural membership is echoed by J. Raz; see his 'Multiculturalism: A Liberal Perspective', *Ethics in the Public Domain*, Oxford: Clarendon Press, 1994. Raz also gives the fact that membership of a cultural group facilitates close

personal relationships as a further reason for thinking that such membership is important. Other key accounts of the significance of cultural membership are in B. Parekh, *Rethinking Multiculturalism*, Cambridge, Mass.: Harvard University Press, 2000; J. Tully, *Strange Multiplicity*, Cambridge: Cambridge University Press, 1995; C. Taylor, 'The Politics of Recognition' in A. Gutmann (ed.), *Multiculturalism and the 'Politics of Recognition'*, Princeton, N.J.: Princeton University Press, 1992.

15 J. Rawls, *A Theory of Justice*, Oxford: Oxford University Press, 1971, p. 440. See also *ibid.*, pp. 92, 107, 443, 543–5. See also J. Rawls, *Political Liberalism*, New York: Columbia University Press, 1993, pp. 106, 203, 318, 319.

16 Kymlicka, *ibid.*, p. 187.

17 See, for example, B. Barry, *Culture and Equality*, Cambridge: Polity Press, 2001, chapter 2 and chapter 8, §4. For critique of Barry see S. Mendus, 'Choice, Chance, and Multiculturalism' in P. Kelly (ed.), *Multiculturalism Reconsidered*, Cambridge: Polity Press, 2002. See also J. Tomasi, 'Kymlicka, Liberalism, and Respect for Cultural Minorities', *Ethics*, vol. 105, 1995; S. Moller Okin, 'Is Multiculturalism Bad for Women?' in J. Cohen (ed.), *Is Multiculturalism Bad for Women?*, Princeton, N.J.: Princeton University Press, 1999; and P. Casal, 'Is Multiculturalism Bad for Animals?', *The Journal of Political Philosophy*, vol. 11, no. 1, 2003.

18 For an overview of the practice and its history see E. Dorkenoo, *Cutting the Rose: Female Genital Mutilation: Its Practice and Its Prevention*, London: Minority Rights Publication, 1994; F.P. Hosken, *The Hosken Report: Genital and Sexual Mutilation of Females*, 4th revised edition, Lexington, Mass.: Women's International Network News, 1994; UN Fact Sheet No. 23, *Harmful Traditional Practices Affecting the Health of Women and Children*. Available on-line: http://www.unhchr.ch/html/menu6/2/fs23.htm, Accessed 17 December 2004.

19 See, for example, B.E. Dawson, 'Circumcision on the Female: Its Necessity and How to Perform It', *American Journal of Clinical Medicine*, vol. 22, no. 6, 1915.

20 UN Fact Sheet No. 23, §I A.

21 Dorkenoo, *ibid.*, p. 31.

22 UN Fact Sheet No. 23, §I A.

23 Dorkenoo, *ibid.*, p. 15.

24 See Dorkenoo, *ibid.*, pp. 13–27.

25 See Dorkenoo, *ibid.*, pp. 36–41.

26 Dorkenoo, *ibid.*, p. 3.

27 Dorkenoo, *ibid.*, p. 101.

28 Dorkenoo, *ibid.*, pp. 115, 118.

29 See Dorkenoo, *ibid.*, pp. 123–8.

30 This is the line taken by the UN: UN Fact Sheet No. 23, §I A.

31 Federal Prohibition of Female Genital Mutilation Act (1995).

32 Prohibition of Female Circumcision Act (1985).

33 Section 268, Criminal Code of Canada, (1997).

34 Prohibition of Female Genital Mutilation Act, New South Wales, Australia.

35 For an extended version of this argument see Barry, *ibid.*, chapter 4, esp. pp. 141–6. For an alternative argument for permitting FGM to be practised on children in the name of liberal toleration see C. Kukathas, 'Cultural Toleration' in W. Kymlicka and I. Shapiro (eds), *Ethnicity and Group Rights: Nomos XXXIX*, New York: New York University Press, 1997; see also C. Kukathas, 'The Life of Brian, or Now for Something Completely Different' in P. Kelly (ed.), *Multiculturalism Reconsidered*.

36 For an excellent review of the UK's recent action with respect to the concluding observations of the UN's 2002 Committee on the Rights of the Child (which also surveys the current state of the UK with respect to children), see Children's Rights Alliance for England, 'The State of Children's Rights in England 2004'. Available on-line: http://www.crae.org.uk/index.html (accessed 11 January 2005).

37 See D. Archard, *Children, Rights and Childhood*, London: Routledge, 1993.

38 As noted by A.J. Simmons, *On The Edge of Anarchy: Locke, Consent, and the Limits of Society*, Princeton, N.J.: Princeton University Press, 1993, p. 120.
39 See *ibid.*, p. 106.
40 See *ibid.*, p. 105.
41 The thesis that (at least some, namely, natural) rights are inalienable is often attributed to John Locke. However, it is worth noting, with A.J. Simmons, that Locke himself nowhere uses the terms 'alienable' or 'inalienable', and that there are grounds for doubt that the position on inalienability often attributed to him has any firm basis in his writings. See *ibid.*, chapter 5, esp. p. 105.
42 *Regina v. Brown, Laskey et al.* For background see the Spanner Trust website: http://www.spannertrust.org. Accessed 27 December 2004.
43 Actual or grievous bodily harm are defined as activities which cause injuries of a lasting nature.
44 Using *volenti non fit injuria* to make the case for the regulation rather than prohibition of FGM is not, however, without problems. For example, a commitment to this principle across the board *prima facie* would make legally permissible privately organised, consensual 'fight clubs' in which men gather for bareknuckle fighting with no rules; or, perhaps, would make duelling legally permissible (this example is taken from J. Horton, 'The Good, The Bad, and The Impartial', *Utilitas*, vol. 8, no. 3, 1996, p. 324, n. 29). There are hard questions here related to the distinction between public and private, self- and other-regarding actions, and how putatively private activities might damage the culture of a society as a whole without harming any individual in particular.
45 For discussion of how Western reactions to FGM can deflect attention from the objectionable ways in which sexual identity is manipulated within Western societies, and perhaps also reveal Western prejudices about traditional communities, see Y. Tamir, 'Hands Off Clitoridectomy', *Boston Review*, vol. 21, no. 3, 1996. Available on-line: http://www.bostonreview.net/BR21.3/Tamir.html. Accessed 27 December 2004.
46 The 'medicalisation' of FGM was recently opposed by the Regional Assembly in Tuscany, who voted against the proposal of Dr Abdul Kadir (a gynaecologist) that doctors in public hospitals be permitted to perform *sunna* on Somali women so as to protect them from health risks created by seeking out non-qualified excisors to perform the procedure (BBC Radio 4, *News Report*, 7.25am, 8 February 2004).
47 See, for example, M. Nussbaum, 'Double Moral Standards?', *Boston Review*, vol. 21, no. 5, 1996. Available on-line: http://www.bostonreview.net/BR21.5/Nussbaum.html. Accessed 27 December 2004.
48 Simmons, *ibid.*, p. 144.
49 For an argument for the prohibition of FGM which invokes the empirical version of this *a priori* claim see C. Chambers, 'Are Breast Implants Better than Female Genital Mutilation? Autonomy, Gender Equality and Nussbaum's *Political Liberalism*', *Critical Review of International Social and Political Philosophy*, vol. 7, no. 3, 2004.
50 Echoing this sentiment, A.J. Simmons states that '[s]urely it would be very difficult to think of any right where transfer was necessarily a sign of profound irrationality, insanity, or loss of control (lack of voluntariness)' (*ibid.*, p. 143). He goes on to describe circumstances in which the alienation or waiving of the right not to be killed, enslaved, or tortured does not stand as a sign of profound irrationality etc. (*ibid.*, pp. 143–4).
51 President Jacques Chirac, Address to the Nation, 17 December 2003. Available on-line: http://newsvote.bbc.co.uk/mpapps/pagetools/print/news.bbc.co.uk/1/hi/world/europe/3330679.stm. Accessed 27 December 2004.
52 However, some polls suggested that up to 40 per cent of France's Muslim population were themselves in favour of the ban. Available on-line: http://newsvote.bbc.co.uk/mpapps/pagetools/print/news.bbc.co.uk/1/hi/world/europe/3474673.stm. Accessed 27 December 2004.
53 'France divided as headscarf ban is set to become law', The Observer, 1 February 2004. Some Jewish and Sikh groups have also voiced their opposition.

54 Surah XXXIII, Verse 59 of the Qur'an states: 'O Prophet! Tell thy wives and thy daughters and the women of the believers to draw their cloaks close around them. That will be better, so that they may be recognized and not annoyed. Allah is ever forgiving, merciful.'

55 See N. Moruzzi, 'A Problem with Headscarves', *Political Theory*, vol. 22, no. 4, 1994.

56 The exact wording of the ban is: 'in primary and secondary public schools, the wearing of signs or clothes through which pupils ostensibly express a religious allegiance is forbidden'. For an excellent reconstruction of the argument for the ban that places it in the context of French political history see C. Laborde, 'Secular Philosophy and Muslim Headscarves in Schools', *Journal of Political Philosophy*, forthcoming.

57 For discussion of recent developments in the controversy see J.R. Bowen, 'Muslims and Citizens: France's Headscarf Controversy', *Boston Review*, vol. 29, no. 1, 2004. Available on-line: http://www.bostonreview.net/BR29.1/bowen.html. Accessed 27 December 2004.

58 For a more sophisticated version of this argument see A.E. Galeotti, *Toleration as Recognition*, Cambridge: Cambridge University Press, 2002, chapter 4.

59 It resonates unpleasantly with a famous anti-immigration speech made by Enoch Powell (then a prominent Conservative MP) in 1968: 'As I look ahead, I am filled with foreboding. Like the Roman, I seem to see "the River Tiber foaming with much blood".'

60 See, for example, E. Badinter: 'Putting a veil on the head, this is an act of submission. It burdens a woman's whole life. Their fathers or their brothers choose their husbands, they are closed up in their own homes and confined to domestic tasks etc.' (quoted in Moruzzi, *ibid.*, p. 662).

61 See, for example, 'France divided as headscarf ban is set to become law', *The Observer*, 1 February 2004; 'Europe focus up to Islam and the veil', *The Guardian*, 4 February 2004; 'When the veil means freedom', *The Guardian*, 20 January 2004.

62 In addition, arguments made by Muslim feminists that Islam does not mandate patriarchal practices would have to be met. See, for example, L. Ahmed, *Women and Gender in Islam*, New Haven: Yale University Press, 1992.

63 Article 2 of the 1958 Constitution reads: 'France is an indivisible, laïque, democratic and social republic. It ensures equality of all citizens before the law with no distinction made on the basis of origin, race or religion. It respects all beliefs.'

64 See Laborde, *ibid.*

65 See, for example, C. Laborde, 'Toleration and Laïcité' in C. McKinnon and D. Castiglione (eds), *The Culture of Toleration in Diverse Societies: Reasonable Tolerance*, Manchester: Manchester University Press, 2003, pp. 162–5.

66 For more on these forms of neutrality see W. Kymlicka, 'Liberal Individualism and Liberal Neutrality', *Ethics*, vol. 99, no. 4, 1989.

67 I am indebted here to the analysis in Laborde, *ibid.*

68 Thanks to John Horton for this point.

69 Laborde, *ibid.*, pp. 170–1.

70 For an introduction see 'Republicanism' in D. Miller (ed.), *The Blackwell Encyclopaedia of Political Thought*, Oxford: Blackwell, 1991. For an account of the evolution of the concept of laïcité through French political history see J. Bauberot, 'The Two Thresholds of Laicization' in R. Bhargava (ed.), *Secularism and Its Critics*, Delhi: Oxford University Press, 1998.

71 The classic text here is J.J. Rousseau, *The Social Contract*, London and Melbourne: Dent, 1973.

72 Brian Barry nicely sets this idea in the context of the Anglo-American philosophical literature on multiculturalism. See Barry, *ibid.*, p. 7.

73 Interview with Margaret Thatcher, 'Aids, Education, and the Year 2000', *Woman's Own*, 31 October 1987, pp. 8–10. Available on-line: http://www.margaretthatcher.org/speeches/displaydocument.asp?docid=106689. Accessed 27 December 2004.

74 J. Tomasi, *Liberalism Beyond Justice*, Princeton, N.J.: Princeton University Press, 2001, p. 76. See also S. Macedo, *Liberal Virtues*, Oxford: Oxford University Press, 1990; W.

Galston, 'Liberal Virtues and the Formation of a Civic Character' in M.A. Glendon and D. Blankenhorn (eds), *Seedbeds of Virtue: Sources of Competence, Character, and Citizenship in American Society*, Lanham, Maryland: Madison Books, 1995.

75 For Tomasi, 'the good political liberal citizen is a person who is skillful at the art of exercising her rights' (*ibid.*, p. 75). On his view, good liberal citizens are capable of conceiving of themselves as rights-holders – and if necessary, capable of pressing their rights – in a way that does not cause damage to, and perhaps even promotes, the projects and pursuits embedded in their non-political identities.

76 For example, see the *Sydney Morning Herald* reporting that 'France imposed the ban in September to reassert the neutrality of its state schools and counter what teachers said was rising Islamist radicalism reflected in the wearing of headscarves, denial of the Holocaust and attacks on Jewish schoolmates' ('First French Pupils Expelled Over Headscarves', *Sydney Morning Herald*, 20 October 2004). Thanks to Bob McKeever for pointing out this piece to me.

77 On this point see J.H. Carens and M. Williams, 'Muslim Minorities in Liberal Democracies: The Politics of Misrecognition' in R. Bhargava (ed.), *Secularism and Its Critics*.

78 See my 'Civil Citizens' in C. McKinnon and I. Hampsher-Monk (eds), *The Demands of Citizenship*, London and New York: Continuum, 2000.

8 Artistic expression

1 S. Rushdie, 'One Thousand Days in a Balloon' in his *Imaginary Homelands*, London: Granta Books, 1991, p. 439.

2 S. Rushdie, 'In Good Faith' in his *Imaginary Homelands*, p. 394.

3 Rushdie, *ibid.*, p. 397.

4 For a more detailed account of the 'Rushdie affair' see J. Horton, 'The *Satanic Verses* Controversy: A Brief Introduction' in J. Horton (ed.), *Liberalism, Multiculturalism and Toleration*, Basingstoke: Macmillan, 1993. See also L. Appignanesi and S. Maitland (eds), *The Rushdie File*, London: Fourth Estate, 1989.

5 A photograph of the painting is available on-line at: http://www.smb.spk-berlin.de/d/exhibition/sensation/harvey.html (accessed 28 April 2005).

6 A photograph of the painting is available on-line at: http://www.artnet.com/Magazine/features/hoving/hoving4-7–10.asp (accessed 28 April 2005).

7 See *Schenck v. United States*, 249 U.S. 47 (1919).

8 J.S. Mill, *On Liberty* in *Utilitarianism*, M. Warnock (ed.), London: Fontana Press, 1962, p. 184.

9 See, for example, S. Akhtar, *Be Careful With Muhammad!*, London: Belleur, 1989.

10 J.S. Mill, *ibid.*, p. 143.

11 See R. Descartes, *Meditations on First Philosophy*, Cambridge: Cambridge University Press, 1996, Meditations 1 and 2.

12 In fact, Mill himself admits that there are some subjects (he mentions geometry and mathematics) with respect to which 'all the argument is on one side' (Mill, *ibid.*, p. 163), but he claims that the exceptions prove the rule.

13 Mill, *ibid.*, pp. 180–1.

14 See J.C. Rees, *John Stuart Mill's 'On Liberty'*, Oxford: Clarendon Press, 1985.

15 Mill, *ibid.*, p. 161.

16 The argument is explicitly invoked by Rushdie in defence of *SV*. See S. Rushdie, 'Is Nothing Sacred?' in his *Imaginary Homelands*.

17 See A. Haworth, *Free Speech*, London and New York: Routledge, 1998. Philosophical accounts of knowledge are sometimes given in terms of justified true belief, but nothing hangs on this characterisation.

18 The 'satanic verses' are to be found in a revision of a biography of Muhammad by an Arabic historian – the *Sirat Rashul Allah* – said to have been written 120–30 years after Muhammad's death. The biographer (Ibn Ishaq) reports a story that Muhammad was anxious to attract the people of Mecca to Islam. As he was reciting to himself this verse of the Qur'an, as revealed to him by the angel Gabriel, 'Have you thought of al-Lat and al-'Uzza and Manat the third, the other' (Sura 53, 19–20; the verse refers to three goddesses worshipped by Meccans), Satan tempted him to add the following 'This are the exalted Gharaniq, whose intercession is approved.' What Muhammad's addition of the verse would signify is his acceptance of the effective intercession of the goddesses, and thus his rejection of monotheism, which – according to the story – led the Meccans to cease the persecution of Muhammad and the first Muslims. The story concludes with Gabriel visiting Muhammad again to upbraid him, as a result of which Muhammad removed the 'satanic verses' from the Qur'an, and the persecution of Muslims resumed. The Muslim scholar Fazlur Rahman argues that this story ought to be accepted as true (see F. Rahman, *Islam*, Chicago: University of Chicago Press, 1979); for scholarly rejection of the story see http://www.islamonline.net/English/In_Depth/mohamed/1424/misconception/article04.shtml (accessed 14 November, 2004).
19 Mill, *ibid.*, p. 182.
20 J. Waldron, 'Rushdie and Religion' in his *Liberal Rights*. Waldron has since stepped back somewhat from this form of aggressive liberalism. See J. Waldron, 'Toleration and Reasonableness' in C. McKinnon and D. Castiglione (eds), *The Culture of Toleration in Diverse Societies: Reasonable Tolerance*, Manchester: Manchester University Press, 2003.
21 See Mill, *ibid.*, chapter 2. It is, however, debatable whether Mill's conception of individuality is best understood as a conception of autonomy.
22 T.M. Scanlon, 'A Theory of Freedom of Expression' in his *The Difficulty of Tolerance*, Cambridge: Cambridge University Press, 2003, p. 15.
23 Scanlon, *ibid.*, p. 16, emphasis added.
24 See T.M. Scanlon, 'Freedom of Expression and the Categories of Expression' and 'Content Regulation Reconsidered', in his *The Difficulty of Tolerance*.
25 Scanlon, 'Freedom of Expression and the Categories of Expression', p. 86.
26 Scanlon, *ibid.*, p. 91.
27 Scanlon, 'Content Regulation Reconsidered', p. 155.
28 Scanlon, 'Freedom of Expression and the Categories of Expression', p. 92.
29 Scanlon, 'Content Regulation Reconsidered', p. 155. The term 'citizen interests' is mine.
30 See Scanlon, 'Freedom of Expression and the Categories of Expression', pp. 90–1.
31 Scanlon, 'Content Regulation Reconsidered', p. 165.
32 Scanlon, 'Freedom of Expression and the Categories of Expression', p. 100.
33 R. Dworkin, 'The Moral Reading and the Majoritarian Premise' in his *Freedom's Law: The Moral Reading of the American Constitution*, Cambridge, Mass.: Harvard University Press, 1996, pp. 15–16.
34 Dworkin, *ibid.*, p. 17.
35 Dworkin, *ibid.*, p. 17.
36 In the Gettysburg Address President Abraham Lincoln defended 'government of the people, for the people, by the people'.
37 Dworkin, *ibid.*, p. 20.
38 Dworkin, *ibid.*, p. 20.
39 *Brown v. Board of Education* 347 U.S. 483 (1954).
40 Dworkin, *ibid.*, p. 24.
41 Dworkin, *ibid.*, p. 25.
42 Note that it is not Dworkin's view – and is not required by the argument from democracy in general – that *political* speech is the primary focus of constitutional protection. Rather, our interests as citizens – that is, as members of a democratic community – are in having freedom of expression across the board. For the more

limited argument that the primary focus of First Amendment freedom of expression is political speech see F. Michelman, 'Conceptions of Democracy in American Constitutional Argument: The Case of Pornography Regulation', *Tennessee Law Review*, vol. 56, no. 291, 1989.

43   See F. Schauer, 'The Second Best First Amendment', *William and Mary Law Review*, vol. 31, no. 1, 1989. The First Amendment reads: 'Congress shall make no law respecting an establishment of religion, or prohibiting the free exercise thereof; or abridging the freedom of speech, or of the press; or the right of the people peaceably to assemble, and to petition the government for a redress of grievances'.

44   L. Doyle, *The Surrendered Wife*, New York: Simon and Schuster, 2001.

45   See Frederick Schauer, 'The Second Best First Amendment', pp. 5–7.

46   Schauer, *ibid.*, p. 2.

47   For a detailed account of Muslim reactions at the time of the controversy see B. Parekh, 'The Rushdie Affair: Research Agenda for Political Phillosophy', *Political Studies*, vol. 38, 1990.

48   See B. Parekh, 'The Rushdie Affair and the British Press: Some Salutary Lessons' in B. Parekh (ed.), *Free Speech*, London: Commission for Racial Equality, 1990.

49   This explains why many Muslims were nonplussed at the suggestion that they simply avoid reading *SV*; for example, 'You are aggrieved that some of us have condemned you without a hearing and asked for the ban without reading the book. Yes, I have not read it, nor do I intend to. I do not have to wade through a filthy drain to know what filth is. My first inadvertent step would tell me what I have stepped into' (S. Shahabuddin in L. Appignanesi and S. Maitland (eds), *The Rushdie File*, p. 47; quoted in P. Jones, 'Respecting Beliefs and Rebuking Rushdie' in J. Horton (ed.), *Liberalism, Multiculturalism, and Toleration*, p. 136, n. 17).

50   See chapter 6, pp. 84–5.

51   Lord Scarman's judgement on the successful 1977 prosecution of *Gay News* for blasphemy, *Gay News*, no. 162, pp. 8–21, March 1979, pp. 10–11.

52   *Ibid.*

53   However, this was not always the case. See D. Edwards, 'Toleration and the English Blasphemy Law' in J. Horton and S. Mendus (eds), *Aspects of Toleration: Philosophical Studies*, London: Methuen, 1985; D. Edwards, 'The History of Blasphemy and the Rushdie Affair' in J. Horton (ed.), *Liberalism, Multiculturalism and Toleration*.

54   Instead, blasphemy was treated as akin to sedition, given the religious foundations of the state. See Edwards, 'Toleration and the English Blasphemy Law', esp. pp. 76–7.

55   See Jones, *ibid.*, p. 122.

56   See Jones, *ibid.*, p. 117 and p. 130.

57   See J. Feinberg, *The Moral Limits of the Criminal Law Vol. 2: Offense to Others*, Oxford: Oxford University Press, 1985, p. 68.

58   Indeed, this was the view of the Law Commission some years prior to publication of *SV*. See The Law Commission, *Working Paper No. 79: Offences Against Religion and Public Worship*, London: HMSO, 1981, and *Criminal Law: Offences Against Religion and Public Worship (Law Com. no. 145)*, London: HMSO, 1985. It was also the view of the Commission for Racial Equality; see M. Day, 'The Salman Rushdie Affair: Implications for the CRE and Race Relations' in B. Parekh (ed.), *Free Speech*, p. 107. A different possibility here is to advocate modification of the account of public reason with which we have been working so as to permit the direct introduction and unmitigated use of arguments and reasons of faith into political debate. See J. Bohman, 'Deliberative Toleration', *Political Theory*, vol. 13, no. 6, 2003. Making this modification is, however, tantamount to the abandonment of liberalism.

59   Indeed, to do so might actually evince disrespect for members' beliefs, insofar as taking a person's beliefs seriously means engaging with them in the 'ordinary rough and tumble of argument' (Jones, *ibid.*, p. 126) which blasphemy law restricts.

60   Parekh, 'The Rushdie Affair', p. 705.

61 T. Modood, 'Muslims, Incitement to Hatred, and the Law' in J. Horton (ed.), *Liberalism, Multiculturalism and Toleration*, p. 146.

62 The clauses in brackets only apply in Northern Ireland.

63 Although the Act itself has not been extended so as to include religious groups, incorporation of the EU's Race Directive (*EC Article 13 Race Directive*) into the Act in 2000 was accompanied by the implementation of a new Employment Directive (*Employment Equality (Religion or Belief) Regulations 2003*) which outlaws religious or belief-based discrimination or harassment in the workplace (the legislation came into force on 2 December 2003). However, the Employment Directive does not protect religious believers from discrimination or harassment outside the workplace.

64 Modood, *ibid.*, p. 146.

65 See also Parekh, *ibid.*, p. 705. Of course, Parekh's claims are open to question.

66 J. Feinberg, 'The Nature and Value of Rights', *Journal of Value Inquiry*, vol. 4, 1970, p. 252.

67 Rushdie, 'In Good Faith', p. 393. Rushdie also thinks, unlike Scanlon, that acts of expression which qualify as works of art *ipso facto* deserve special protection in law. See Salman Rushdie, 'Is Nothing Sacred?' in his *Imaginary Homelands*.

68 Scanlon, 'Content Regulation Reconsidered', p. 155.

69 Scanlon, 'A Theory of Freedom of Expression', p. 16.

70 Waldron, 'Toleration and Reasonableness', p. 23.

71 J. Cohen, 'Freedom of Expression' in D. Heyd (ed.), *Toleration: An Elusive Virtue*, p. 183.

9 Pornography and censorship

1 R. West, *The Clarion*, 14 November 1913.

2 See A. Dworkin on the 'Take Back the Night' movement, 'Pornography and Grief' in D. Cornell (ed.), *Feminism and Pornography*, Oxford: Oxford University Press, 2000. See also A. Dworkin, *Pornography: Men Possessing Women*, London: The Women's Press, 1984. For an account of the tortuous course of US Supreme Court decisions regarding pornography, obscenity, and censorship see J. Feinberg, *The Moral Limits of the Criminal Law* Vol. 2: *Offense to Others*, Oxford: Oxford University Press, 1985, chapter 12.

3 To say that this view is the zeitgeist is not, however, to say that most people approve of or are indifferent towards pornography. In particular, there is evidence to suggest that a large majority of women in the UK believe that pornography is offensive, degrading to women, and causes sexual violence against women (see C. Itzin and C. Sweet, 'Women's Experience of Pornography: UK Magazine Survey Evidence' in C. Itzin (ed.), *Pornography: Women, Violence, and Civil Liberties*, Oxford: Oxford University Press, 1993). If this evidence about what women in the UK believe about pornography is reliable then women's participation in the political zeitgeist *vis-à-vis* the regulation of pornography shows them to be remarkably tolerant.

4 Of course, some sexually explicit material designed in part to produce arousal can also aim to propagate truths; for example, the Marquis de Sade's book *One Hundred and Twenty Days of Sodom* (New York: Grove Press, 1987) can be seen both as a piece of pornography and as a novel with propositional content (insofar as it serves as a commentary on class and hypocrisy in eighteenth-century France). Such pieces – insofar as they have genuine propositional content – are hard cases for any definition of pornography to be used in law.

5 Those interested in the causal debate might start with the following pieces: E. Donnerstein, D. Linz and S. Penrod, *The Question of Pornography: Research Findings and Policy Implications*, New York: The Free Press, 1987; D. Copp and S. Wendell (eds), *Pornography and Censorship*, Buffalo, NY: Prometheus Books, 1983, 'Part 2:

Social Scientific Surveys'; C. Itzin (ed.), *Pornography: Women, Violence and Civil Liberties*, 'Part 3: Pornography and Evidence of Harm'.

6 See B. Williams *et al.*, *Obscenity and Film Censorship: An Abridgement of the Williams Report*, Cambridge: Cambridge University Press, 1981.

7 See Feinberg, *ibid.*, chapter 12.

8 Feinberg, *ibid.*, p. xiii.

9 R. Dworkin, 'Do We Have a Right to Pornography?' in his *A Matter of Principle*, Oxford: Clarendon Press, 1986, p. 354.

10 R. Dworkin, 'Reverse Discrimination' in his *Taking Rights Seriously*, London: Duckworth, 1977, p. 234.

11 'Individual rights are political trumps held by individuals. Individuals have rights when, for some reason, a collective goal is not a sufficient justification for denying them what they wish, as individuals, to have or to do, or not a sufficient justification for imposing some loss or injury on them' (R. Dworkin, 'Introduction' in his *Taking Rights Seriously*, p. xi). See also Dworkin, 'Do We Have a Right to Pornography?', p. 359.

12 Dworkin, 'Do We Have a Right to Pornography?', p. 353.

13 See R. Dworkin, 'Women and Pornography', *New York Review*, 21 October 1993, p. 41.

14 For a similar – but *ad hominem* – challenge to Dworkin see R. Langton, 'Whose Right? Ronald Dworkin, Women, and Pornographers', *Philosophy and Public Affairs*, vol. 19, no. 4, 1990.

15 C. MacKinnon, 'Francis Biddle's Sister' in her *Feminism Unmodified*, Cambridge, Mass.: Harvard University Press, 1987, p. 178. See also C. MacKinnon, 'Not a Moral Issue', *ibid.*, p. 155.

16 See C. MacKinnon, 'Difference and Dominance: On Sex Discrimination' in her *Feminism Unmodified*. For analysis see A.S. Laden, 'Radical Liberals, Reasonable Feminists', *The Journal of Political Philosophy*, vol. 11, no. 2, 2003.

17 MacKinnon, 'Not a Moral Issue', p. 148. See also C. MacKinnon, *Only Words*, Cambridge, Mass.: Harvard University Press, 1993, p. 25.

18 None of the ordinances became law. For an account of the legislative debates see C. MacKinnon, 'The Roar on the Other Side of Silence' in D. Cornell (ed.), *Feminism and Pornography*. See also A. Dworkin and C. MacKinnon, *In Harm's Way: Pornography Civil Rights Hearing*, Harvard: Harvard University Press, 1998.

19 MacKinnon, *Only Words*, pp.121–2, n. 32.

20 Note, however, that the ordinance allows that 'the use of "men, children, or transsexuals" in the place of "women" is also pornography' (MacKinnon, *ibid.*, p. 122, n. 32).

21 For an argument against this restrictive definition see Feinberg, *ibid.*, p. 145.

22 See the papers in Part V, D. Cornell (ed.), *Feminism and Pornography*.

23 MacKinnon, *ibid.*, p. 71.

24 C. MacKinnon, '"More Than Simply a Magazine": Playboy's Money' in her *Feminism Unmodified*, p. 140.

25 MacKinnon, 'Not a Moral Issue', p. 156.

26 MacKinnon, 'Francis Biddle's Sister', pp. 181–2.

27 See MacKinnon, *ibid.*, p. 193.

28 R. Dworkin, *ibid.*, p. 40.

29 See H. Steiner, *An Essay on Rights*, Oxford: Blackwell, 1994.

30 R. Dworkin, *ibid.*, p. 38.

31 MacKinnon, 'Not a Moral Issue', p. 156.

32 R. Dworkin, *ibid.*, p. 38.

33 R. Dworkin, *ibid.*, p. 41.

34 R. Dworkin, *ibid.*, p. 40.

35 R. Dworkin, *ibid.*, p. 42.

36 R. Dworkin, *ibid.*, p. 41.

37 For MacKinnon's response to Dworkin, and Dworkin's response to MacKinnon's response, see 'Pornography: An Exchange', *New York Review*, 3 March 1994.

38 J.L. Austin, *How to Do Things With Words*, London: Oxford University Press, 1962.
39 R. Langton, 'Speech Acts and Unspeakable Acts', *Philosophy and Public Affairs*, vol. 22, no. 4, 1993. In this paper she also argues that pornography subordinates women in virtue of its perlocutionary effects; however, I do not address this argument.
40 Langton, *ibid.*, pp. 319, 324; italics in original.
41

> Nobody heard him, the dead man,
> But still he lay moaning:
> I was much further out than you thought
> And not waving but drowning.
>
> Poor chap, he always loved larking
> And now he's dead
> It must have been too cold for him his heart gave way,
> They said.
>
> Oh, no no no, it was too cold always
> (Still the dead one lay moaning)
> I was much too far out all my life
> And not waving but drowning.
>   (Stevie Smith, 'Not Waving but Drowning').

42 It goes without saying that the conventions supplying the felicity conditions for marrying by uttering 'I do' can change so as to secure illocutionary enablement for this class of people with respect to the act of marrying through the utterance 'I do'. This is what the pro-gay marriage lobby aims at.
43 Langton, *ibid.*, pp. 323–4. Langton's reference to the 'move of protest' relates to Linda Marchiano's account of her coercion and abuse in the making of *Deep Throat* (L. Marchiano, *Ordeal*, Secaucus, N.J.: Citadel Press, 1980), which was subsequently marketed in some contexts as pornography, and so became pornography. See Langton, *ibid.*, p. 321–2.
44 Although Langton indicates that she thinks her analysis does lend support to pro-censorship arguments, she does not herself – at least in this paper – advocate censorship. See Langton, *ibid.*, pp. 329–30.
45 For critique of Langton on grounds unrelated to the consequences of her analysis for questions of censorship see D. Jacobson, 'Freedom of Speech Acts? A Response to Langton', *Philosophy and Public Affairs*, vol. 24, 1995.
46 Langton, *ibid.*, p. 304.
47 See Langton, *ibid.*, p. 325.
48 Langton makes this quite explicit. See *ibid.*, pp. 305, 329.
49 Langton, *ibid.*, p. 305.
50 Langton, *ibid.*, p. 329.
51 See, for example, A. Dworkin, *Pornography: Men Possessing Women*.
52 See J. Hornsby, 'Free and Equal Speech', *Imprints*, vol. 1, no. 2, 1996.
53 See T. Modood, 'Muslims, Incitement to Hatred, and the Law' in J. Horton (ed.), *Liberalism, Multiculturalism and Toleration*, Basingstoke: MacMillan, 1993.

10 Holocaust denial

1 I would like to thank Gideon Calder, and audiences at the LSE Department of Government seminar, the LSE Department of Philosophy seminar in Philosophy and Public Policy, and the University of Brighton Philosophy Society, for useful

comments on this chapter. Thanks are also due to Charles Boundy and Tony Bruce at Routledge for legal advice.

2 P. Levi, *If This Is A Man*, London: Abacus, 1987.

3 See J.S. Mill, *On Liberty in Utilitarianism*, M. Warnock (ed.), London: Fontana Press, 1962, chapter 1.

4 'Tell Me Everything', Holocaust History Organisation. Available on-line: http://www.holocaust-history.org/short-essays/general.shtml ccessed 12 August 2004. Another excellent introductory resource is the *Holocaust Encyclopaedia* (hosted by the United States Holocaust Memorial Museum). Available on-line: http://www.ushmm.org/wlc/en. Accessed 23 August 2004. The statistics given in this section are taken from the *Encyclopaedia*.

5 M. Shermer and A. Grobman, *Denying History*, Berkeley: University of California Press, 2000, p. 101. I use this definition of the Holocaust in order to provide a tight focus on the activities of Holocaust deniers, whose attentions are overwhelmingly devoted to this aspect of the Nazi atrocities. Use of this definition should not be taken to indicate ignorance of, or a demotion of concern for, the other victims of the Nazis.

6 See H. Bresheeth, S. Hood and L. Jansz, *The Holocaust for Beginners*, Cambridge: Icon Books, 2000, p. 62.

7 See http://www.holocaust-history.org/short-essays/final-solution.shtml (accessed 12 August 2004); http://www.holocaust-history.org/hitler-final-solution/index.shtml (accessed 12 August 2004).

8 See http://www.holocaust-history.org/short-essays/wannsee.shtml (accessed 12 August 2004).

9 For more on the history of European anti-semitism see S. Friedlander, *Nazi Germany and the Jews*, Vol. 1, New York: HarperCollins, 1997. For more on the Holocaust see R. Hilberg, *The Destruction of the European Jews*, New York: Holmes and Meier, 1985; L. Yahil, *The Holocaust*, Oxford: Oxford University Press, 1990; L. Dawidowicz, *The War Against the Jews*, New York: Holt, Rinhart and Winston, 1975.

10 See http://www.holocaust-history.org/short-essays/nuremberg.shtml (accessed 16 August 2004).

11 For example, the Office of Special Investigations in the US Justice Department, and Simone Wiesenthal's Nazi Documentation Centre in Vienna.

12 Shermer and Grobman, *ibid.*, p. 100, emphasis in original.

13 See D. Lipstadt, *Denying the Holocaust*, London: Penguin Books, 1993, pp. 21–9. See also P. Vidal-Naquet, *Assassins of Memory*, New York: Columbia University Press, 1992, pp. 18–19; A.E. Mathis, 'Holocaust, Denial of' in P. Knight (ed.), *Conspiracy Theories in American History: An Encyclopaedia*, Santa Barbara, CA: ABC-CLIO, 2003. Also available on-line: http://www.holocaust-history.org/denial/abc-clio/index.shtml. Accessed 13 August 2004.

14 See Lipstadt, *ibid.*, pp. 31–48.

15 D.J. Goldhagen, *Hitler's Willing Executioners: Ordinary Germans and the Holocaust*, New York: Alfred Knopf, 1996.

16 As attested to by the Historikerstreit (the Historians' Controversy) in Germany in the 1980s during which historians and public intellectuals battled over the best inter-pretation of Germany's Nazi past – in particular, over the uniqueness of the Holocaust – and the significance of this interpretation for Germany's current and future political identity. See *New German Critique*, no. 44, 1988, Special Issue on the Historikerstreit.

17 See, for example, J.E. Young, *Writing and Rewriting the Holocaust*, Bloomington: Indiana University Press, 1988, and S. Friedlander, *Memory, History and the Extermination of the Jews of Europe*, Bloomington: University of Indiana Press, 1993. For critique of the work of historians in different national contexts see L. Dawidowicz, *The Holocaust and the Historians*, Cambridge, Mass.: Harvard University Press, 1981.

18   For a comprehensive account see Lipstadt, *ibid*. Extensive bibliographies of HD literature
     can be found on-line at http://purl.oclc.org/NET/holbib.html and http://purl.oclc.org/
     NET/holbib2.html. Accessed 18 August 2004.
19   Available on-line: http://www.ihr.org/leaflets/gaschambers.shtml. Accessed 16 August
     2004.
20   For a dismissal of Faurisson's 'conclusions' see N. Fresco, 'The Denial of the Dead:
     On the Faurisson Affair', *Dissent*, Fall 1981.
21   See Shermer and Grobman, *ibid*., pp. 80–4; Lipstadt, *ibid*., pp. 37–8.
22   The petition also stated that Faurisson was denied access to public libraries, but this is
     false. He was denied access to the Centre de Documentation Juive Contemporaine,
     but this is a private foundation with the right to refuse access to whomever it wishes.
     Thus, it does not follow that Faurisson's rights were violated by their exclusion of him.
     See Vidal-Naquet, *ibid*., p. 162, n. 10.
23   See, for example, Vidal-Naquet, 'On Faurisson and Chomsky' in his *Assassins of
     Memory*.
24   N. Chomsky, 'Some Elementary Comments on the Rights of Freedom of Expression'.
     Available on-line: http://www.zmag.org/chomsky/articles/8010-free-expression.html.
     Accessed 16 August 2004.
25   R. Faurisson, *Mémoire en défense contre ceux qui m'accusent de falsifier l'histoire*
     (Memoir of defence against those who accuse me of falsifying history), Paris: La
     Vielle Taupe, 1980.
26   Chomsky, 'Some Elementary Comments on the Rights of Freedom of Expression', p. 3
27   For Chomsky's response, and further thoughts on Faurisson's freedom of expression, see
     N. Chomsky, 'His Right to Say It'. Available on line. http://zena.secureforum.com/
     7not/mmag/ullarticles1.ctm. Accessed 16 August 2004.
28   Quoted in United Nations document CCPR/C/58/D/550/1993, paragraph 2.6.
     Available on-line: http://www.unhchr.ch/tbs/doc.nsf/MasterFrameView/4c47b59ea
     48f7343802566f200352fea?Opendocument. Accessed 16 August 2004.
29   See http://www.unhchr.ch/tbs/doc.nsf/MasterFrameView/4c47b59ea48f7343802566
     f200352fea?Opendocument. Accessed 16 August 2004.
30   On the accuracy of Irving's self-publicity in this respect see R.J. Evans, *Lying About
     Hitler*, New York: Basic Books, 2001, pp. 15–18. See also *passim* for the best
     existing account of Irving's distortions and lies, of the trial, and of its immediate
     aftermath.
31   Lipstadt, *ibid*., p. 180.
32   Lipstadt, *ibid*., p. 181.
33   See Evans, *ibid*., pp. 28–9.
34   *The Irving Judgement*, London, 2000, pp. 335–9.
35   *The Irving Judgement*, pp. 346–7. On Irving's anti-semitism witness his statement
     that, 'I'm going to form an Association of the Auschwitz survivors, survivors of the
     Holocaust and other liars, or the ASSHOLS' (*The Guardian*, 12 January 2000).
36   Evans, *ibid*., p. 70.
37   See the Anti-Defamation League update on Irving at http://www.adl.org/learn/ext_
     us/irving_up.asp. Accessed 23 August 2004.
38   See H. Steiner, *An Essay on Rights*, Oxford: Blackwell, 1994.
39   See http://www.holocaust-history.org/pamphlets/zundel/who-is-zundel-1.pdf. Accessed
     16 August 2004.
40   For a good summary of the details of these laws see 'Combating Holocaust Denial
     Through Law in the United Kingdom', Appendix B, JPR Report No. 3, 2000,
     Institute for Jewish Policy Research. Available on-line: http://www.jpr.org.uk/
     Reports/CS_Reports/no_3_2000/index.htm. Accessed 17 August 2004.
41   See 'Combating Holocaust Denial Through Law in the United Kingdom', pp. 11–13.
42   The wording of the proposed bill was:

> A Bill to make it a criminal offence to claim, whether in writing or orally, that the policy of genocide against the Jewish people committed by Nazi Germany did not occur.
>
> 1(1) The Public Order Act 1986 is amended as follows.
>
> 1(2) In section 18 there shall be inserted the following subsection –
>
> 5 (a) For the purpose of this section, any words, behaviour or material which purport to deny the existence of the policy of genocide against the Jewish people and other similar crimes against humanity committed by Nazi Germany ('the Holocaust') shall be deemed to be intended to stir up racial hatred.
>
> 2(1) This Act may be cited as the Holocaust Denial Act 1997.
>
> 2(2) This Act extends to England and Wales only.

The bill passed to committee stage, but was not allowed sufficient parliamentary time to proceed any further. The Institute for Jewish Policy Research counselled against any such bill. See 'Combating Holocaust Denial Through Law in the United Kingdom'.

43 The term is taken from W.V. Quine, *The Web of Belief*, New York: Random House, 1978.

44 See Shermer and Grobman, *ibid.*, pp. 114–7.

45 For discussion see R. Gaita, *A Common Humanity*, London: Routledge, 1998, pp. 157–86.

46 *The Times* stated that the trial would address, 'whether one of the blackest chapters of 20th century history actually happened, or is a figment of imaginative and politically motivated Jewry' (A. Hamilton, 'Academic Buccaneer vs Bookish Schoolmaster', *The Times*, 12 January 2000, p. 3). However, as the presiding judge Charles Gray made clear, 'What was at issue . . . was Irving's methodology and historiography, not what happened back in the 40s' (C. Dyer, 'Judging History', *The Guardian* (G2), 1 April 2000, p. 10; material quoted in Evans, *ibid.*, pp. 35–8).

47 Indeed, Tariq Modood cites HD as paradigmatic of the harm of group defamation from which he argues that Muslims ought to be protected in law. See T. Modood, 'Muslims, Incitement to Hatred, and the Law' in J. Horton (ed.), *Liberalism, Multiculturalism and Toleration*, Basingstoke: Macmillan, 1993, p. 145.

48 T.M. Scanlon, 'Freedom of Expression and the Categories of Expression' in his *The Difficulty of Tolerance*, Cambridge: Cambridge University Press, 2003, p. 92.

49 Scanlon, *ibid.*, p. 92.

50 United Nations document CCPR/C/58/D/550/1993, paragraph 2.2.

51 See 'Combating Holocaust Denial Through Law in the United Kingdom', §2, pp. 3–4; §5, pp. 11–13.

52 Paradoxically, if deniers have a right to access to the Academy then the speech act argument for the legal prohibition of HD might gain more currency in virtue of the fact that membership of the Academy normally bestows authority on the member with respect to their subject, and often much else. I shall not consider this consequence any further.

53 Thanks to Philip Cook for this suggestion.

54 See Lipstadt, *ibid.*, chapter 10.

55 See http://www.ihr.org. Accessed 19 August 2004. For an account of the history and personnel of the IHR see Shermer and Grobman, *ibid.*, pp. 43–8; Lipstadt, *ibid.*, chapter 8.

56 See http://www.ihr.org/main/journal.shtml. Accessed 19 August 2004.

57 See http://www.ihr.org/main/about.shtml. Accessed 19 August 2004.

58 See Lipstadt, *ibid.*, pp. 144–53.

59 See Evans, *ibid.*, pp. 141–2.
60 Weber was news editor for National Vanguard, the publication of the US neo-Nazi group the National Alliance, and has described Jews as 'the traditional enemies of truth'. See Shermer and Grobman, *ibid.*, pp. 46–8.
61 See Shermer and Grobman, *ibid.*, p. 79.
62 See J.C. Zimmerman, *Holocaust Denial: Demographics, Testimonies and Ideologies*, Lanham, Maryland: University Press of America, 2000, p. 123.
63 For Irving's version of relativist history see Evans, *ibid.*, p. 34.
64 See D. Hayes, 'Intellectuals and Education: The Role of the University', *Critical Review of International Social and Political Philosophy*, vol. 6, no. 4, 2003, p. 131. For – ironically – an argument made by a historian that comes close to this conclusion see K. Jenkins, *Re-thinking History*, London: Routledge, 1991 (thanks to Gideon Calder for directing me to this piece).
65 Vidal-Naquet, *ibid.*, p. xxiv.
66 R. Barnett, *Beyond All Reason: Living with Ideology in the University*, Buckingham: SRHE/Open University Press, 2003, p. 18.
67 See R. Barnett, *Realizing the University in an Age of Supercomplexity*, Buckingham: SRHE/Open University Press, 2000.
68 J. Panton, 'What are Universities For? Universities, Knowledge, and Intellectuals', *Critical Review of International Social and Political Philosophy*, vol. 6, no. 4, 2003, pp. 148–9.
69 See Hayes, *ibid.*, p. 134.
70 See Panton, *ibid.*, p. 151.
71 T.M. Scanlon, 'Content Regulation Reconsidered' in his *The Difficulty of Tolerance*, p 155
72 See A. Hudson, 'Intellectuals for Our Times', *Critical Review of International Social and Political Philosophy*, vol. 6, no. 4, 2003.
73 See R. Barnett, 'Academics as Intellectuals', *Critical Review of International Social and Political Philosophy*, vol. 6, no. 4, 2003.
74 For examples of the contributions public intellectuals can make, see A.M. Melzer, J. Weinberger, and M.R. Zinman (eds), *The Public Intellectual: Between Philosophy and Politics*, Lanham, Maryland: Rowman and Littlefield Publishers, 2003.
75 For similar thoughts, see Hayes, *ibid.*, p. 137; see also Panton, *ibid.*, pp. 154–5.

Bibliography

Many of the best recent materials on toleration have been produced by the Morrell Studies in Toleration Programme in the Department of Politics at the University of York. See J. Horton, and S. Mendus (eds), *Aspects of Toleration: Philosophical Studies*, London and New York: Methuen, 1985; S. Mendus and D. Edwards (eds), *On Toleration*, Oxford: Clarendon Press, 1987; S. Mendus (ed.), *Justifying Toleration: Conceptual and Historical Perspectives*, Cambridge: Cambridge University Press, 1988; S. Mendus, *Toleration and the Limits of Liberalism*, Basingstoke: Macmillan, 1989; J. Horton and S. Mendus (eds), *John Locke: A Letter Concerning Toleration In Focus*, London and New York: Routledge, 1991; J. Horton (ed.), *Liberalism, Multiculturalism and Toleration*, Basingstoke: Macmillan, 1993; J. Horton and S. Mendus (eds), *Toleration, Identity and Difference*, Basingstoke: Macmillan, 1999; and S. Mendus (ed.), *The Politics of Toleration*, Edinburgh: University of Edinburgh Press, 1999.

Other significant recent collections are D. Heyd (ed.), *Toleration: An Elusive Virtue*, Princeton, N.J.: Princeton University Press, 1996; T.M. Scanlon, *The Difficulty of Tolerance*, Cambridge: Cambridge University Press, 2003; and C. McKinnon and D. Castiglione (eds), *The Culture of Toleration in Diverse Societies: Reasonable Tolerance*, Manchester: Manchester University Press, 2003.

Ahmed, L., *Women and Gender in Islam*, New Haven: Yale University Press, 1992.
Akhtar, S., *Be Careful With Muhammad!*, Belleur: London, 1989.
American Anthropological Association Executive Board, 'Statement on Human Rights' (submitted to the UN Commission on Human Rights), *American Anthropologist*, vol. 49, no. 4, 1974: 539–43.
Anschutz, R.P., *The Philosophy of J.S. Mill*, Oxford: Clarendon Press, 1953.
Appignanesi, L. and Maitland, S. (eds), *The Rushdie File*, London: Fourth Estate, 1989.
Archard, D., *Children, Rights and Childhood*, London: Routledge, 1993.
Ashcraft, R., *Revolutionary Politics and Locke's 'Two Treatises of Government'*, Princeton, N.J.: Princeton University Press, 1986.
Austin, J.L., *How to Do Things With Words*, London: Oxford University Press, 1962.
Baghramian, M., *Relativism*, London: Routledge, 1994.
Baghramian, M. and Ingram, A. (eds), *Pluralism: The Philosophy and Politics of Diversity*, London: Routledge, 2000.

Barnett, R., *Realizing the University in an Age of Supercomplexity*, Buckingham: SRHE/ Open University Press, 2000.

——*Beyond All Reason: Living with Ideology in the University*, Buckingham: SRHE/Open University Press, 2003.

——'Academics as Intellectuals', *Critical Review of International Social and Political Philosophy*, vol. 6, no. 4, 2003: 108–22.

Barry, B., *Theories of Justice*, London: Harvester-Wheatsheaf, 1989.

——*Liberty and Justice: Essays in Political Theory II*, Oxford: Clarendon Press, 1991.

Bauberot, J., 'The Two Thresholds of Laicization' in R. Bhargava (ed.), *Secularism and Its Critics*, Delhi: Oxford University Press, 1998.

Bellamy, R. and Mason, A. (eds), *Political Concepts*, Manchester: Manchester University Press, 2003.

Bentham, J., *An Introduction to the Principles of Morals and Legislation*, London: Methuen, 1996.

Berlin, I., *Four Essays on Liberty*, Oxford: Oxford University Press, 1969.

——*The Crooked Timber of Humanity*, H. Hardy (ed.), London: John Murray, 1990.

Berlin, I. and Williams, B., 'Pluralism and Liberalism: A Reply', *Political Studies*, vol. XLII, no. 2, 1994: 306–9.

Bhargava, R. (ed.), *Secularism and Its Critics*, Delhi: Oxford University Press, 1998.

Bohman, J., 'Deliberative Toleration', *Political Theory*, vol. 13, no. 6, 2003: 757–79.

Bowen, J.R., 'Muslims and Citizens: France's Headscarf Controversy', *Boston Review*, vol. 29, no. 1, 2004.

Bresheeth, H., Hood, S., and Jansz, L., *The Holocaust for Beginners*, Cambridge: Icon Books, 2000.

Broome, J., 'Is Incommensurability Vagueness?' in R. Chang (ed.), *Incommensurability, Incomparability and Practical Reason*, Cambridge, Mass.: Harvard University Press, 1997.

Carens, J.H. and Williams, M., 'Muslim Minorities in Liberal Democracies: The Politics of Misrecognition' in R. Bhargava (ed.), *Secularism and Its Critics*, Delhi: Oxford University Press, 1998.

Carter, S.L., *The Dissent of the Governed*, Cambridge, Mass.: Harvard University Press, 1998.

Casal, P., 'Is Multiculturalism Bad for Animals?', *The Journal of Political Philosophy*, vol. 11, no. 1, 2003: 1–22.

Chambers, C., 'Are Breast Implants Better than Female Genital Mutilation? Autonomy, Gender Equality and Nussbaum's *Political Liberalism*', *Critical Review of International Social and Political Philosophy*, vol. 7, no. 3, 2004: 1–33.

Chang, R. (ed.), *Incommensurability, Incomparability and Practical Reason*, Cambridge, Mass.: Harvard University Press, 1997.

Chomsky, N., 'Some Elementary Comments on the Rights of Freedom of Expression'. Available on-line: http://www.zmag.org/chomsky/articles/8010-free-expression.html. Accessed 16 August 2004.

——'His Right to Say It'. Available on-line: http://zena.secureforum.com/Znet/zmag/ allarticles1.cfm. Accessed 16 August 2004).

Cohen, J., 'Moral Pluralism and Political Consensus' in D. Copp, J. Hampton and J.E. Roemer (eds), *The Idea of Democracy*, Cambridge: Cambridge University Press, 1993.

——'A More Democratic Liberalism', *Michigan Law Review*, vol. 92, 1994: 1503–46.

——'Freedom of Expression' in D. Heyd (ed.), *Toleration: An Elusive Virtue*, Princeton, N.J.: Princeton University Press, 1996.

Copp, D. and Wendell, S. (eds), *Pornography and Censorship*, Buffalo, New York: Prometheus Books, 1983.

Copp, D., Hampton, J. and Roemer, J.E. (eds), *The Idea of Democracy*, Cambridge: Cambridge University Press, 1993.

Cornell, D. (ed.), *Feminism and Pornography*, Oxford: Oxford University Press, 2000.

Crowder, G., 'Pluralism and Liberalism', *Political Studies*, vol. XLII, no. 2, 1994: 293–305.

Cullity, G. and Gaut, B., *Ethics and Practical Reason*, Oxford: Clarendon Press, 1997.

Dawidowicz, L., *The War Against the Jews*, New York: Holt, Rinehart and Winston, 1975.

——*The Holocaust and the Historians*, Cambridge, Mass.: Harvard University Press, 1981.

Dawson, B.E., 'Circumcision on the Female: Its Necessity and How to Perform It', *American Journal of Clinical Medicine*, vol. 22, no. 6, 1915: 520–3.

de Sade, M., *One Hundred and Twenty Days of Sodom*, New York: Grove Press, 1987.

Descartes, R., *Meditations on First Philosophy*, Cambridge: Cambridge University Press, 1996.

Devlin, P., *The Enforcement of Morals*, London: Oxford University Press, 1965.

Donnerstein, E., Linz, D. and Penrod, S., *The Question of Pornography: Research Findings and Policy Implications*, New York: The Free Press, 1987.

Dorkenoo, E., *Cutting the Rose: Female Genital Mutilation: Its Practice and Its Prevention*, London: Minority Rights Publication, 1994.

Doyle, L., *The Surrendered Wife*, New York: Simon and Schuster, 2001.

Dupré, J., 'Normal People', *Social Research*, vol. 65, no. 2, 1998: 221–48.

Dworkin, A., *Pornography: Men Possessing Women*, London: The Women's Press, 1984.

——'Pornography and Grief' in D. Cornell (ed.), *Feminism and Pornography*, Oxford: Oxford University Press, 2000.

Dworkin, A., and MacKinnon, C., *In Harm's Way: Pornography Civil Rights Hearing*, Harvard: Harvard University Press, 1998.

Dworkin, G. (ed.), *Mill's On Liberty: Critical Essays*, Lanham, Maryland: Rowman and Littlefield, 1997.

Dworkin, R., *Taking Rights Seriously*, London: Duckworth, 1977.

——*A Matter of Principle*, Oxford: Clarendon Press, 1986.

——'Women and Pornography', *New York Review*, 21 October 1993: 36–42.

——*Freedom's Law: The Moral Reading of the American Constitution*, Cambridge, Mass.: Harvard University Press, 1996.

——'Do Liberal Values Conflict?' in M. Lilla, R. Dworkin and R. Silvers (eds), *The Legacy of Isaiah Berlin*, New York: New York Review of Books, 2001.

Eagleton, T., 'Defending the Free World', *The Socialist Register*, 1990: 85–95.

Edwards, D., 'Toleration and the English Blasphemy Law' in J. Horton and S. Mendus (eds), *Aspects of Toleration: Philosophical Studies*.

——'The History of Blasphemy and the Rushdie Affair' in J. Horton (ed.), *Liberalism, Multiculturalism and Toleration*, London and New York: Methuen, 1985.

Estlund, D., 'Making Truth Safe for Democracy' in D. Copp, J. Hampton and J.E. Roemer (eds), *The Idea of Democracy*, Cambridge: Cambridge University Press, 1993.

Evans, R.J., *Lying About Hitler*, New York: Basic Books, 2001.

Faurisson, R., *Mémoire en défense contre ceux qui m'accusent de falsifier l'histoire*, Paris: La Vielle Taupe, 1980.

Feinberg, J., 'The Nature and Value of Rights', *Journal of Value Inquiry*, vol. 4, 1970: 243–60.

——*The Moral Limits of the Criminal Law* Vol. 1: *Harm to Others*, Oxford: Oxford University Press, 1984.

——*The Moral Limits of the Criminal Law* Vol. 2: *Offense to Others*, Oxford: Oxford University Press, 1985.

——*The Moral Limits of the Criminal Law* Vol. 3: *Harm to Self*, Oxford: Oxford University Press, 1986.

——*The Moral Limits of the Criminal Law* Vol. 4: *Harmless Wrongdoing*, Oxford: Oxford University Press, 1988.

Foster, L. and Herzog, P. (eds), *Defending Diversity: Contemporary Philosophical Perspectives on Pluralism and Multiculturalism*, Amherst: University of Massachusetts Press, 1994.

Fraser, N., 'Solidarity or Singularity? Richard Rorty between Romanticism and Technocracy' in A. Malachowski (ed.), *Reading Rorty*, Oxford: Blackwell, 1990.

Fresco, N., 'The Denial of the Dead: On the Faurisson Affair', *Dissent*, Fall 1981.

Friedlander, S., *Nazi Germany and the Jews*, Vol. 1, New York: HarperCollins, 1997.

——*Memory, History and the Extermination of the Jews of Europe*, Bloomington: University of Indiana Press, 1993.

Gaita, R., *A Common Humanity*, London: Routledge, 1998.

Galeotti, A.E., *Toleration as Recognition*, Cambridge: Cambridge University Press, 2002.

Galston, W., 'Liberal Virtues and the Formation of a Civic Character' in M.A. Glendon and D. Blankenhorn (eds), *Seedbeds of Virtue: Sources of Competence, Character, and Citizenship in American Society*, Lanham, Maryland: Madison Books, 1995.

Geras, N., *Solidarity in the Conversation of Humankind: The Ungroundable Liberalism of Richard Rorty*, London: Verso, 1995.

Glendon, M.A. and Blankenhorn, D, (eds) *Seedbeds of Virtue: Sources of Competence, Character, and Citizenship in American Society*, Lanham, Maryland: Madison Books, 1995.

Goldhagen, J., *Hitler's Willing Executioners: Ordinary Germans and the Holocaust*, New York: Alfred Knopf, 1996.

Goodin, R.E. and Pettit, P. (eds), *A Companion to Contemporary Political Philosophy*, Oxford: Blackwell, 1995.

Gowans, C.W. (ed.), *Moral Disagreements: Classic and Contemporary Readings*, London: Routledge, 2000.

Gray, J., *Isaiah Berlin*, London: HarperCollins, 1995.

——*Mill on Liberty: A Defence*, London: Routledge, 1996.

——'Where Pluralists and Liberals Part Company' in M. Baghramian and A. Ingram (eds), *Pluralism: The Philosophy and Politics of Diversity*, London: Routledge, 2000.

Gutmann, A. (ed.), *Multiculturalism and the 'Politics of Recognition'*, Princeton, N.J.: Princeton University Press, 1992.

Haddock, B. and Sutch, P. (eds), *Multiculturalism, Identity and Rights*, London: Routledge, 2003.

Harman, G., 'Moral Relativism Defended', *The Philosophical Review*, vol. 84, 1975: 3–22.

Harris, I., *The Mind of John Locke*, Cambridge: Cambridge University Press, 1994.

Harrison, G., 'Relativism and Tolerance', *Ethics*, vol. 86, 1976: 122–35.

Hart, H.L.A., *Law, Liberty and Morality*, London: Oxford University Press, 1963.

Hatch, E., 'The Good Side of Relativism', *Journal of Anthropological Research*, vol. 53, 1997: 371–81.

Haworth, A., *Free Speech*, London and New York: Routledge, 1998.

Hayes, D., 'Intellectuals and Education: The Role of the University', *Critical Review of International Social and Political Philosophy*, vol. 6, no. 4, 2003: 123–38.

Hernnstein, R.J. and Murray, C., *The Bell Curve: Intelligence and Class Structure in American Life*, New York: Simon and Schuster, 1996.

Heyd, D. (ed.), *Toleration: An Elusive Virtue*, Princeton, N.J.: Princeton University Press, 1996.

Hilberg, R., *The Destruction of the European Jews*, New York: Holmes and Meier, 1985.

Hill Jnr., T.E., *Autonomy and Self-Respect*, Cambridge: Cambridge University Press, 1991.

——'The Stability Problem in Political Liberalism', *Pacific Philosophical Quarterly*, vol. 75, 1994: 333–52.

Himmelfarb, G., *On Liberty and Liberalism: The Case of John Stuart Mill*, New York: Knopf, 1974.

Honderich, T. (ed.), *The Oxford Companion to Philosophy*, Oxford: Oxford University Press, 1995.

Hornsby, J., 'Free and Equal Speech', *Imprints*, vol. 1, no. 2, 1996.

Horton, J. (ed.), *Liberalism, Multiculturalism and Toleration*, Basingstoke: Macmillan, 1993.

——'The Satanic Verses Controversy: A Brief Introduction' in J. Horton (ed.), *Liberalism, Multiculturalism, and Toleration*, Basingstoke: Macmillan, 1993.

——'Three (Apparent) Paradoxes of Toleration', *Synthesis Philosophica*, vol. 9, fasc. 1, 1994: 7–19.

——'Toleration as a Virtue' in D. Heyd (ed.), *Toleration: An Elusive Virtue*, Princeton, N.J.: Princeton University Press, 1996.

——'The Good, The Bad, and The Impartial', *Utilitas*, vol. 8, no. 3, 1996: 307–28.

——'Liberalism and Multiculturalism: Once more unto the breach' in B. Haddock and P. Sutch (eds), *Multiculturalism, Identity and Rights*, London: Routledge, 2003.

Horton, J. and Mendus, S. (eds), *Aspects of Toleration: Philosophical Studies*, London and New York: Methuen, 1985.

——(eds), *John Locke: A Letter Concerning Toleration In Focus*, London and New York: Routledge, 1991.

——(eds), *Toleration, Identity and Difference*, Basingstoke: Macmillan, 1999.

Hosken, F.P., *The Hosken Report: Genital and Sexual Mutilation of Females*, 4th revised edition, Lexington, Mass.: Women's International Network News, 1994.

Hudson, A., 'Intellectuals for Our Times', *Critical Review of International Social and Political Philosophy*, vol. 6, no. 4, 2003: 33–50.

Itzin, C. (ed.), *Pornography: Women, Violence, and Civil Liberties*, Oxford: Oxford University Press, 1993.

Itzin, C., and Sweet, C., 'Women's Experience of Pornography: UK Magazine Survey Evidence' in C. Itzin (ed.), *Pornography: Women, Violence, and Civil Liberties*, Oxford: Oxford University Press, 1993.

Jacobson, D., 'Freedom of Speech Acts? A Response to Langton', *Philosophy and Public Affairs*, vol. 24, no. 1, 1995: 64–79.

Jay, A. (ed.), *The Oxford Dictionary of Political Quotations*, Oxford: Oxford University Press, 2001.

Jenkins, K., *Re-thinking History*, London: Routledge, 1991.

Jones, P., 'Respecting Beliefs and Rebuking Rushdie' in J. Horton (ed.), *Liberalism, Multiculturalism, and Toleration*, Basingstoke: Macmillan, 1993.

Kant, I., *The Moral Law: Kant's Groundwork of the Metaphysic of Morals*, tr. H.J. Paton, London: Unwin Hyman, 1989.

——*The Metaphysics of Morals*, Gregor, M. (ed.), Cambridge: Cambridge University Press, 1996.

Kelly, E. and MacPherson, L., 'On Tolerating the Unreasonable', *The Journal of Political Philosophy*, vol. 9, no. 1, 2001: 38–55.

Kelly, P. (ed.), *Multiculturalism Reconsidered*, Cambridge: Polity Press, 2002.

Knight, P. (ed.), *Conspiracy Theories in American History: An Encyclopaedia*, Santa Barbara, CA: ABC-CLIO, 2003.

Korsgaard, C., *Creating the Kingdom of Ends*, Cambridge: Cambridge University Press, 1996.

Kroll, R., Ashcraft, R. and Zagorin, P. (eds), *Philosophy, Science, and Religion in England 1640–1700*, Cambridge: Cambridge University Press, 1992.

Kukathas, C., 'Cultural Toleration' in W. Kymlicka and I. Shapiro (eds), *Ethnicity and Group Rights: Nomos XXXIX*, New York: New York University Press, 1997.

——'The Life of Brian, or Now for Something Completely Different' in P. Kelly (ed.), *Multiculturalism Reconsidered*, Cambridge: Polity Press, 2002.

Kymlicka, W., Liberalism, *Community and Culture*, Oxford: Clarendon Press, 1989.

——'Liberal Individualism and Liberal Neutrality', *Ethics*, vol. 99, no. 4, 1989: 83–105.

——*Contemporary Political Philosophy*, 2nd edition, Oxford: Oxford University Press, 2002.

Kymlicka, W. and Shapiro, I. (eds), *Ethnicity and Group Rights: Nomos XXXIX*, New York: New York University Press, 1997.

Laborde, C., 'Toleration and Laïcité' in C. McKinnon and D. Castiglione (eds), *The Culture of Toleration in Diverse Societies: Reasonable Tolerance*, Manchester: Manchester University Press, 2003.

——'Secular Philosophy and Muslim Headscarves in Schools', *Journal of Political Philosophy*, forthcoming.

Laden, A.S., 'Radical Liberals, Reasonable Feminists', *Journal of Political Philosophy*, vol. 11, no. 2, 2003: 133–52.

Langton, R., 'Whose Right? Ronald Dworkin, Women, and Pornographers', *Philosophy and Public Affairs*, vol. 19, no. 4, 1990: 311–59.

——'Speech Acts and Unspeakable Acts', *Philosophy and Public Affairs*, vol. 22, no. 4, 1993: 293–330.

Larmore, C., *Patterns of Moral Complexity*, Cambridge: Cambridge University Press, 1987.

——*The Morals of Modernity*, Cambridge: Cambridge University Press, 1996.

Levi, P., *If This Is A Man*, London: Abacus, 1987.

Lilla, M., Dworkin, R. and Silvers, R. (eds), *The Legacy of Isaiah Berlin*, New York: New York Review of Books, 2001.

Lipstadt, D., *Denying the Holocaust*, London: Penguin Books, 1993.

Locke, J., *A Letter Concerning Toleration*, J. Tully (ed.), Indianapolis: Hackett Publishing Co., 1983.

Macedo, S., *Liberal Virtues*, Oxford: Oxford University Press, 1990.

MacIntyre, A., *After Virtue*, London: Duckworth, 1981.

Mackie, J.L., *Ethics: Inventing Right and Wrong*, London: Penguin Books, 1977.

MacKinnon, C., *Feminism Unmodified*, Cambridge, Mass.: Harvard University Press, 1987.

——*Only Words*, Cambridge, Mass.: Harvard University Press, 1993.

Malachowski, A.R. (ed.), *Reading Rorty*, Oxford: Blackwell, 1990.

Mandle, J., *What's Left of Liberalism?*, Lanham, Maryland: Lexington Books, 2000.

Marchiano, L., *Ordeal*, Secaucus, N.J.: Citadel Press, 1980.

Marshall, J., *John Locke: Resistance, Religion and Responsibility*, Cambridge: Cambridge University Press, 1994.

Mathis, A.E., 'Holocaust, Denial of' in Knight, P. (ed.), *Conspiracy Theories in American History: An Encyclopaedia*, Santa Barbara, CA: ABC-CLIO, 2003.

Matravers, M. and Mendus, S., 'The Reasonableness of Pluralism' in C. McKinnon and D. Castiglione (eds), *The Culture of Toleration in Diverse Societies: Reasonable Tolerance*, Manchester: Manchester University Press, 2003.

McClosky, H.J., *John Stuart Mill: A Critical Study*, London: Macmillan, 1971.

McKinnon, C., 'Exclusion Rules and Self-Respect', *Journal of Value Inquiry*, vol. 34, no. 4, 2000: 491–505.

——'Civil Citizens' in C. McKinnon and I. Hampsher-Monk (eds), *The Demands of Citizenship*, London and New York: Continuum, 2000.

——*Liberalism and the Defence of Political Constructivism*, New York: Palgrave Macmillan, 2002.

——'Rights: Their Basis and Limits' in R. Bellamy and A. Mason (eds), *Political Concepts*, Manchester: Manchester University Press, 2003.

McKinnon, C. and Castiglione, D. (eds), *Toleration: Moral and Political*, Special Issue of *Res Publica*, vol. 7, no. 3, 2001.

——(eds), *The Culture of Toleration in Diverse Societies: Reasonable Tolerance*, Manchester: Manchester University Press, 2003.

McKinnon, C. and Hampsher-Monk, I. (eds) *The Demands of Citizenship*, London and New York: Continuum, 2000.

Meckled-Garcia, S., 'Toleration and Neutrality: Incompatible Ideals?' in C. McKinnon and D. Castiglione (eds), *Toleration: Moral and Political*, Special Issue of *Res Publica*, vol. 7, no. 3, 2001: 293–313.

Melzer, A.M., Weinberger, J., and Zinman, M.R. (eds), *The Public Intellectual: Between Philosophy and Politics*, Lanham, Maryland: Rowman and Littlefield, 2003.

Mendus, S. (ed.), *Justifying Toleration: Conceptual and Historical Perspectives*, Cambridge: Cambridge University Press, 1988.

——*Toleration and the Limits of Liberalism*, Basingstoke: Macmillan, 1989.

——'Locke: Toleration, Morality and Rationality' in J. Horton and S. Mendus (eds), *John Locke: A Letter Concerning Toleration In Focus*, London and New York: Routledge, 1991.

——(ed.), *The Politics of Toleration*, Edinburgh: University of Edinburgh Press, 1999.

——'Choice, Chance, and Multiculturalism' in P. Kelly (ed.), *Multiculturalism Reconsidered*, Cambridge: Polity Press, 2002.

Mendus, S. and Edwards, D. (eds) *On Toleration*, Oxford: Clarendon Press, 1987.

Mill, J.S., *On Liberty in Utilitarianism*, M. Warnock (ed.), London: Fontana Press, 1962.

——*The Subjection of Women*, Massachusetts: MIT Press, 1970.

——*Considerations on Representative Government*, Buffalo, New York: Prometheus Books, 1991.

Miller, D. (ed.), *The Blackwell Encyclopaedia of Political Thought*, Oxford: Blackwell, 1991.

Modood, T., 'Muslims, Incitement to Hatred, and the Law' in J. Horton (ed.), *Liberalism, Multiculturalism, and Toleration*, Basingstoke: Macmillan, 1993.

Moller Okin, S., *Justice, Gender and the Family*, New York: Basic Books, 1989.

——'Is Multiculturalism Bad for Women?', in J. Cohen (ed.), *Is Multiculturalism Bad for Women?*, Princeton, N.J.: Princeton University Press, 1999.

Moruzzi, N., 'A Problem with Headscarves', *Political Theory*, vol. 22, no. 4, 1994: 653–72.

Mulhall, S. and Swift, A., *Liberals and Communitarians*, Oxford: Blackwell, 1996.

Munoz-Darde, V., 'Should the Family be Abolished, then?', *Proceedings of the Aristotelian Society*, vol. XCXIX, part 1, 1999.

Nicholson, P., 'Toleration as a Moral Ideal' in J. Horton and S. Mendus (eds), *Aspects of Toleration*, London and New York: Methuen, 1985.

Nozick, R., *Anarchy, State and Utopia*, Oxford: Blackwell, 1974.

Nussbaum, M., 'Double Moral Standards?', *Boston Review*, vol. 21, no. 5, 1996.

O'Neill, O., *Towards Justice and Virtue: A Constructive Account of Practical Reasoning*, Cambridge: Cambridge University Press, 1996.

Panton, J., 'What are Universities For? Universities, Knowledge, and Intellectuals', *Critical Review of International Social and Political Philosophy*, vol. 6, no. 4, 2003: 139–56.

Parekh, B., 'The Rushdie Affair: Research Agenda for Political Phillosophy', *Political Studies*, vol. 38, 1990: 695–709.

——(ed.), *Free Speech*, London: Commission for Racial Equality, 1990.

——*Rethinking Multiculturalism*, Cambridge, Mass.: Harvard University Press, 2000.

Plamenatz, J., *The English Utilitarians*, Oxford: Blackwell, 1958.

Popper, K., 'Toleration and Intellectual Responsibility' in S. Mendus and D. Edwards (eds), *On Toleration*, Oxford: Clarendon Press, 1987.

Quine, W.V., *The Web of Belief*, New York: Random House, 1978.

Rachels, J., 'Subjectivism' in P. Singer (ed.), *A Companion to Ethics*, Oxford: Blackwell, 1991.

Raphael, D.D., 'The Intolerable' in S. Mendus (ed.), *Justifying Toleration: Conceptual and Historical Perspectives*, Cambridge: Cambridge University Press, 1988.

Rawls, J., *A Theory of Justice*, Oxford: Oxford University Press, 1971.

——*Political Liberalism*, New York: Columbia University Press, 1993.

——*John Rawls: Collected Papers*, Cambridge, Mass: Harvard University Press, 1999.

——*Justice as Fairness: A Restatement*, Cambridge, Mass.: Harvard University Press, 2001.

Raz, J., 'On the Nature of Rights', *Mind*, vol. XCIII, 1984: 194–214.

——*The Morality of Freedom*, Oxford: Clarendon Press, 1986.

——'Facing Diversity: The Case of Epistemic Abstinence', *Philosophy and Public Affairs*, vol. 19, no. 1, 1990: 3–46.

——*Ethics in the Public Domain*, Oxford: Clarendon Press, 1994.

1997.

Rees, J.C., *John Stuart Mill's 'On Liberty'*, Oxford: Clarendon Press, 1985.

Robson, J.M., *The Improvement of Mankind: The Social and Political Thought of John Stuart Mill*, Toronto: University of Toronto Press, 1968.

Rogers, G.A.J. (ed.), *Locke's Philosophy: Content and Context*, Oxford: Clarendon Press, 1994.

——*Contingency, Irony, Solidarity*, Cambridge: Cambridge University Press, 1989.

——*Objectivity, Relativism and Truth*, Cambridge: Cambridge University Press, 1991.

——*Philosophy and Social Hope*, London: Penguin Books, 1999.

Rosenblum, N., *Membership and Morals: The Personal Uses of Pluralism in America*, Princeton, N.J.: Princeton University Press, 1998.

Roth, P., *The Plot Against America*, London: Jonathan Cape, 2004.

Rousseau, J.J., *The Social Contract*, London and Melbourne: Dent, 1973.

Rushdie, S., *Imaginary Homelands*, London: Granta Books, 1991.

Sandel, M., *Liberalism and the Limits of Justice*, Cambridge: Cambridge University Press, 1982.

Scanlon, T.M., *The Difficulty of Tolerance*, Cambridge: Cambridge University Press, 2003.

Schauer, F., 'The Second Best First Amendment', *William and Mary Law Review*, vol. 31, no. 1, 1989: 1–22.

Schneewind, J.B. (ed.), *Mill: A Collection of Critical Essays*, London: Macmillan, 1969.

Sher, G., *Beyond Neutrality: Perfectionism in Politics*, Cambridge: Cambridge University Press, 1997.

Shermer, M. and Grobman, A., *Denying History*, Berkeley: University of California Press, 2000.

Shweder, R.A., 'The Astonishment of Anthropology' in C.W. Gowans (ed.), *Moral Disagreements: Classic and Contemporary Readings*, London: Routledge, 2000.

Simmons, A.J., *On The Edge of Anarchy: Locke, Consent, and the Limits of Society*, Princeton, N.J.: Princeton University Press, 1993.

Singer, P. (ed.), *A Companion to Ethics*, Oxford: Blackwell, 1991.

——*Practical Ethics*, Cambridge: Cambridge University Press, 1993.

Steiner, H., *An Essay on Rights*, Oxford: Blackwell, 1994.

Strauss, L., *The Rebirth of Classical Political Rationalism*, Chicago: University of Chicago Press, 1989.

Tamir, Y., 'Hands Off Clitoridectomy', *Boston Review*, vol. 21, no. 3, 1996.

Taylor, C., *Philosophy and the Human Sciences: Philosophical Papers* Vol. II, Cambridge: Cambridge University Press, 1985.

——*Human Agency and Language: Philosophical Papers* Vol. 1, Cambridge: Cambridge University Press, 1985.

Ten, C.L., *Mill On Liberty*, Oxford: Clarendon Press, 1980.

Tomasi, J., 'Kymlicka, Liberalism, and Respect for Cultural Minorities', *Ethics*, vol. 105, 1995: 580–603.

——*Liberalism Beyond Justice*, Princeton, N.J.: Princeton University Press, 2001.

Tully, J., *An Approach to Political Philosophy: Locke in Contexts*, Cambridge: Cambridge University Press, 1993.

——*Strange Multiplicity*, Cambridge: Cambridge University Press, 1995.

Vidal-Naquet, P., *Assassins of Memory*, New York: Columbia University Press, 1992.

Waldron, J. (ed.), *Theories of Rights*, Oxford: Oxford University Press, 1984.

——'Locke: Toleration and the Rationality of Persecution' in J. Horton and S. Mendus (eds), *John Locke: A Letter Concerning Toleration In Focus*, London and New York: Routledge, 1991.

——*Liberal Rights: Collected Papers 1981–1991*, Cambridge: Cambridge University Press, 1993.

——'Rights' in R.E. Goodin and P. Pettit (eds), *A Companion to Contemporary Political Philosophy*, Oxford: Blackwell, 1995.

——'Toleration and Reasonableness', C. McKinnon and D. Castiglione (eds), *The Culture of Toleration in Diverse Societies: Reasonable Tolerance*, Manchester: Manchester University Press, 2003.

Walzer, M., *Spheres of Justice: A Defence of Pluralism and Equality*, Oxford: Blackwell, 1983.

Warnock, M., 'The Limits of Toleration' in S. Mendus and D. Edwards (eds), *On Toleration*, Oxford: Clarendon Press, 1987.

Wenar, L., 'Political Liberalism: An Internal Critique', *Ethics*, vol. 106, 1995: 32–62.

Williams, B., Morality: *An Introduction to Ethics*, Harmondsworth: Penguin Books, 1972.

——'Tolerating the Intolerable' in S. Mendus (ed.), *The Politics of Toleration*, Edinburgh: Edinburgh University Press, 1999.

Williams, B. *et al.*, *Obscenity and Film Censorship: An Abridgement of the Williams Report*, Cambridge: Cambridge University Press, 1981.

Wong, D.W., *Moral Relativity*, Berkeley: University of California Press, 1984.

——'Coping with Moral Conflict and Ambiguity' in L. Foster and P. Herzog (eds), *Defending Diversity: Contemporary Philosophical Perspectives on Pluralism and Multiculturalism*, Amherst: University of Massachusetts Press, 1994.

Yahil, L., *The Holocaust*, Oxford: Oxford University Press, 1990.

Young, J.E., *Writing and Rewriting the Holocaust*, Bloomington: Indiana University Press, 1988.

Zimmerman, J.C., *Holocaust Denial: Demographics, Testimonies, and Ideologies*, Lanham, Maryland: University Press of America, 2000.

Index

aboriginal groups 105
abortion 82
act-utilitarianism 47
acts/omissions 12
L'affaire du foulard 112–18
affronts to the senses 83
Africa 106, 107
agreement motive 48
all-male clubs 6
Alliance for Marriage 6, 82
American Anthropological Association 38
Amish 102
Amsterdam 3–4
analytic/synthetic truths 43–4
anger 84
animal rights 82
annoyance 84
anthropology 37–9, 45
anti-foundationalism 43–4
anti-patriarchy 114, 115
anti-semitism 25, 153, 156, 157, 165
anti-utopianism 58
anxiety 84
appearance/reality 43–4
artistic expression: see freedom of
    expression
Aryan race 154
Asians 5
audience interests 125–6, 164, 170
Auschwitz-Birkenau 154
Austin, J.L. 145–6, 151–2
Australia 107
Austria 4, 160
authority 148–50, 151
autonomy **62–6**; female genital
    mutilation 109; Holocaust denial
163–4; laïcité 116; pornography
138–9; significant interests 125

bare knowledge offence 87–9, 139
Barnett, Ronald 169
Barry, Brian 47–50, 180n.38, 189n.34
Basques 94
Belgium 160
The Bell Curve (Herrnstein and Murray)
    25
Belzec 155
Bentham, Jeremy 54
Berlin, Isiah 58–62, 182n.16, 182n.21,
    182n.28, 182n.29
black people 4, 5
blasphemy 129–35
Body Count 185n.12
boredom 84, 86
Bowers v. Hardwick (1986) 5
Brady, Ian 120
British National Party (BNP) 4
Brooklyn Museum 121
Broome, John 181n.3
Brown v. Board of Education (1954) 6, 127–8
burdens of judgement 71–3, 74, 75, 77–8,
    82, 116
bushido 56, 181n.10
bystander interests 125, 165

Canada 107
Caribbean people 4
Carto, Willis 167
Categorical Imperative 97–8
censorship: see pornography
Chang, Ruth 181n.7, 181n.9
Charles II 8

Chase, Alexander 18
Chelmno 155
childbirth 106
children: protection from harm 108–9, 138, 148; rights 91, 107, 189n.35; *see also* headscarves
Chirac, Jacques 112–13, 115
Le Choc du Mois 158
Chomsky, Noam 157–8
Church/state 8–9
circumcision: *see* female genital mutilation
citizenship: *laïcité* 115–17; pornography 139; significant interests 125, 126; *see also* democracy
clash of rights 144, 145
class 30–1
clitoridectomy 106
coercion: evaluative beliefs 27; female genital mutilation 112; headscarves 115; law 11; master/slave 148–50; religion 9; salvation 176n.28
Cohen, Joshua 135
commitment 19
communitarianism 95–6, 187n.47
communities of meaning 101, 103–5
competitive pluralism 62–6
comprehensive liberalism 68, 184n.45
conflicts 6–7, 48
consensus 69–70
consent , physical harm and 109, 110–12
consequences of judgement 71–2
consitutional consensus 70
constructivism 183n.5
contemporary problems 13–17
conversion 48
'Cop Killer' (Body Count) 185n.12
Council of Europe survey 4
Countryside Alliance 82
creationism 50
crimes against humanity 158
cultural membership 102–5; instrumental good 188n.10; intrinsic good 103–4, 114, 188n.10, 189n.14
culture critics 44–7
culture , solidarity and 44–6

damaged status 137–8
Deep Throat (film) 197n.43

defamation 132–4, 164–5
democracy: abandonment 47; freedom of expression 126–8, 135, 194n.42; government authority 7–10; Holocaust denial 162–3; pornography 139–45
Denmark 4
Denying the Holocaust (Lipstadt) 159
difference 14, 69
dignity 90, 92
disgust and revulsion 83–4
dislike/disapproval: incommensurability 57–8; strong opposition 23–5; weak opposition 19–20; wide opposition 27–33
dogmatism 48
doubt 47–50
duties of justice 97–8
Dworkin, Andrea 142–3
Dworkin, Ronald: democracy 126–8, 135; interest-based rights 92; legal moralism 140–1, 143–4

Eagleton, T. 179n.26
Einsatzgruppen 154, 155
embarrassment 84
Employment Directive 195n.63
Enlightenment 116
epistemological scepticism 35, 47–50, 51
equal opportunities 96
equal rights 96
erotica 143
ethnic minorities 4
evaluative beliefs 49–50
evaluative disapproval 23–7, 177n.8
evaluative incomparability 53–5, 65
Evans, Richard 159–60
evolution, theory of 50
excision 106
exclusion 46
Exclusion Bill 8
experiments in living 109

factual beliefs 49–50
fallibility 47–50; freedom of expression 122–3; Holocaust denial 161; pornography 138
Farrakhan, Louis 25, 178n.13
Faurisson, Robert 156–8, 167
fear 84

Federal Marriage Amendment 5–6, 82
Feinberg, Joel 83–9, 134, 140, 186n.18,
    186n.24
female genital mutilation 105–12,
    189n.34, 190n.43, 190n.44, 190n.45,
    190n.49
feminism 96, 138, 191n.61
Final Solution 155
Fortuyn, Pim 4
France 4, 112–18, 156–8, 160
freedom of expression: classic arguments
    121–9, 138–9; democracy 126–8;
    fallibility 122–3; Holocaust denial
    157–8, 163–4, 166; inequality 143–5;
    'second best' 128–9; significant
    interests 125–6, 134; truth, argument
    from 123–4
freedom of speech: democracy 128–9;
    inequality 143–4; interest-based rights
    90, 96; locutions 145–6, 150–1;
    Muslim quote 119
friendship/money 55
Frist, Bill 5
frustration 84

gay marriages 5–6, 28–30
Gay News 130
'Gayssot Act' 1990 158
genocide: see Holocaust denial
genocide, intention to commit 156
Germany 160, 166
ghettoes 155
Giuliani, Rudolph 121
Göering, Hermann 155
Goldhagen, Daniel 156
good/bad 178n.20
good life 116
Goodridge v. MA Dept of Public Health 5–6
governments , authority of 7–10
Gray, John 59, 182n.29
groups: defamation 164–5; libel 132–3;
    rights 94; special rights 101–2; see
    also cultural membership

harm: intelligible 80; offence and 82–9;
    politically salient 80; rights-based
    harm 81–2, 89–95; rights-based harm
    worries 95–8; social construction of
    inequality 140–5; utility and 12–13

Hart, H.L.A. 13
Harvey, Marcus 120–1
Hayes, Dennis 169
headscarves 112–18
health care 93
Herrnstein, Richard 25
Heydrich, Reinhard 155
hijab 112–18
Hindley, Myra 120–1
Hirsi Ali, Ayaan 4
history 156, 157, 167, 168
Hitler, Adolf 25, 39, 156
Hitler's Willing Executioners (Goldhagen)
    156
Holland 3–4
Holmes, Justice 121–2
Holocaust denial: in the Academy
    166–71, 200n.52; audience interests
    170; democracy 162–3; fallibility 161;
    Faurisson case 156–8; freedom of
    expression 166; Irving case 158–60,
    163; law and 160–6, profound offences
    163–4, 166; revisionism 156; 'second
    best' 163; significant interests 162,
    163; speech act theory 165–6,
    200n.52; truth 161–2, 168–9
Holocaust Denial Act 1997 199n.42
Holocaust facts 154–6
The Holy Virgin Mary (Ofili) 121
homophobia 29–30
homosexuality , criminalising 5
Horton, John 32–3, 83, 177n.2, 180n.47
hostility 64–5
human nature/cultural nurture 43–4
human rights 38, 106, 158
humiliation 84
hunting with dogs 82

illocutionary speech 145–8, 150–1, 165
immigrant groups 102–3
immigration policies 4
imperfect social duties 97–8
importance, tolerance and 14
inalienable rights 109–10, 190n.40
incitement to violence 12–13, 163
inclusivity 16
incommensurability: autonomy and
    competitive pluralism 62–6; negative
    liberty 58–62; opposition 33–4;

reasonableness 74–6; theses of 52–6, 66, 75, 181n.3, 181n.7, 181n.10; toleration from 57–8
incomparability, evaluative 53–5, 65
incompatibility, practical 53, 55–6, 65
incompossibility 76–9
individual rights 196n.11; excessive 95–6; groups 102–4; liberalism 82, 88, 89–98; limits 173; political trumps 92, 196n.11
inequality: liberty and 144–5; social construction 140–5
infibulation 106
Institute for Historical Review (IHR) 167
instrumental good 188n.10
integration 102
interest-based rights 90–2, 134–5
International Covenant on Civil and Political Rights 158
International Military Tribunal 155
intrinsic good 103–4, 114, 188n.10, 189n.14
Iran 120
ironists 46–7
Irving, David 158–60, 163, 167
Islam: censorship see The Satanic Verses (Rushdie); circumcision 108; dogmatism 48; headscarves 112–18; special rights 101–2; treatment of women 4
Islam, pornography and: harm and offence 82–9; incompossibility 76–9; liberal rights 94–5; profound offences 85, 87–8; shock 84
Israel 42, 157, 160, 166
Italy 4

James II 8
Japan 56
jihad, avoiding 7–13
Jospin, Lionel 113
The Journal of Historical Review (JHR) 167
Judaism 101–2, 108; see also Holocaust denial
judgmental regulation 126
'Justice as Fairness' (Rawls) 74–5
justification 26–7
'justification principle' 40–3

Kant, Immanuel 40, 68, 92, 183n.5, 187n.37, 188n.54
Kantianism 97–8
Khatami, Mohammed 120
Khomeini, Ayatollah 120
Kristallnacht 154
Kymlicka, W. 102, 103–4, 105, 188n.7

Lady Chatterley's Lover (Lawrence) 120
laïcité 115–17
Langton, Rae 145–50, 197n.42, 197n.44
language , offensive 86
Larmore, Charles 181n.3
law: coercion 11; Holocaust denial 160–6; legal moralism 88–9, 140–1, 143–4, 162–3; political liberalism 68–70; see also pluralism
Lawrence, D.H. 120
Lawrence v. Texas (2003) 5
legitimacy 71
A Letter Concerning Toleration (Locke) 7–10, 176n.23
Levi, Primo 153
libel 132
liberalism: harm and offence 82–9; new challenges 172–4; non-liberalism and 16; as political 68–70; rights 81–2, 89–97
liberty 144–5; inequality 144–5; Liberty Principle 11–13; negative 58–62; negative liberty 58–62, 109, 182n.28; positive liberty 60–1; protection of 153
On Liberty (Mill) 10–13
Lipstadt, Deborah 156, 159
Locke, John 7–10, 68, 176n.20, 190n.40
locutions 145–8
London Charter (1945) 158
love and affection 108
loyalty 116–17
Loyola, Ignatius de 45

McCalden, David 167
Mackie, J.L. 39–40
MacKinnon, Catharine 141–5, 150
Major, John 3
majority, tyranny of 7–13, 153
male circumcision 108–9
male supremacy 142
Marchiano, Linda 197n.43

marriages 5–6, 28–30, 82, 146–7, 197n.42
Massachusetts 5–6
master/apprentice 170–1
master/slave 148–50, 180n.30
master-value 53, 54, 57
Matravers, Matt 49–50
Mendus, Susan 49–50
mercy 178n.16
metaphysical scepticism **35–43**;
    explantation of 35–6; relativism
    37–43; subjectivism 35–6
Midnight's Children (Rushdie) 119
Mill, John Stuart: comprehensive liberalism
    68; exceptions 192n.12; fallibility 47,
    122; liberty 153; truth 123, 124;
    tyranny of the majority 10–13, 154
Minneapolis Ordinance 142–3
'Model Ordinance' 142–3, 147
Modood, Tariq 132–3, 151, 200n.47
modus vivendi 69–70
Montaigne, Michel de 52
morality: judgement 34, 51 m ; moral
    independence 141, 145; moralistic
    legal paternalism 140; neutral 22;
    pluralism 162–6; prudence 15–16,
    43–4, 45, 57; *see also* relativism
motivation 183n.6
Muhammad 119–20, 124, 131–2, 193n.18
multiculturalism: debates 101; female
    genital mutilation 105–12;
    headscarves 112–18
Murray, Charles 25
Myra (Harvey) 120–1

National Front 167
National Health Service 93
negative liberty 58–62, 109, 182n.28
neo-fascism 25
neutrality 116
'new populist' movements 4
Nicholson, Peter 22–3, 31
Nietzsche, Friedrich 45, 180n.30
1984 (Orwell) 39, 46
non-rejection, tolerance and 14, 15
normative argument 76
Norway 4
'Not Waving but Drowning' (Smith)
    197n.41
Nuremberg Trials 155, 158

obligations 97–8
Obscene Publications Act 1959 120, 140
offence: categories of 83–4; harm and
    82–9
offensive nuisances 85–7
Ofili, Chris 121
Old Order Amish 102
O'Neill, Onora 97, 188n.53
open-mindedness 178n.20
opposition: incommensurability 65;
    interpretations of 18–19; prospects
    33–4; strong 18–19, 23–7, 29; weak
    18–23, 29; wide 19, 27–33
opposition, tolerance and 14–15
Orwell, George 39, 46, 67
other-regarding actions 12–13
overlapping consensus 69–70, 183n.16,
    184n.33

Palestine 42
Panton, James 169
paradox of toleration 19, 20, 31–3, 172
Parekh, Bhikhu 132, 133–4
participant interest 125
patriarchy 114, 115, 142, 191n.61
Patriot Act (2001) 90, 185n.28
Penguin Books 159, 165
perfect duties of justice 97–8
perfectionism 62, 65, 68
perlocutionary speech 145–8
personal property rights 93, 94
philosophy 39–43
physical harm 108; consent 109, 110–12
pluralism: competition 62–6;
    reasonableness 74–6; *see also*
    incommensurability
poets 44–7
Poland, invasion of 154–5
police 4, 5
political community 127–8
Political Liberalism (Rawls) 74–5
political refugees 4
political stability 114
Poor Clares 55, 56, 65, 181n.11
pornography: classic arguments 138–9;
    damaged status of women 137;
    definitions 140, 142–3; general
    attitudes 195n.3; harm 140–50;
    inequality 140–5; non-moralistic

arguments 144–5; significant interests 139; silencing women 145–50; speech act theory 145–8, 164–5; truth 138, 195n.4
positive liberty 60–1
postmodernism 45
power: inequality 15, 142, 188n.52; master/slave 148–50; overlapping consensus 69–70
practical incompatibility 53, 55–6, 65
practical reason: assumptions 183n.17; burdens of judgement 75; failure of 10; normative argument 76; pragmatism 43; reasonableness 68; role of 184n.40; self-respect 104; subjectivism 36; wide opposition 32, 172
pragmatism 35, 43–7, 50–1
priests 7–10
privacy: bare knowledge offence 87–8; ironists 47; libel 132; rights 5–6, 109, 110; secularism 115–16; sensitivity 47
'The Problem of the Gas Chambers' (Faurisson) 156–8
problems, contemporary 13–17
profound offences 84–9; Holocaust denial 163–4, 166; public sex acts 185n.12; responses to 130–2
prohibition/regulation 111–12
promises 91
property rights 187n.45
prudence 15–16, 43–4, 45, 57
Public Order Act 1986 199n.42
public reason 71–2
public sex acts 86, 185n.12
public transport 86
pungent smells 86

Qur'an 4, 113, 191n.53

race relations: blasphemy and 129–35; equality 6; immigration policies 4; intolerance perceptions 5
Race Relations Act 1976 133
racism: evaluative disapproval 25–7; inactive racists 20–2, 26, 31; segregation 6, 127–8; survey 4; workplace 195n.63
Raphael, D.D. 26
rationality , arguments from 7–10

Rawls, John: assumptions 70–1, 75, 183n.17; liberalism 68–70; overlapping consensus 183n.16, 184n.33; pluralism 74–6; property rights 187n.45; reasonableness 70–3; rights 93; scepticism 73–4; self-respect 104
Raz, Joseph: autonomy and competitive pluralism 62–6; evaluative incomparability 55; interest-based rights 91; intrinsic good 189n.14; legal duty 68
reasonableness: assumptions 70–1, 75, 183n.17; clarifications 73–6; incompossibility 76–9; opposition 34; political liberalism 68–70; toleration from 70–3
Rees, J.C. 13
regulation/prohibition 111–12
relativism: anthropology 37–9, 45; in Berlin 58–9; explantation of 36–7, 50; Holocaust denial 168; philosophy 39–43
religion: blasphemy 129–35; conversion 48; employment 195n.63; enforcing uniformity 7–10; gay marriages 28–30; headscarves 112–18; mockery 86; reasonableness 75–6
remainder 6
republican argument 114, 115–17
requirement, tolerance as 14, 15–16
resentment 84
resources, sustaining 49
responsible opposition 28, 30–2
Restoration 7–10
restraint 20–2
revisionism 156, 157, 167
rights: compossibility 94; generations 93–4; interest-based 90–2; liberalism 89–95
rights-based harm 81–2, 89, 185n.2
Roman Catholicism 75–6
romanticism: see anthropology
Rorty, Richard 43–7, 59, 180n.32
Rushdie, Salman 119, 120, 151, 165
Russell, Bertrand 35
Rye House plot 8

sado-masochism 110–12
Sandel, Michael 179n.19
'satanic verses' 193n.18

Satanic Verses (Rushdie): authority 151; defamation 133–4; democracy 126, 128, 135; fallibility 122–3; group libel 132–3; Muslim reaction 120, 194n.49; profound offence 130–2; publication of 119; 'second best' 129; significant interests 126, 134–5; synopsis 119–20; truth 124
Saudi Arabia 88
Scanlon, T.M. 125–6, 134
scepticism 35–7; epistemological 35, 47–50, 51; metaphysical 35–6; opposition 33; pragmatism 35, 43–7, 50–1; reasonableness 73–4
Schauer, Frederick 128–9
schools 4, 102
'second best' 128–9, 139, 163
Second World War 156
secularism 113, 115–16
segregation 6, 127–8, 154
self-determination 94
self-regarding actions 12–13
self-respect 103–4, 187n.38
Sensation (collection) 121
sense of justice 70–2, 82
September 11 attacks 48, 90
sexual discrimination 141–2
Shaftesbury, Earl of 8
shame 84
shock 84
Shoguns 56, 181n.13
Shweder, Richard A. 38
significant interests: freedom of expression 125–6; Holocaust denial 162, 163; pornography 139; *The Satanic Verses* 134–5
Sikhs 101
silencing 122, 145–50
Simmons, A.J. 112, 190n.49
skittishness 87–8
Smith, Stevie 197n.41
Smith, Winston 49
socio-economic rights 93, 94
sodomy 5
solidarity 44–6, 69
Somalia 91, 107
'Some Elementary Comments on the Rights of Freedom of Expression' (Chomsky) 157–8
Soviet Union, invasion of 155

Spain 160
Spanner case 110–11
special rights 90–1, 101–2
Stasi Commission 113
state neutrality 116
Sterne, Laurence 178n.20
strong opposition 18–19, 29
strong poet 179n.24
subjectivism 35–6
subliminal advertising 126
Sunday shopping 14–15
sunna 106, 108–9
supererogatory acts 97–8
sustainable resources 49
Switzerland 160

taste 177n.9
Taylor, Charles 104
Tebbit, Norman 101
Thatcher, Margaret 117
threatening behaviour 86
Tinnuni, Julin 117–10, 192n.74
transitivity 62, 182n.30
transparency 50–1
truth: analytic/synthetic 43–4; arguments for 123–4; Holocaust denial 161, 168–9; pornography 138, 195n.4; *The Satanic Verses* 124
tyranny of the majority 7–13, 153

unemployment rates 4
United Nations High Commission for Human Rights 106
United Nations Human Rights Committee 158
United Nations Universal Declaration Universal Human Rights 38
universal rights 90–1
universal suffrage 93
universities 166–71
USA: Bill of Rights 127, 128–9; Constitution 126–7; FGM (female genital mutilation) 107; gay marriages 5–6; Holocaust denial 167; 'Model Ordinance' 142–3, 147; Patriot Act 90, 185n.28; pornography 140; profound offences 88
utilitarianism 12–13, 47, 54
utopianism 58

validity/invalidity 178n.3
value pluralism: autonomy 62–6;
    incommensurability 52–8; negative
    liberty 58–62
Van Gogh, Theo 3–4
Vidal-Naquet, P. 168–9
Viking/Penguin 119, 120
violence 5
virtue 22–3, 31, 32–3, 97
volenti non fit injuria 109, 110, 111,
    190n.43
Voltaire 157
Waldron, Jeremy: coercion 9;
    incompatibility 76–9; interest-based
    rights 90, 91, 134–5; open-mindedness
    178n.20; truth 124
'Wannsee Conference' (1942) 155
war crimes 155
Warnock, Mary 20, 23–4

we-intentions 44–6
weak opposition 18–23, 29, 177n.2
Weber, Mark 167
Wenar, Leif 75–6
West, Rebecca 137
wide opposition 19, 27–33
William of Orange 8
Williams, Bernard 31–2, 39, 182n.29
women: clash of rights 144, 145; silencing
    145–50; status see damaged status;
    status of 4; unemployment rates 4
Wong, David 36–7, 40–3, 179n.17
World Health Organisation 107
World Trade Center 48

xenophobia 4

Zionist conspiracy 156, 157